Shakespeare

& the Greek

Romance

Carol Gesner

Shakespeare & the Greek Romance

A STUDY OF ORIGINS

The University Press of Kentucky

Lexington   1970

Standard Book Number: 8131–1220–6

Library of Congress Catalog Card Number: 70–11509

Copyright © 1970 by The University Press of Kentucky

A statewide cooperative scholarly publishing agency serving Berea College, Centre College of Kentucky, Eastern Kentucky University, Kentucky State College, Morehead State University, Murray State University, University of Kentucky, University of Louisville, and Western Kentucky University.

Editorial and Sales Offices: Lexington, Kentucky 40506

Contents

Preface

It is common knowledge among literary scholars that Greek romance was an important factor in shaping Renaissance narrative and drama. Boccaccio drew on its materials for *Il Filocolo* and *The Decameron;* Cervantes admitted to competing with Heliodorus in *Persiles y Sigismunda.* The influence of Greek romance has been recognized in the work of Lyly, Sidney, and Greene; and the significance of Heliodorus has been studied. That many of Shakespeare's plays embody Greek romance materials has long been known, but there has been need for a single work that draws together the facts of the relationship. The whole question of the influence of Greek romance on Renaissance literature in England and on the continent has yet to be investigated. Investigation of that scope is beyond the limits of this work, which attempts only to collect what is known of the Greek romance materials in Shakespeare's plays, with the hope that such a focus will clarify some of the backgrounds of his composite art as well as bring about more understanding of the total relationship of the Greek romance to Renaissance literature. Since Shakespeare wrote in neither a cultural nor an intellectual vacuum, it has seemed desirable to describe briefly the Greek romance tradition as it may be observed historically and in the works of Boccaccio and Cervantes. Details of other writings, both Continental and English, which embody Greek romance materials have been collected and are mentioned briefly in the text or in the notes where they seem to be appropriate. I hope that this method will serve to relate Shakespeare to the overall Greek romance tradition in literature and to demonstrate how wide and pervasive the tradition has been.

The danger in books such as this is in centering the eye too closely upon the objective, and thus failing to bring into view other factors which should be considered in drawing a balanced conclusion. My purpose here is to present evidence that Greek romance is a major fabric of Renaissance narrative and drama, and that many of the marvelous adventures and titillating plot motifs and patterns, especially those calculated to induce surprise and horror or to create a spectacular effect, derive from the novel of the Greek decadence. While what follows may seem to emphasize the afterlife of the Greek romance at the expense of other literary genres, the reader is fairly warned that Greek romance did not work alone, but is only one bright thread in a complicated web which includes materials supplied by other classical genres, folklore, legend, myth, and chivalric romance. Since Greek romance has been the one literary type most frequently overlooked, it has seemed necessary to center full attention on it and to supplement the discussion of the text with substantial bibliographic detail so that the weight of evidence may serve to demonstrate the popular as well as the academic approval of the romances during the period *c.* 1300–1642. This method should help to substantiate the thesis that Greek romance has been a much underrated factor in the development of fiction and drama, while at the same time drawing together the body of materials that relate specifically to Shakespeare.

This work began as long ago as 1951, the result of a stimulating lecture by Professor Waldo McNeir of the University of Oregon, who has encouraged me by publishing the discussion of *Cymbeline*. A version of this work eventually emerged as a Louisiana State University doctoral dissertation, under the guidance of Professor William John Olive. President-Emeritus Francis S. Hutchins and Vice President-Emeritus Louis Smith of Berea College have made it possible to broaden the scope of the dissertation by granting me leave of absence from my teaching duties during the fall semester of 1964. They have further assisted me with research grants during the summers of 1964, 1965, and 1966. During the summer of 1968 assistance was extended to me by Yale University.

Miss Faunice Hubble of the Berea College Library has been especially gracious in helping me locate materials, as have officials of the libraries of Columbia, Oxford, and Yale Universities. M. Roger Pierrot of the Bibliothèque Nationale has answered bibliographic queries. My thanks must go to colleagues at Berea College: Professor Charles Pauck has assisted me with some German texts; Professor-Emeritus Charlotte Ludlum has read the portion of the manuscript dealing with historical aspects of the classical romances; Dr. William Schafer has read the manuscript and made many suggestions, as has Professor Thomas Stroup of the University of Kentucky. A final critical reading by Professor F. David Hoeniger of the University of Toronto not only helped me with many details of style and arrangement, but offered encouragement when it was most needed. Finally I must thank Marie Tychonievich Clendenin and Judy Clouse of Berea College for typing the manuscript, and Doubleday and Company for permission to quote from Moses Hadas's translation of Xenophon of Ephesus. The sections dealing with *The Tempest* and *Cymbeline* were published originally as *"The Tempest* as Pastoral Romance" in *The Shakespeare Quarterly* 10 (1959), and *"Cymbeline* and the Greek Romance: A Study in Genre" in *Studies in English Renaissance Literature,* ed. Waldo F. McNeir (Baton Rouge, La., 1962). The editors of *The Shakespeare Quarterly* and the Louisiana State

University Press have given me permission to include them, somewhat revised and augmented, in this volume.

My friend and colleague Professor Eleanor Brooks (Berea College 1937–1966) gave me much encouragement during the early phases of research and composition. Her death in 1966 left me heir not only to her students and to her courses, but to many of her books. For these reasons I dedicate the work to her memory and also to the others who have assisted me along the way.

Shakespeare

& the Greek

Romance

Chapter One

The Greek
Romances

AN INTRODUCTION

The Greek romances of the early Christian era have
been called the twilight of Greek literature, the descent
from Olympus, and have been relegated to the literary
scrap heaps as childish in substance and wanting in
truth. This adverse criticism results from their marvel-
ously improbable action and the puppetlike quality of
their protagonists, as well as from their amorality, their
elaborate language, and self-conscious, somewhat Eu-
phuistic style. Even a superficial knowledge of the permanent values of the true Olympians—Homer, Sopho-
cles, Aeschylus—testifies to the truth of this harsh
judgment. But the Greek romances form a tremendous
storehouse for many of the primary plots and motifs of
fiction. They are forerunners of the modern novel and
the direct ancestors of the historical novel and the *voyage imaginaire*. It is in them that we find the origin of
the one indispensable of romantic fiction, the heroine.[1]
In Greek letters they have a very real importance in that
they form a direct link between Greek literature and
Oriental civilization, perhaps the only literary ground,

except the beast fables, in which Greek met non-Greek and received rather than dispersed. As hybrids they fill an exotic corner in the history of letters; at the same time they have a workaday importance to the student of the English Renaissance, for they have been a pervasive influence on drama and fiction since their earliest publication, and a knowledge of them is essential to a full understanding of the Renaissance literary milieu. Heliodorus, Longus, Achilles Tatius, and *Apollonius of Tyre* all were published in English translations between 1483 and 1597, and other romances were accessible in Greek manuscripts. The impact of these books on the English novel was important,[2] and they exerted a considerable influence in the drama as well.[3] A study of them, both as a type of literature and as a reflection of a civilization, is thus of genuine value.

Nineteenth-century scholars believed that the romances developed from a synthesis of love and travel stories through the direct agency of the rhetorical schools vigorous in Greece during the period of the early Roman empire.[4] But twentieth-century discoveries of papyrus fragments of a number of hitherto unknown romances have pushed back the dating of their origin. The most important of these fragments contains the Ninus story,[5] dated on paleographic evidence during the second century B.C.[6] It seems likely that the romances developed, perhaps as a kind of popular historical biography, from local legends in centers of Greek culture in the Mediterranean world, for the titles of some—*Babylonica, Ephesiaca, Aethiopica*—celebrate places.[7] Apparently they derive from the lower intellectual levels pushing against and being influenced by the upper levels. After the conquests of Alexander the Great, Assyrians, Babylonians, Jews, and Phrygians wrote fanciful tales of their legendary heroes, perhaps through a desire for cultural preservation. A need to defend religious or cultural values threatened by the new Christian order may also have been a factor in their composition, for in the romances we find interest in the pagan pantheon as well as in the pagan philosophical systems.[8] In them also are marks left by the New Comedy and such hero cycles as those of Ninus and Alexander.[9] In Greek literature, the *Odyssey* itself could have supplied their authors with the basic separation plot or travel story. The *Argonautica*, in a technical sense an epic, is also a versified romantic novel.[10] Further, the collection of *Milesian Tales* by Aristides of Miletus and the *Love Romances* of Parthenius must have had some germinal influence on the romances.

The Ninus fragment is the first true romance of which we have any remains and is probably the direct progenitor of the erotic romances and possibly of the romantic biographies of the early Christian era. The hero, Ninus, is the legendary founder of Ninevah. The heroine is probably Semiramis, who may have had historical reality in the person of Sammu-ramut, the wife of the Assyrian king, Shamshi-Adad. In the popular mind she was transformed from an earthly queen to a goddess of love and war,[11] taking a substantial place in the Babylonian mythology. Thus the fragment confronts us with the transformation of historical persons (at least in the case of Semiramis) to mythological figures, and thence to characters in a novel.

At first glance the Ninus fragment would appear to be a romantic biography, since Semiramis can to some extent be identified with a historical person. In truth, it is barefaced attachment of famous names to fiction. The Ninus story makes no pretense at historicity. Evidence of this is the fact that the viciously erotic nature of Semiramis in Babylonian mythology has been transformed to that of a young girl of incredible shyness and undoubted chastity, and the powerful Ninus of legend has become a youth in his teens.

Except in the epitome in the *Bibliotheca* of Photius

(c. 870–871), *The Wonderful Things Beyond Thule*[12] (second or third centuries A.D.) of Antonius Diogenes is lost. From Photius we know that the romance was written in twenty-four books and that Dinias, the hero, related his adventures with Dercyllis, the heroine, to a friend. In centering on a pair of lovers who travel to marvelous places—the vicinity of the North Pole, the underworld, the land of the Amazons—the story falls into the true Greek romance pattern: that pattern which Northrup Frye classifies as the "quest," a wish fulfillment, escape romance of adventure which usually falls into episodic, processional structure built on a theme of a perilous journey.[13] Such a plot usually develops in three stages: the perilous journey, minor adventures, a crucial struggle often leading to the death of the hero or to a condition near death, and final discovery and recognition of the hero by a welcoming people. The hero is often highborn, a great deliverer, or can be identified more or less with a god or a Messiah figure. In the great crisis he experiences a real or a ritual death followed by rebirth or recognition or both. In Greek romance the "quest" usually is begun when a pair of youthful lovers—frequently married—are separated. Their desire for reunion usually motivates the journey. The minor episodic adventures frequently include storm and shipwreck, followed by various combinations of narrow escapes and humiliations at the hands of brigands, pirates, brothel keepers, poisoners, and kidnappers. Usually the hero and heroine experience imprisonment, slavery, and attempted seduction. The great crisis frequently comes to the heroine rather than to the hero: As a result of some misfortune she falls into an unconsciousness so deep that it is mistaken for death. Eventually she is restored to the hero, most often at the conclusion of the romance in a triallike recognition scene in which all mysteries and mistakes are explained and all loose threads are knitted up again.

The *Babylonica*[14] (second or third century A.D.) of Iamblichus is a fully developed love romance with a similar journey structure and most of the adventure motifs which became the accepted conventions in the later, better-known romances. The motif of apparent death is repeated four times: twice in a deathlike trance induced by poison, once by mistaken identity, and once when the hero and heroine hide in a tomb and are mistaken for fresh corpses. The importance of developing this motif is not to be overestimated, for it is represented in all the later Greek romances except *Daphnis and Chloe* and it is a motif frequently adapted by Renaissance writers. Like *The Wonderful Things Beyond Thule*, the *Babylonica* is extant only in an epitome of Photius.[15]

Chaereas and Callirhoe[16] of Chariton of Aphrodisia is the first romance to survive intact, although there is no sure reference to the author in either ancient or Byzantine writers. Papyrus fragments discovered in Egypt date it about A.D. 150.[17] Much of Chariton's emphasis is on historical background and historical figures. Thus it demonstrates a straight line of development from the Ninus fragment, in which historical figures serve as protagonists, to the technique of the modern novelists who use historical background and figures to add interest and color. Chariton's historical personages serve as they would in a novel by Sir Walter Scott: They are accessories to the story, almost painted backdrops before which the heroes and heroines work out their destinies, rather than figures of the plot. Chariton's historical accuracy is manipulated, as is Scott's, to serve his own artistic purpose. For example: Hermocrates, the general of Syracuse who defeated the Athenians in the naval battle of 414 B.C., is represented as the father of the heroine. Chariton makes him a contemporary of the great Persian King Artaxerxes (*c.* 404—*c.* 359 B.C.), who actually came into royal power only after Hermocrates had died. A very convincing background is created by the use of such figures and by frequent mention of the wars between Syracuse and Athens, the wars of the Greeks and the Persians, and the military genius of Cyrus the Great. But chiefly the illusion of history is created by the hero's active engagement in the revolt of the Egyptians against Persian domination.

It is in *Chaereas and Callirhoe* that we first experience what might be called the prevailing plot motivation in Greek romance, the will of the gods, and the typical Greek romance personality patterns: a strong-willed, resourceful heroine; a slightly effeminate, hot-tempered, timid hero. Further, this pair are so miraculously handsome that the ignorant frequently mistake them for gods—the Messianic quality of the hero of a "quest" romance. They are of course typically highborn, although their aristocratic connections are frequently revealed only at the conclusions of the romances.

Habrocomes and Anthia, or the *Ephesiaca*[18] (second or third centuries A.D.), by Xenophon of Ephesus, comes to us in a manuscript of five books which may represent only the epitome of a much longer work, for the speeches are short—even laconic—and the shifting of scene from one group of characters or one event to another is very rapid, both rather abnormal characteristics for the genre. Xenophon does not pretend to be writing history, but otherwise he follows the accepted pattern of the Greek romances, perhaps deliberately imitating Chariton.

The ultimate source of *Apollonius of Tyre*[19] is unknown or lost, but many scholars agree that it must have been a pagan Greek romance of about the same period as the *Ephesiaca*.[20] It is usually conceded that the earliest Latin version of *Apollonius* was probably made during the sixth century—whether as an adaptation or as a translation is disputed.[21] In any case, the authorship is unknown.

The narrative opens with the rape of a princess by her father, King Antiochus. To keep suitors from her, the king devises a riddle for them to solve. Those who fail to find the solution die. A young nobleman, Apollonius of Tyre, finds the answer, but must flee. During the course of his adventures he marries a beautiful girl who apparently dies during a storm at sea while bearing him a daughter. He is separated from the wife by mistaken death and from the daughter by leaving her with foster parents to be reared. The events that follow are typical of other Greek romances, and the general resemblance to the *Ephesiaca* is pronounced, except that the titillating adventures involve the daughter Tharsia as well as the apparently dead wife. *Apollonius*, thus, has two heroines, both typical of the genre in their characterizations, although the husband-father hero differs from his counterparts in other Greek romances by being characterized as a manly, scholar-prince rather than as a beautiful, emotionally unstable adolescent.

The weird beginning in the incest story is unique among the Greek romances, which conventionally open with the meeting and separation of a pair of lovers. The unpleasant episode does serve, however, to underscore two important characteristics of the genre: their fundamentally Oriental nature and their frequent association with historical persons or events. Historically, King Antiochus the Great (277–187 B.C.) actually ruled in Asia Minor, but the incest story is probably slander on his memory.[22] History is further suggested in the flight of Apollonius from Tyre when he fears Antiochus's treachery, for Tyre did pass to the control of Antiochus the Great in 221 B.C.

With the *Aethiopica*[23] (c. third century A.D.) of Heliodorus of Emesa, the Greek romance came of age. The motifs and conventions that found their primitive expressions in Ninus reached their final form in the *Aethiopica*, which is in fact the monument to its class, an apotheosis of Greek romance which embodies all that its predecessors suggested. Far the longest of the Greek romances, it rambles through ten books before the lovers live happily ever after.

The *Aethiopica* is particularly interesting for its structure: for Heliodorus borrowed from epic poetry and the stage the technique of beginning *in medias res* and then filling in necessary information about the earlier action by means of the tale within the tale or the flashback. As each new character enters the action he relates his previous history and those portions of the history of the protagonists that are known to him. Thus the episodes dramatically advance the action of the plot. The author does not assume omniscience; the reader learns what he needs to know by living with the action and is theoretically kept in a state of suspense about the identities and the purposes of the characters until all the *dramatis personae* have entered and told their stories. Unfortunately, the suspense is often more theoretical than real; for when Heliodorus has one character relate the story of his life, which includes relating the life of his friend, and the life of the friend includes relating the life of the friend's friend, the stories of the second teller and the original teller are suspended in midair while the third is told. The result is soporific, a triple inversion involving intolerable literary gymnastics.

In spite of the structural originality, the plot materials of the *Aethiopica* do no more than maintain and reinforce the conventional essentials of the earlier Greek romances. Even the traditionally garbled historical background is there: Egypt during the period of domination by the Persians. Facts about Ethiopia are very different. In the *Aethiopica* it is an imaginary country where anything can happen, where Chariclea, a Negro princess, can be born white and where the miraculous is foretold in dreams, Heliodorus's favorite oracles.

Two elements of the plot would seem on first reading to be new to the genre: the exposure of Chariclea as an infant and the very prolonged trial-like conclusion. The exposure, however, was suggested in *Apollonius of Tyre* when the infant Tharsia was left with unloving foster parents to be reared and the grand reunion scene is on close examination only an extended and exaggerated version of the shorter recognition and reunion scenes which concluded the other romances.

A distinctive quality of the *Aethiopica* is the philosophic coloring of Neo-Pythagorean doctrine which had emerged during the early years of the Christian Church in a futile attempt to stem the tide that was running against paganism. The teachings embodied in Philostratus's biography of Apollonius of Tyana are held by two minor characters in the romance, and much reverence is paid to the gymnosophists of Ethiopia,[24] whom Apollonius of Tyana had visited for instruction.

Except for *Apollonius of Tyre*, the *Aethiopica* has been the most popular of all the Greek romances. Perhaps this is to be expected, since it epitomizes the genre in all its faults and virtues, and as such, where there would be a demand for a romance of this class, there would be an especial demand for the *Aethiopica*. But of all the Greek romances, only one, the *Lesbiaca*, or *Daphnis and Chloe*[25] (third century A.D.) of Longus, stands undisputed as literature. The others are now merely curiosities, bypaths for a patient scholar or a literary historian. *Daphnis and Chloe* alone escapes the fault so characteristic of popular fiction, that of being so much of its age that it is lost to any other age. It is the only Greek romance to attain the stature of genuine literary merit, and it stands to our day as a modest, but permanent, contribution to fiction.

The singular excellence of *Daphnis and Chloe* comes chiefly from its pastoral setting, which in itself is unique in the extant Greek romances. Like the others, it centers on a pair of lovers and includes the harrowing excitements of pirates and war, the traditional supernatural direction of the gods, trial scenes, kidnappings, recognition, and reunion. But unlike the others, the lovers (unique in remaining unmarried until the end of the story) experience all these adventures quietly at home. They take no journey, save a very short one to the nearby city. They lead their simple pastoral lives while adventures of the world come to them. As a result, Longus' romance achieves a unity which the others lack. The others give impressions of kaleidoscopic impermanence and long, uncertain time sequence. The action of *Daphnis and Chloe*, save for a few paragraphs, takes but one full year and a half. The theater of the usual Greek romance is the wide Mediterranean world;[26] *Daphnis and Chloe* is confined to the island of Lesbos. The action becomes tightly knit and unified by the pastoral background. The breathless jumping from one catastrophe to another, characteristic of the genre, is thus avoided. A few mishaps come in upon the lovers from the outside world, but the pair have still their sheep and goats to water, their cheeses to press, their vineyards to harvest.

Daphnis and Chloe is the best plotted of all the Greek romances. Its single theme, love, and the unified pastoral background serve to tighten the reins and keep it within reasonable bounds. The separation of hero and heroine, a motif common to the others, creates a serious plot defect in *Chaereas and Callirhoe* and in the *Ephesiaca*, for the reader is constantly shifting attention from one set of characters to another, and must keep straight the threads of two stories as they develop in a series of ill-connected episodes. *Apollonius of Tyre* actually has three lines of development in the main plot: the separate careers of Apollonius, his wife, and his daughter. The plot of the *Aethiopica*, so deliberately snarled by the involution of the chronology, is further complicated by the separation of the lovers. But *Daphnis and Chloe* is all one piece. The lovers are not far apart for any length of time, and the chronological sequence develops in such order that we are always aware of the passing of days and seasons. The plot is motivated by Eros, but unlike the Olympians of the other romances, he seldom acts except through natural agents. It is his will rather than his hand that causes characters to be in the right places at the right times for events to occur.

The quality of innocence and childhood which hovers over this pair of lovers—and Chloe is the one exception to the pattern of a strong-willed heroine in Greek romance—is also singular in the genre. The heroes and heroines of the other romances are chaste—indeed, more so than Daphnis who deliberately takes a lesson so that he will know what to do—but theirs is not the chastity of innocence; it is the chastity of conscious choice. Callirhoe is not innocent in her love for Chaereas, although she is chaste even when she finds herself in the awkward position of having two husbands. Anthia and Habrocomes experience and understand passion. The two women of *Apollonius of Tyre* are pure beyond question, but they understand the difference between good and evil, and are fortunately so constituted as to choose good. Theagenes and Chariclea are physically chaste to the end of their adventures, but the chastity is almost a mockery. It is no more than a postponement of physical love for a calculated benefit; they make capital of it. Daphnis and Chloe are chaste without realizing what chastity is; they experiment with love with no understanding of its nature, its physical expression, or their resulting emotions. The young lovers are innocent, though Longus is a jaded sophisticate finding amusement in the observation of childhood, and this note of decadence seems a forecast that the development of the genre had run its course.

Finally, *Clitophon and Leucippe*[27] is almost a mockery

of the other romances in its exaggeration of their qualities and in its slight tone of depravity. It has been said that the idealism of Heliodorus inspired Achilles Tatius to make a parody of the genre,[28] a logical conclusion under the old presumption that the romance dated from *c.* A.D. 300.[29] Recently discovered papyrus fragments dating from the second century invalidate many old conclusions,[30] including this one. It is no longer possible to view Achilles Tatius as the end of a line of development in the Greek novel, but for the purposes of critical examination, it is convenient to treat it last, since its decadent qualities take it out of the mainstream, while at the same time its similarities make it impossible to classify it with any other genre.

For his chief ingredients, Achilles Tatius follows the pattern of other Greek romances. The materials are so typical of the entire group that they require no comment, save for one element: the gnawing worm of decadence which infects them. The conventional plot compounded of voyage and separation begins with a new motif. After the first declarations of love are made, Leucippe agrees to admit Clitophon to her bedchamber, an act unthinkable to any of the heroines of the other romances. The travel of the pair is motivated by the need to escape resulting parental wrath. The motif of chastity dominant throughout the other romances is twisted and flouted by the actions and speeches of both hero and heroine of *Clitophon and Leucippe*. They are never able to lift love above a purely physical plane. One long passage contains a formal debate of the relative merits of love between man and boy and man and woman. The decadence is illustrated by the details of Leucippe's apparent death as a sacrifice of the pirates: The heroine of the romance lies all day in a closed coffin with a bloody sheep gut tied to her stomach, and her lover has sight of her with her abdomen apparently split open and empty of its entrails. Typical of the Greek romance heroes, he faints, but here with good reason.

If only for convenience in discussion, *Clitophon and Leucippe* stands at the end of a series which can be traced from the pseudohistoric Ninus fragment through the heroics of the *Aethiopica.* In Achilles Tatius the typical aristocratic background and tone of the romances turns surprisingly bourgeois; the high moral conception of the characters becomes so cynical as to seem like parody, while the conventional motifs are embellished with details calculated to shock or disgust.

But "This is a long preamble of a tale!"—or of a study, the avowed purpose of which is to show how the Greek romances lived again during the Renaissance. Were the romances better known, the study might begin like Heliodorus *in medias res* with the invention of printing, but for all their popularity in the past, except for *Daphnis and Chloe* and *Apollonius of Tyre*—ironically the two which are least representative—these romances are not frequently read today. After the third century of the Christian era the Greek romances were more or less forgotten, but the revival of literary studies during the Byzantine period brought with it among scholars an increasing interest in the novels. During the ninth, tenth, and eleventh centuries they were widely read,[31] and in the twelfth century imitations were made by Nicetas Eugenianus, Eustathius Makrembolites, Constantinius Manasses, and Theodorus Prodromus.[32]

Chapter Two

The

Continental

Tradition

THE MEDIEVAL BACKGROUND

The twelfth-century imitations of the Greek romances kept the spirit of the genre alive through the Middle Ages and into the Renaissance. Indeed, their example had never been altogether extinguished, for some of it is obviously embedded in the chivalric cycles. The best known of the Greek romances in the Middle Ages, *Apollonius of Tyre*, was actually reworked in the twelfth-century epic of Jourdain de Blaie and related to the Charlemagne cycle.[1] The constant and chaste love of the Hellenistic couples is similar to the somewhat more spiritual love of the courtly tradition, although the motif of adulterous love in the Medieval tales is never present in the affairs of the central characters of the Greek novels: albeit, horrible examples of unchaste love often occur among minor characters. Despite the difference, it is likely that the Greek romances are among the sources of *Floire and Blancheflor, Aucassin and Nicolette, Partonopeus de Blois, Ipomédon, Blancandin,*

Guillaume de Palerme, Escoufle, Floriant and Florette, Galeran de Bretagne, Jean and Blonde, and *Cléomadès.*[2]

Even the pairing of the names of lovers which so frequently creates the titles of the romances is a tradition that can be clearly traced from the Hellenistic *Clitophon and Leucippe, Theagenes and Chariclea* (a commonly used alternative title for the *Aethiopica*), and *Daphnis and Chloe,* to the Byzantine *Hysmine and Hysminias, Charicles and Drusilla;* and then on to the Medieval *Floire and Blancheflor, Aucassin and Nicolette, Troilus and Criseyde.* Episodic structure, long journeys, and separated lovers are common to both Greek and chivalric cycles. The chastity tests which Medieval ladies sometimes had to endure, although they go back even to Levitical law (Numbers 5: 11–31) and the ancient myth of the Stygian fountain which disgraced the guilty by rising, were also required of Heliodorus's Chariclea (trial by fire) and Achilles Tatius's Leucippe (trial by water). The bodily marks and identifying tokens which often reveal lost relatives in courtly romance (Book V of the *Amadis* cycle) are similar to the black birthmark and rich tokens of Chariclea and to the articles left with Longus's Daphnis and Chloe at their exposure as infants. The exposure motif (related also to the stories of Moses and Romulus and Remus) also reappears: for example, in the abandonment of Amadis in a box placed in a stream, the story of Esplandian carried off and suckled by a lioness, and the exposure of Palmcrin on a mountain covered with palms and olive trees.

The courtly tradition of falling in love at first sight, often in a church or at a religious ceremony, which we read of in Boccaccio's *Filostrato* (*c.* 1340) and in Chaucer's *Troilus and Criseyde* (*c.* 1377),[3] has ancient counterparts in the meeting of Chariton's Chaereas and Callirhoe at a ceremony dedicated to Aphrodite,

Xenophon's Habrocomes and Anthia at the ceremonies of Artemis, and Heliodorus's Theagenes and Chariclea at solemnities in Delphi. Love sickness follows in all these cases, physical reactions so severe that victims frequently must take to their beds. Apollonius and his wife meet at a banquet rather than at a religious house, but she is so stricken with love for him that she soon takes to her bed. Daphnis and Chloe of Longus who had known each other from early childhood, nevertheless, are ill when erotic love develops between them. Such love sickness is a common motif in ancient literature. Besides the romance lovers, we read of it in *Hippolytus* —Phaedra pines with fever, paleness, loss of appetite, and frenzied speech for her husband's son. Theocritus and Ovid also wrote of the ravages, as do the authors of the Medieval courtly romances: *Piramus and Thisbe, Cligès, Lancelot, Athis and Profilias,* and *Amadas and Ydoine.*[4]

An episode in Iamblichus's *Babylonica* is clearly prophetic of the courts of love of the Middle Ages: At the temple of Venus situated on an island at the confluence of the Tigris and the Euphrates rivers, Mesopotamia, the youngest daughter of a priestess of Venus, gives gifts to three lovers. The first receives a cup from which she often drank. The second receives a chaplet of flowers she had worn about her brow. The third receives a kiss. The lovers argue over which has received the greatest token and plead the case before an amatory judge, who decides in favor of the kiss.

The firmly established tradition continued into the Renaissance. Even a superficial study of the publication record of the Greek romances from *c.* 1470 to 1642 reveals enormous popularity. *Apollonius of Tyre* was apparently the first to be printed, about 1470. From then on the romances appeared frequently in both Latin and vernacular translations and in scholarly Greek editions.

The geographical distribution of their publishers was widespread, running east and west from Kolozvar to London, north and south from Copenhagen to Valencia. Thus it has seemed important to investigate their effect on the letters of the period. As a result of the investigation it seems sound to assert that wherever the fiction or drama of the period contains the stock-in-trade of the plots of Greek romance—abduction, abandonment, mistaken death or identity, restoration of lost heirs or relatives, robbers, shipwreck, pirates, sudden shifts in fortune, all coupled with epiphanies, disguises, oaths, dreams—the Hellenistic novel must be considered before the roots of such literature can be fully untangled, bearing always in mind that the motifs have a kind of universal quality and appear also in various combinations in Euripidean romance and the New Comedy.[5] But Hellenistic novels are especially to be considered if such motifs are coupled with one or more of the primary plots apparently derived from the Greek novels: the separation plot, the potion plot, the slandered bride plot, and the stock pastoral plot. Within these, most often in the separation and the pastoral plots, is frequently the motif—or myth—of the royal or highborn child cast away or exiled in infancy. Often he is fostered by a shepherd or another of humble birth.

The separation romance frequent in Western literature—Hero and Leander, Pyramus and Thisbe, Tristan and Isolde—is the basic structure of all extant Greek romances except *Daphnis and Chloe.*

The separation plot frequently evolves into the potion romance which parallels the central situation of *Romeo and Juliet,* its sources and analogues: Two lovers (usually married) are endangered by a rival for the lady. As a means of escape, a sleeping potion is obtained from a friend or a physician. The heroine drinks it and is buried as if dead. The hero visits the tomb believing her dead. The oldest known versions of this plot, to my knowledge, are the *Ephesiaca* and the *Babylonica.*[6]

Sometimes the separation plot evolves into the slandered bride plot—the "Ariodante and Genevra" episode of *Orlando Furioso:* Two lovers, either engaged to be married or very recently married, are separated when a jealous rival for the lady conspires with her own servant to trick the hero into believing that his lady receives another lover in her chamber. Brutal accusation follows. In the ancient prototype, *Chaereas and Callirhoe,* the lady apparently dies as a result of a blow struck in anger by the "hero." In the Renaissance versions the blow is usually psychic. The results are apparent death of the lady after a deep swoon, or after she is placed in mortal jeopardy. Eventually she is cleared and the couple are usually married.

Although Vergil was probably the fountainhead from which the Renaissance pastoral writers drew much of their materials, the Greeks—Theocritus, Moschus, Bion, and Longus—are not to be overlooked. As to Longus, Edwin Greenlaw has shown that *Daphnis and Chloe* supplied the chief elements in a stock pastoral plot used by Sidney, Spenser, and Shakespeare:[7] A child of unknown parentage (usually a girl) is reared by shepherds or is living in pastoral seclusion. A lover, who may be a foundling or a highborn man in guise of a shepherd or a forester, is introduced. A rival lover, usually a rude, bumbling, cowardly person, complicates the love story and functions as a foil for the hero. He often supplies the comic elements. Melodramatic incidents (such as the attack of a lion or a bear) give the hero an opportunity to prove his prowess. In a captivity episode the heroine is abducted and the hero comes to the rescue. It finally develops that the heroine is of high birth and may marry the hero.

Aside from such plot materials, collections of tales in

a framework—one of the characteristic Renaissance genres—may also owe some debt to Greek romance.[8] The *Aethiopica* contains the story of Chariclea's past and the histories of several minor characters set within the framework of a separation plot. *Clitophon and Leucippe* begins in Sidon with Clitophon's relation of his separation story as he and a friend examine a painting of Europa and the bull (the place and the painting symbolic of the story that follows). *Daphnis and Chloe* is an interpretation of a painting. *The Wonderful Things Beyond Thule* (or *Dinias and Dercillas*) is an account of adventures recorded on cypress tablets found in a coffer near a tomb. But since the framework device for fiction is at least as old as a Twelfth Dynasty Egyptian papyrus[9] —to say nothing of the *Arabian Nights*—it is unsound to push the idea of ultimate debt too far.

Further, the Greek romances are characterized by the rhetorical style developed during the Second Sophistic period. Frequent use is made of highly artificial oxymoron, antithesis, homeopathy, alliteration, assonance, unnatural illustrations, declamations, and soliloquies. In fact, most of the distressing stylistic traits of *Euphues* are employed frequently throughout the romances. Stage terms and references to drama often occur. Wherever this elaborate style is coupled with Greek romance motifs and stock plots, there has probably been some direct influence. It is dangerous, however, to push this kind of source hunting too far.

BOCCACCIO: IL FILOCOLO AND THE DECAMERON

The impression left by the Hellenistic romances on Renaissance letters takes at least two forms. In some works it is obviously present, but at secondhand or thirdhand, remote, almost traditional in treatment and effect. In some, quite obvious firsthand influence occurs in the

form of imitation by borrowing. Boccaccio's earliest
long work, *Il Filocolo*[10] (*c.* 1337–1339), is a prime example of the derived influence; Cervantes's *Persiles y Sigismunda*, of the direct. The first prose romance in Italian
literary history, *Il Filocolo* has long been recognized as
in essence pure Greek romance filtered through the me-
dium of the courtly love tradition. Boccaccio apparently derived most of it from the story of "Floris and
Blancheflor," found in a thirteenth-century French version[11] which several scholars believe can be traced ultimately to a Greek origin.[12] J. H. Reinhold sees it as an
evolvement from the *Aethiopica* and *Apollonius of Tyre*
in combination with materials from the book of Esther
and Apuleius's story of Cupid and Psyche[13] (a separation
romance with overtones of folklore and mythology).
Those who disagree assign to it a Byzantine, Arabic, or
Persian origin.[14] Since recent scholarship has recognized so clearly the Oriental elements in the Greek romances, one opinion does not necessarily rule out the
other. The materials of the romance in Boccaccio's time
were part of the repertoire of the Provençal troubadours and were known to the famous Rambaldo di Va-
queiras. In *Il Filocolo* Boccaccio himself says the romance was well known in Naples when he wrote.[15]

As Boccaccio tells the tale (his version not yet translated into English): A Roman nobleman and his wife, a
descendant of Julius Caesar, travel to a shrine in Spain.
Hearing false reports that the Romans have pillaged a
city, the king of Spain attacks the party and kills the
nobleman. The wife survives and is protected by the
Spanish queen. On the day the queen gives birth to
Florio, the Roman noblewoman dies in giving birth to
Biancofiore. As the children are reared together love
develops. Since Biancofiore's high ancestry is unknown,
the king wishes to destroy their feelings. Thus he sends
Florio to study philosophy at Montorio. At parting Bian-

cofiore gives Florio a magic ring which will tell him of her safety. The king next falsely accuses her of trying to poison him. She is condemned to the stake. Warned by his ring and by Venus, Florio, disguised, rescues Biancofiore, then returns to his studies. Biancofiore is sold by the king to merchants who take her to Alexandria, where she is resold to an admiral of the Sultan of Babylon and guarded in a tower with women destined for the sultan. When Florio is told that Biancofiore is dead he tries to kill himself on her false tomb, but is saved by his mother who tells him the truth. Florio then sets out as "Filocolo" (sometimes translated "Pilgrim of Love" and sometimes "Love's Labor") to find his lady. During a sea journey a tempest blows him to Italy where he meets the beautiful Fiammetta as she presides over a court of love.[16] Florio eventually reaches Alexandria, bribes the guard, and is carried to Biancofiore in a hamper of flowers. Discovered by the admiral, they are condemned to the stake. Venus intervenes and makes them invulnerable to the flames and the admiral is reconciled by their courage. It then develops that he is Florio's uncle. The lovers are married and journey home. Passing through Italy they discover Biancofiore's noble origin, and at the Lateran Florio is converted to Christianity. Finally they reach Spain. The old king is dead and Florio ascends the throne. The couple live happily ever after.[17]

The story is clearly a development of the meandering Medieval tales and is no less tedious to read. Nevertheless, the essential fabric of Greek romance is also present in the plot and in the theme: the persistence of natural, or instinctive, love in spite of all obstacles. Biancofiore's false death and Florio's weeping at her tomb recall Rhodanes at Sinonis's false tomb in the *Babylonica*, Chaereas and Habrocomes at the tombs of the living Callirhoe and Anthia. Chariclea, Leucippe, and the wife and daughter of Apollonius are all mistakenly mourned as dead by the heroes of the romances. Apollonius sees a mock tomb of his daughter as Florio sees Biancofiore's mock tomb. Sea journeys lead to the return of the ladies in each case, except in the *Babylonica* and the *Aethiopica,* in which the miracles are effected by land. The fire that fails to consume Florio and Biancofiore recalls the flame that could not touch the lovers of the *Aethiopica* or the hero of the *Ephesiaca.* The false charge made against Biancofiore that she tried to poison the king has ancient counterparts in the false charges that Sinonis and Rhodanes poisoned a man, that Chariclea poisoned an old woman, and the false murder charge that led to Habrocomes's attempted crucifixion. The storms and dreams of *Il Filocolo* move also through the Greek romances, and the magic ring of Florio has its ancient counterpart in the "Pantarbo" of Chariclea. Florio's disguise as a merchant has earlier examples in Leucippe's disguise as a slave, Chariclea's as a beggar. Xenophon's Anthia was taken like Biancofiore to be sold at Alexandria to a powerful Oriental. Chariton's Callirhoe experienced the captivity of a harem. The revelation of Biancofiore's descent from the Julian line and the fact that her lover is the son of a king is reminiscent of the revelation in the *Aethiopica* that Chariclea is the daughter of the royal family of Ethiopia and her lover of the line of Achilles. Further, Biancofiore's relationship to the Julian family stands in the Greek romance tradition of linking fiction and historical personages.

The episode of Florio at the court of love has a forerunner in the *Babylonica.* Even its admission to the tale as an episode unrelated to the main currents of the romance—aside from the exact precedent in the *Babylonica*—has precedent in the unrelated episodes of Aegialeus and Thelixinoe and Hippothoos and Hyperanthes in the *Ephesiaca,*[18] as well as in the five irrelevant tales, the debate on Alcibiadean love, the account of the discovery of Tyrian dye, and the interpolation of myths and ekphrases in *Clitophon and Leucippe*. Five narratives, varying from fable to war, are inserted in *Daphnis and Chloe*. The episodic structure of the *Aethiopica*—although in most instances the episodes are pertinent to the plot—further maintains and teaches the tradition.

Passages of psychological realism mix frequently in *Il Filocolo* with magic and prophetic dreams, with mythology and supernaturally caused events. As in the Greek romances, the world is realistic, but the gods are the ruling agents who often shape the events of the plot. The Venus who intervenes to warn Florio of danger and to save him and Biancofiore at the stake also intervened to marry Callirhoe to Chaereas and then to make her a second marriage with Dionysius. Similarly, Pan, Eros, and the nymphs concern themselves in the affairs of Daphnis and Chloe. Eros motivated the love of Habrocomes and Anthia; and Helios, Apollo, and Artemis untangle the threads as their story develops. Sometimes in *Il Filocolo* the gods seem to be a traditional or rhetorical motif. For example, the love of Florio and Biancofiore results from Venus's wish to have one as lovely as Biancofiore to serve her. She sends Cupid to instill the love which could have developed quite realistically and naturally as a result of the two youngsters' being reared together and reading together the love poems of Ovid. Similarly, in *Daphnis and Chloe,* the shepherd and goatherd who became foster parents of the children are motivated in a dream of the nymphs and Eros to send their charges to the pasture to tend the herds and flocks, an act which needed no supernatural motivation, for it is exactly the work which country parents could be expected to ask of their children. Although at the conclusion of *Il Filocolo* the lovers turn Christian, the pagan deities preside until then because, says Nicolas

Perella, of Boccaccio's "inordinate ambition to emulate the ancients and the wish to lend epic resonance to . . . [the] tale."[19]

Fortune is another presiding deity in *Il Filocolo*, perceived as a kind of personification, a metaphor or rhetorical device, to give form to the abstract or the unexpected. She accounts for the peripety of the plot, coincidence, and unexpected shifts in circumstance. When a character in *Il Filocolo* says that Fortune is envious or wrathful, he means that he is not having his way with life. Fortune is the force unamenable to man's will, and as a force apparently free from God's will, can take the form of a cruel goddess, a mythical personification of the negative dimension of life. For example, the slaying of Biancofiore's father is attributed to bad fortune. Further, when Florio and Biancofiore are finally united in the tower, Fortune "plots" another misadventure for them, sending the admiral to the tower to find them together. In short, Fortune plays the role of chance, that which is unpredictable by reason and has no particular relationship to order. Similarly, in Greek romance Fortune plays a heavy role. Fortune is said to be responsible for the flight of Clitophon and Leucippe that leads to all their trouble. She is responsible also for any moral choices the characters make. The exposure of the infant Chariclea is a surrender to Fortune, although Providence rescues her. Through Fortune the gods bring Theagenes and Chariclea together at Delphi, drive their ship in a storm to the haunts of the robbers, lead to the captivity of the lovers and their eventual restoration to the king and queen of Ethiopia. In *Daphnis and Chloe* Fortune is less powerful, but the word is used as an equivalent to "estate" or "condition in life." Nevertheless, it is the degree of Fortune that saved the infant Daphnis and caused his older siblings to die so that he would be welcomed back by his parents.[20] In *Chaereas and Callirhoe* when the heroine is carried off in a ship by pirates she says, "Cruel Fortune . . . thou didst make my lover to be my murderer . . . thou didst surrender me to the hands of tomb robbers and didst bring me forth from the tomb to the sea and didst set over me sea-robbers more awful than the very waves."[21] Later we learn that while Callirhoe was speaking Fortune was bringing her to Dionysius who was to be her second husband.

Biancofiore's beauty creates a sense of awe in all who behold her. She seems to the merchants to whom she has been sold to be clothed in celestial splendor. Perella attributes this to the tradition of the *dolce stil novo* which Boccaccio knew so well,[22] but the motif can also be traced to Greek romance. Chariton's Callirhoe is mistaken by the Ionians for the goddess Aphrodite; Anthia and Habrocomes are mistaken for deities when they first arrive at Rhodes. When Chariclea is first seen by the pirates she tends Theagenes's wounds after the shipwreck, and the pirates ask how a deity could kiss a corpse with such passion. It is Biancofiore's beauty, not her virtue, which makes her worthy of release from the tower. This placing of high value on physical beauty also has ancient precedent. When Callirhoe is sold as a slave her master refuses to treat her as one because of her beauty. When Anthia is about to be slain by order of her wicked captor, she cries, "Alas, everywhere that fatal beauty proves a snare. . . . Because of that beauty Habrocomes has died in Tyre, and I die here."[23] The servant stays his hand because he reflected that he would be perpetrating a crime to kill one so fair as Anthia.

Il Filocolo is frequently censured for its excessive rhetoric; its digressive, episodic character; its excursions into mythology and theology; and its long descriptive passages. Artistically the criticism is just; gener-

ically it may be some evidence that in *Il Filocolo*
Boccaccio was consciously writing Greek romance, although the story materials were no doubt traditionally
derived. The Hellenistic romances abound in descriptive
passages of works of art, geography, cities, storms, and
other natural phenomena. Achilles Tatius and Longus
both open their novels with formal and extended descriptions of paintings. The *Aethiopica* includes descriptions of floods and wind conditions of the Nile, details
of home and family life of the Delta nomads and the
troglodytes of Ethiopia. The narrative of *Clitophon and
Leucippe* is often interrupted by descriptions of cities,
geographical peculiarities, and accounts of myths. Even
the theological discourse of the monk Ilario who con-
verts Florio to Christianity has an earlier counterpart in
the discourse and philosophical teachings of the gymnosophists of the *Aethiopica*.

One of Boccaccio's achievements in *Il Filocolo* has
been to give the ancient legend an artistic and literary
dignity that it lacked in the oral and written sources,
bringing to it allusions and echoes of the Old and New
Testaments, Vergil, Ovid, Dante, the Medieval romances,
and the *dolce stil novo* poets. That the original Greek
romances had such pretensions is no doubt true, but the
results smacked more of Alexandrine pedantry than of
art, albeit Perella thinks that Boccaccio failed "to
achieve an artistic harmony or unity of parts."[24] Essentially, *Il Filocolo* lifts and ennobles the Greek romance
tradition, if only in the treatment of the theme of natural or instinctive love and the persistence of such love
against all obstacles erected by an unfriendly universe
or a convention-bound social system. Important to the
theme is the idea that the lady's beauty creates good,
has a refining effect, and elevates to virtue. Greek romance treats the instinctive love of young people for
each other, but seldom lifts it from a physical level. In

Il Filocolo love includes the joy of sensual pleasure, but combines it with touching affection, capacity for self-sacrifice, and all-consuming passion. The result is spiritual achievement and a lifting to virtue, not the mere conventional physical chastity that the lovers usually preserve for each other in Greek romance.

Like *Il Filocolo*, Boccaccio's *Decameron*[25] (1353) includes many Greek romance materials, but here more remotely, less consistently, derived less obviously from the original materials than those of *Il Filocolo*.[26] For example, in "Andreuccio da Perugia" (II, 5) a young man experiences a series of misadventures that end in the macabre. He is tricked by looters into being locked in a tomb, and in terror falls upon a newly buried corpse, weeps, and faints. A second set of tomb robbers liberates him. This smacks strongly of the horrors of the *Babylonica*, the *Ephesiaca*, or *Chaereas and Callirhoe*, any one of which could have furnished the live burial motif. In the latter two, both victims of live burial are rescued by grave robbers, as is Andreuccio.[27]

"Madonna Beritola" (II, 6) seems to be almost pure Greek romance in its separation plot as well as in some of its incidents: A sudden reversal of political fortune causes a gentleman to be imprisoned and his young wife to flee with her child. During her travels she gives birth to an infant, takes a sea journey, and after pirates capture the ship and crew and steal her children, finds herself marooned alone on a desert island. To console herself, the lady suckles a pair of newborn kids. In time she is rescued and treated kindly as an upper servant. After many years she is reunited with her children, who had been sold as servants, and with her husband whom she had thought dead. At the conclusion of the story the children are happily married and the family returns to its former estate.

This separation plot is reminiscent of *Apollonius of*

Tyre (an infant is lost during a sea journey), and the pastoral interlude of the bereft mother's suckling the kids is Longus in reverse (a sheep and a goat nurse the infants Daphnis and Chloe when they are abandoned). The separation, recognition, reunion, and highly desirable marriages of the children are typical of Greek romance. Any one of them could have suggested the conventional pattern.[28]

"The Sultan of Babylon" (II, 7) features a shipwrecked beauty, the daughter of a king, anything but a Greek romance heroine in her willingness to couple— whether to save her life or for pleasure—with those who desire her. After a series of lively nights and harrowing adventures (sea voyages, shipwreck, seduction, murders, kidnapping, a recognition scene, deception—all such vicissitudes being attributed to Fate as in the Greek novel), she is finally returned to her father who had believed her dead. She tells him a tale strangely like the adventure of the wife in *Apollonius of Tyre:* After being shipwrecked Princess Alatiel was rescued by strangers and given refuge in a Christian convent (the wife of Apollonius finds refuge in a temple of the chaste Diana), until she could be returned safely to her father. The sultan believes the story and thinks she has preserved her virtue through her long separation from the court. So believing, he marries her to the king.

Except for her lack of chastity, the Princess Alatiel is a typical Greek romance heroine in her beauty, her adventures, her ready wit and willingness to practice deception in order to save herself. Any of the romances, especially the *Ephesiaca,* but excepting *Daphnis and Chloe,* could have furnished the materials for the story. The interlude in which the princess is courted by her first rescuer—before she has lost her maidenhood and was still unwilling—is similar to the episode in *Chaereas and Callirhoe* in which the heroine is courted honorably by a man to whom she has been sold as a slave.[29]

"Bernabo da Genoa" (II, 9), long recognized as a source of the wager plot in *Cymbeline,* is another separation romance. The wager plot and its complications are not of the Greek romances, but the wanderings of the misused lady in masculine disguise to preserve her chastity, her sea voyage, her service with the great, the general belief that she is dead, the attack upon her instigated by a mistaken husband are all conventional patterns in the Hellenistic novel. The attack is also interesting as a cultural transformation. Chaereas, Apollonius, and Theagenes each strikes or kicks his lady (Apollonius strikes his daughter). Bernabo simply orders a servant to kill the wife. That is, the culture of the Renaissance placed the destructive blow at secondhand, hardly an advance in civilization, since the order of death would indicate some reflection, and the blow of the early Greek "heroes" was always the result of a spontaneous, hot-tempered reaction to circumstantial evidence. In each case the "hero" acts in anger for reasons that later prove to be mistaken.[30]

In "King Guglielmo . . . [and] Gerbino" (IV, 4) the grandson of the King of Sicily is desired by the daughter of the King of Tunis, although she has never seen him, on the basis of his reputation for beauty, prowess, and courtesy. He returns the love for the same reasons. The heroine, nevertheless, is married by her father to the King of Granada. The lover turns pirate and attacks the ship carrying the lady to her new home. When he seems to be winning, the Saracens cut the lady's veins and throw her overboard. The lover recovers the body, weeps, buries it. He returns home in sorrow and is decapitated in front of his grandfather for his act of piracy.

This tragic story contains the conventional separation plot (modified by the fact that the lovers had never met) as well as the typical sea journey and pirate raid (also modified by the hero's role as a pirate). In *Clito-*

phon and Leucippe a minor character, Callisthenes, falls in love with a girl on the basis of a good report of her. He turns pirate when her father refuses his offer. In the same novel the hero on shipboard sees the heroine on another ship beheaded by her captors. Her torso is cast into the sea. Clitophon recovers the body and treats it as Gerbino did, only to learn later that the decapitation was a trick and that Leucippe still lived. In the Boccaccio story the heroine's death is genuine and the hero beheaded. This would seem to be an example of Greek romance materials, perhaps remotely or traditionally derived: the stock plot, the stock incidents, but both modified to new directions and minus the happy ending.[31]

"Cimone" (V, 1) has many Greek romance elements, but the typical separation is not of lovers, but of a "lover" and the woman whom he desires. Sea journey, sea battle, sudden shifts of fortune, storm, imprisonment, kidnapping, and the final happy union of the couple make up the plot which is compounded of materials that could have been derived from almost any of the Greek romances except *Daphnis and Chloe*. The central idea is the motif of the hero's being transformed by love: Before he meets Efigenia, Cimone is a rough, brutish fellow. Love refines him in manners as well as in spirit. This is similar to the subplot of Callisthenes and Calligone in Books II and VIII of Achilles Tatius in which the abduction of a lady leads to the transformation of the pirate who kidnapped her.[32]

"Gostanza . . . [and] Martuccio Gomito" (V, 2) is a separation romance in which each lover believes the other dead. The hero joins a pirate gang and the heroine attempts suicide, takes a sea journey, and is washed up on a friendly shore where she is given kind treatment and shelter which preserves both her life and her chastity—all very much in the manner of the adventures of the wife in *Apollonius of Tyre*. Eventually there is recognition and reunion. One incident of the plot is the imprisoned hero's assisting his captor against an enemy. This motif appears in the *Babylonica* as well as in "Huon of Bordeaux."[33]

"Pietro Boccamozza" (V, 3) is another separation romance: Lovers flee parents who object to their union. They are separated by a robber band and meet with other misadventures before they are happily married.[34]

"Gisippus . . . [and] Titus" (X, 8) is believed by Wolff to be a retelling of a lost Greek romance which probably came to Boccaccio from the Old French "Athis et Prophilias."[35] When he sees the heroine, the hero falls in love at first sight. His sufferings are similar to those of Habrocomes in the *Ephesiaca* and Theagenes in the *Aethiopica*, both of whom fall in love at first sight and find similar ways to express it. Emphasis is placed on chaste love. Mistaken identity helps to win the lady. The separation theme is modified: Two friends, Titus and Gisippus, are separated, and the minor hero, Gisippus, meets with miserable conditions that lead to his dressing as a beggar (as does Chariclea in the *Aethiopica*), to murders, and imprisonment. Like Rhodanes of the *Babylonica*, Habrocomes, and Chaereas, Gisippus is condemned to crucifixion, but is saved in time as are the earlier heroes. No special emphasis is placed on sea journey in this tale, yet both heroes and heroine travel from Athens to Rome, suggesting that Boccaccio's tale may be a contracted form of an original which was a typical Greek romance.

This story has been one of the most popular in the *Decameron*. It was translated by Matteo Bandello (*Titi Romani Egesippiq. Atheniensis, amicorum historia, etc.*, 1509) and retold by Sir Thomas Elyot in the *Boke Named the Governour* (chapter xii, 1531). Edward Lewicke paraphrased it in English (*History of Titus and*

Gisippus, 1562), and Oliver Goldsmith inserted it in a miscellany as "The Story of Alcander and Septimus" (*Bee*, October 6, 1759). It became the subject of an old French play by Alexandre Hardy (*Gésippe, ou Les Deux Amis*, 1624–1628).[36] Further, there is some evidence that it is a source of Lyly's *Euphues*.[37] Thus, if Greek literature is behind the tale, it has achieved important places in Italian, French, and English literature as well,[38] demonstrating clearly the pervasive influence the Hellenistic romances have exercised on the history of Western fiction.[39]

If in *Il Filocolo* Boccaccio demonstrated that the old Greek separation plot and its hackneyed motifs could be used in the services of the courtly-chivalric mode for such a theme as love ennobling to virtue and as a vehicle for artistic display of the highest in the literary tradition, in the *Decameron* he often reversed the process and used the same narrative motifs against a background that is frequently bourgeois or less, and in stories which sometimes have no purpose more serious than the very good one of entertaining the reader and teaching the morality of nature. In *The Decameron* Boccaccio lifted from Greek romance materials the Hellenistic requirement that they pretend to high purpose and aspire to high levels of literary or heroic preciosity. He demonstrated that such fiction could exist even as comedy or as farce, and in the service of joyous natural love, freely given rather than prudently withheld.[40] Much of *The Decameron* derives from sources other than Greek romance, and doubtless many of the romance elements in the collection are ubiquitous in fiction and in folklore, but the great popularity of *The Decameron*, as demonstrated by its publication record, and its frequent use of materials related to or derived from Greek romance, undoubtedly called attention to the Greek romances themselves, perhaps furthering the cause of their early publication and demonstrating to other writers various ways to employ them in literature.

CERVANTES: CONTEMPORARIES, PERSILES Y SIGISMUNDA AND THE NOVELAS EXEMPLARES

Much of the romantic adventure fiction of the sixteenth and seventeenth century in Spain, which had evolved through the older chivalric cycles, is a kind of showcase for the display of Greek romance motifs in Renaissance letters. Only six years after Ludovico Dolce's Italian translation of Books V through VIII of *Clitophon and Leucippe* (1546), Alfonso Nuñez de Reinso published in Spanish *Clareo y Florisea* (Venecia, 1552),[41] the Dolce material from Achilles Tatius, somewhat distorted, with added introductory matter and twenty more chapters of adventure, including a descent into Hell after the manner of Book VI of the *Aeneid*. *Apollonius of Tyre* had been known in Spanish since the thirteenth-century "Libro de Apolonio"[42] and appeared in the *Patrañuelo* of Juan de Timoneda by 1576. Longus was apparently unknown in Spanish throughout the period, but Heliodorus was known in two translations, the first published in 1554, *Historia Ethiopica . . . por un segreto amigo de su patria*, etc., and reissued in 1563, 1581, and 1615. The second by Ferñada de Mena, *La historia de los leales amantes*, etc., published in 1587, was reissued in 1614, 1615, and 1616.[43]

According to Jess Gerding, the influence of the Greek novels can be noted as the sentimentality of such works as Juan Rodrígues de la Cámara's *Siervo libre de amor* (*c*. 1430) and Diego de San Pedro's *Cárcel de amor* (1450) begins to combine with Heliodoran type adventure.[44] Diego de San Pedro even tried to give the impression that his novels had Greek originals.[45] The pattern can be traced in Juan de Segur's *Lucindaro y Medusina*

(1548), wherein allegory is coupled with two ill-fated lovers who experience the usual hectic misfortunes—even a voyage to an underseas kingdom—which readers of Hellenistic novels expect.

Almost all the Greek romance conventions appear in Lope de Vega's *El peregrino en su patria* (1604).[46] Ruth Horne classifies it as a late Renaissance imitation of the Greco-Byzantine adventure romance and thinks it derives from Heliodorus in plot and structure.[47] Like the *Aethiopica*, the romance opens *in medias res* with a pair of lovers suddenly separated, the victims of shipwreck. Similarly, the pasts of lovers are not made clear before Books III and IV. The characterizations follow the model of quick-witted strength in the heroine that is Chariclea, and the somewhat vapid, ready-to-weep hero that is Theagenes.

De Vega's charming play *La dama boba* (1613) includes a young woman who delights in novels and poems, and fancies herself an intellectual. She prefers the romance of "Eliodoro, griego poeta divino" above all others. The *Aethiopica* is extolled as: ". . . una historia amorosa,/ digna de aplauso y teatro./ Hay dos prosas diferentes:/ poética y historial;/ la historia lisa y leal,/ cuente verdades patentes,/ . . . la poética es hermosa."[48] When her father gives an account of her favorite books, those which have occasioned the infirmity of female intellectualism, the *Aethiopica* has first place with the " 'Rimas' de Lope de Vega, 'Galatea' de Cervantes, el Camoes de Lisboa," trailing behind.[49]

De Vega's *Novelas a la señora Marcía Leonarda* (1621) reveal the Greek romance stereotypes and actually mention "Eliodoro" and "Leucipe y el enamorado Clitofonte" as the source of the "tantos accidentes, tantos amores y peligros" in "Las Fortunas de Diana."[50]

Doubtless some of the Greek romance material that appeared in Renaissance Spain was derived indirectly, as was the Boccaccio material, from other literary and even verbal sources. Some of course was probably due to their actual publication and general accessibility to a willing audience conditioned to an enjoyment of their endless peripeties and romantic excesses by similar earlier favorites, the chivalric cycles.[51] The popularity that would make possible Lope's casual references in works written primarily for entertainment was reinforced further in Spain by the sixteenth-century preoccupation with rediscovering the classics. Alonso López Pinciano, an influential critic of the age, in *Philosophia Antigua Poética* (Madrid, 1595) actually classified Heliodorus and Achilles Tatius with the *Iliad* and the *Aeneid*, and saw them as the link between the classical epic and the chivalric romance.[52] Such double endorsement, by the intellectual as well as by the uncritical audience,[53] does much to explain Cervantes's haste to advertise in the prologue of the *Novelas exemplares*, which appeared in 1613, the same year as *La dama boba*, that his forthcoming romance *Persiles y Sigismunda*[54] was to be *"libro que se atreve a competir con Eliodoro."*[55]

Scholars have long recognized the importance of the *Aethiopica* in the genesis of the *Persiles*,[56] and even without Cervantes's own reference to Heliodorus the initiated reader of the romances senses the relationship almost at once, for it is markedly present in the opening episodes, and before long one is aware of structural similarity as well as coincidence in details. Briefly, Cervantes's romance (unavailable in English since the translation of 1854) opens with the hero Periandro in great danger as a captive of pirates who are suddenly shipwrecked. Periandro is rescued by Prince Arnaldo of Denmark, who had been cruising the North Sea in search of Auristela, who Periandro says is his sister. Disguised as a maiden, Periandro is sold to barbarians who inhabit an island where Auristela is thought to be.

The barbarian Bradimiro at once falls in love with the disguised hero.

Auristela, disguised as a man, is on the same island with her nurse. When the time comes to settle the fate of the captives, a battle ending in general slaughter erupts among the barbarians. The island is set ablaze, but the hero and the heroine are saved by a Spaniard who conducts them to a cave. They pass the night by hearing his life story. Eventually all set out, ostensibly for Rome, for Auristela has vowed a pilgrimage to the holy city. During the course of their travels Periandro and Auristela experience all the usual Greek romance adventures, including an interlude at the court of the island king, Polycarpo, where a complicated love intrigue occurs. The hero, heroine, and a variety of companions whom they have met along the way, finally move out of the mysterious north and travel through Portugal, Spain, France, and Italy. In Rome it is finally revealed that Periandro and Auristela are really Prince Persiles of Iceland and Princess Sigismunda of Friesland, and not brother and sister at all. Auristela-Sigismunda's vow fulfilled, they are married and return home.

Throughout the course of their travels the young couple frequently meet strangers who interrupt the movement of the narrative with long accounts of their lives. As the strangers come and go, as perils and disasters strike and strike again, the young couple persist in complete and chaste fidelity to each other and to the fulfillment of the vow to reach the holy city.

Similarly, the *Aethiopica* plunges the reader suddenly into harrowing adventures: On the banks of the Nile a band of robbers find a shipwrecked youth and a maiden of unmatched beauty. As the robbers are about to claim them, a rival band attacks and the couple are taken to an island retreat where they are protected in a cave by a young Greek, Cnemon, who tells them his life history as a means of passing the tedium of the night. The hero says that he and the lady are brother and sister, Theagenes and Chariclea. Suddenly the first robber band returns and abducts Chariclea. Theagenes and his new friend set out in search of her. The young couple, frequently separated, travel over North Africa, meeting with the usual Greek romance adventures and spending some time at the court of Arsace, wife of the satrap, where a complicated love intrigue develops. In time the couple reach Ethiopia and it is revealed that Chariclea is the long-lost princess and heiress to the throne. She and Theagenes are then married.

During the course of the wanderings they have experienced all the anticipated adventures of the genre. From time to time during the period of their mishaps, they meet with strangers who interrupt the narrative with tales of important events and life histories. A significant structural difference between the *Aethiopica* and the *Persiles*, however, is that the tales which interrupt the Heliodorus narrative, although they might at first reading seem to be mere digressions, do prove relevant long before the conclusion of the romance by making clear the past of the lovers and by revealing the reason for their journey to Ethiopia. In this way Heliodorus is a better craftsman than Cervantes, who makes no attempt to relate the interpolated episodes, except to proclaim them stories told by those who meet the young couple during their adventures.[57]

The similarity between the dramatically conceived openings *in medias res* and the narrative structures—travel tales interrupted by episodes which are vast recitals of past events in the lives of the fellow travelers—is obvious at once. So also is the vast range of the geography: in the *Aethiopica*, from Greece to Ethiopia, the far south of the known world; and in *Persiles*, from the unexplored reaches of the North Sea to Spain and Italy.

In both romances the geographically exotic areas have a far-away-and-long-ago quality. The North Sea of Cervantes is filled with mysterious islands peopled by anthropaphagi, pagans, enchantresses. The Ethiopia of Heliodorus contains side by side within its borders naked philosophers of a Neo-Pythagorean persuasion and a high-minded ambivalently civilized king who is not only friendly toward the humane philosophers, but is priest to a sun and moon cult which demands human sacrifice. Withal, both novelists become fairly realistic when their characters are on home territory. The latter half of *Persiles*, an account of travel adventures through Spain, France, and Italy, contains passages as accurate and as true to life as those which detail the roads and villages of *Don Quixote*, although the scenes in France and Italy are never as convincing as those which deal with Spain. Similarly, the familiar parts of Greece and the Nile Delta of the *Aethiopica* contain passages of homely realism on flood conditions, the lives of the Delta nomads, and pirates of the marshes.[58] Both heroines are crown princesses of remote regions, which facts, coupled with the misty geography, help make possible the air of destiny which envelops the central characters and gives to the romances a flavor of pseudohistory so typical of the Greek novels as a genre.

Further study of the two romances shows that many details are duplicated, although almost always with minor differences.[59] In both romances the lovers are so ravishingly beautiful that they are thought to be divinities. They are also completely chaste and completely faithful to each other, regardless of difficulties or of separation. Chariclea and Auristela-Sigismunda both vow chastity until they achieve their goals, and although both travel for many months unchaperoned and in the company of their lovers, they keep their vows and are never tempted by their beloveds to break them. Both pairs of lovers travel as brother and sister, at times in disguise. Each heroine is forced to defend her virtue by pretending to accept another lover, but each puts off an unwelcome marriage by asking for time to fulfill a religious vow. Further, both heroines weep over the heroes when they believe the conditions of their beloveds are hopeless, and both experience physical illness from love, as do both heroes.

Their characterizations are also similar in the note of duplicity in each couple. In spite of the aura of absolute perfection thrown over them, Theagenes and Chariclea, Persiles and Sigismunda, invariably lie themselves out of any situation, often before they have an opportunity to know whether a lie might do damage or be useful in saving their skins.[60] As to social status, both couples have much in common. Although the royal parentage of Periandro and Auristela is shrouded in mystery until the conclusion of the novel, the air about them, their abilities and bearing, tell any initiated reader of their high births. No one is surprised to learn at the conclusion of the novel that Periandro is really a prince and that Auristela is a princess. The identity of Chariclea as the Crown Princess of Ethiopia is made mysterious for a large part of the *Aethiopica*, but is revealed long before the end of the romance. Theagenes's descent from Achilles is made clear early to the reader.

As Chariclea travels with the "Pantarbe," a precious jewel given to her by her mother, Auristela receives a cross of diamonds and pearls from her nurse. Theagenes performs a feat of great strength in subduing a bull at a public ceremony. In a similar situation, Periandro-Persiles overpowers a savage horse. The barbarized Spaniard Antoino of *Persiles* corresponds to the barbarized Greek Cnemon in the *Aethiopica*. Both are fugitives as a result of crimes of violence. Both conduct the heroes and heroines to safety in caves and there relate to them their life histories. Both set out with the young couples and become party to their further adventures. Hipolita of *Persiles*, like Arsace in the *Aethiopica*, is degraded by unrequited love for the hero. Both women fume at the futility of their efforts to seduce the heroes; both try every means to gratify their voluptuous passions. Hipolita asks a sorceress to break Auristela's health; Arsace tries to poison Chariclea through the agency of an old crone.

In the *Aethiopica* dreams, portents, revelations, love potions, and witchcraft performed by an old hag to raise the dead, increase the suspense and excitement. In *Persiles* we read of revelations through dreams and portents. Numerous references to lycanthropy occur, and the old witch Cenotia attempts to secure Auristela for King Polycarpo as Cybele the procuress of the *Aethiopica* tries to secure Theagenes for Arsace, the powerful wife of the satrap.

In both romances blind chance seems to be back of the misfortunes. In Heliodorus it accords with the pagan idea of "Fortuna" as a malignant force creating hardship and adversity. Cervantes as a Catholic writer trusted ultimately in "Providence" to provide a happy issue out of all the afflictions which beset the wanderers, but he imitates also a pagan concept of fortune behind the trials which test the lovers. Both romances philosophize frequently: Heliodorus preaches gymnosophism; Cervantes, Christianity. In fact the Christian coloring of *Persiles* is so strong that it can be interpreted as an effort to do for romantic fiction what Tasso had done for the epic: that is, to write a Christian novel after the model of the ancients as Tasso had written a Christian epic in *Gerusalemne liberata*. The fact that *Persiles* is so positively Christian in coloring and philosophy clearly distinguishes it from Reinso's adaptation of Achilles Tatius and Lope de Vega's *El peregrino*. The wanderings of the characters from north to south move them from the pagan north to Christian Rome and allegorically from paganism to the middle point of the world in the relation of their souls to God.[61]

Rudolph Schevill, who has written of the relationship between *Persiles* and the *Aethiopica,* warns however that Cervantes's work had more than one source, and that Vergil's *Aeneid* may have played a more influential role even than the Greek novel.[62] The romances of chivalry (which probably descended themselves from the Greek romances through the Byzantine imitations), contemporary rogue stories, histories of voyages and discoveries also helped to form Cervantes's artistic methods in *Persiles.*[63] As to the *Aeneid,* Schevill finds Books IV and V major influences, especially in the love intrigue which occurs at the court of King Polycarpo, an affair that seems to be somewhat similar to the love of Aeneas and Dido, although in "skeletal" form: Periandro reaches the court of King Polycarpo in time to participate in games. The Princess Sinforosa falls in love with the stranger. Soon Auristela, who has been separated from the hero, is shipwrecked on the shore of Polycarpo's country. The king—who like Queen Dido has been widowed—falls in love with her. Except that the sexes are reversed, this is the Dido-Aeneas story. Sinforosa confesses her love for Periandro to his "sister" Auristela, as Dido confessed her love to her sister Anna. For a while Auristela is very ill because of lovesickness and the machinations of the Jewish woman Judith. Auristela is visited in her illness by Periandro and reassured. Letters change hands. Periandro is asked to tell the history of his wanderings. Sinforosa pays acute attention to every word. In order to preserve themselves inviolate for each other, after a clouded entanglement of intrigue and counterintrigue, we find the lovers planning an escape and Polycarpo—like Dido—

setting fire to the palace. In the midst of the uproar, Sinforosa and Polycarpo climb a tower and see the strangers escape.[64]

Schevill's opinion that the Polycarpo interlude has strong Vergilian roots (although it completely lacks the Vergilian emotional intensity) has much to substantiate it. At the same time the episode embodies interesting analogies with *Apollonius of Tyre:* Prince Apollonius is washed up on a foreign shore after a storm wrecks his ship. He finds his way to the city where he attracts the attention of the king by his skill at playing ball. Invited to dinner at the court, Apollonius charms the king's daughter with his skill on the lyre. She falls ill with love for him. During her illness Apollonius visits her. Letters change hands and rival suitors for the princess must be dealt with before the pair are married.

Cervantes could hardly have escaped knowing either Vergil or the Apollonius romance. Aside from the fact that *Apollonius of Tyre* was available in Spanish by 1576 and in Italian, which he seems to have read with ease,[65] as early as 1486, there is some evidence that the romance was more or less in the general literary domain. Besides the thirteenth-century "Libro de Apolonio," there exists a twelfth-century manuscript (No. 9783) in the Bibliotheca Nacional containing the Latin *Historia Apollonii.* Book IV of Alfonso el Sabio's *Grande e General Estoria* (*c.* 1270) mentions the Apollonius story; and in the fourteenth-century Gower's *Confessio Amantis*, of which Book VIII is the Apollonius romance, was translated into Portuguese by Roberto Paym, and later into Spanish prose by Juan de Cuenca. Ballads published in 1524 and 1566 name "Apollonio." A fifteenth-century prose version *Historia de los Siete Sabios y del rey Apolonio*[66] is no longer extant.

The fact is that strong similarity exists between *Apollonius of Tyre* and the story of Dido and Aeneas in

Vergil. The ancient romance may well have been dependent on Vergil for the episode, but to try to untangle the relationship between the epic and the romance, or the roots of the Cervantes episode, seems vain.

Some reflections of the Apollonius tradition seems to appear in the *Novelas exemplares:*[67] Preciosa of "La gitanilla" is the lost child of a nobleman, identified finally by some trinkets and a birthmark, as well as by innate superiority in intelligence, beauty, and behavior, all of which bespoke her good birth in spite of her rearing by gypsies. In this she resembles Chariclea of the *Aethiopica* (identified by trinkets and a birthmark and carrying always, in spite of a simple rearing, an aura of high ancestry) and Tharsia, the lost daughter of Prince Apollonius. Both Preciosa and Tharsia remain triumphantly high bred, moral, and chaste, despite having to earn their livings by singing and dancing. Both perform before their fathers, are at last recognized, and finally honorably married.[68]

The theme is repeated with variations in "La ilustre fregona" and in "La Señora Cornelia." In "La española inglesa" the motif is repeated within a separation romance: The kidnapped child of a Spanish nobleman, reared gently because of her beauty and virtue, is loved by the son of her captor. The love sickness syndrome, separation by sea journey, a rival lover, a poison attack on the heroine, recognition and reunion of the heroine with her parents, identification by birthmark, and the apparent death of the hero all keep it firmly in the Greek romance tradition.

In "Las dos doncellas" two girls dress like boys and travel to seek their lovers. "El amante liberal" is a brief, but complete, Greek romance: Leonisa, a maiden of incomparable beauty, is loved by Ricardo, although she does not at first return his love. An incursion of Turks leads to their captivity as slaves, separation, sea journey, and shipwreck. During the course of their adventures the heroine triumphantly preserves her honor intact, although all who see her beauty desire to reap it. For a time she believes the hero dead—again the traditional motif in reverse. United in captivity, the couple are involved in a complicated love intrigue.[69] Ricardo is hotly desired by Halima, the wife of the "cadi" who is to deliver Leonisa to the "Grand Turk." The hero puts off her advances for a time by claiming a course of devotion for the recovery of his freedom—again a reversal of the motif in which the Greek romance heroine gains time from an unwelcome suitor with the excuse of a religious vow. It is planned that during a sea journey— significantly in the environs of Alexandria—Leonisa will be declared suddenly dead at sea, and the cadi's wife Halima will be cast overboard in her stead. The cadi will, thus, be free of his wife and will also be free to enjoy the heroine himself rather than turn her over to the harem of the Grand Turk. The plans are foiled by an attack of pirates, but after a nobly conducted battle, Ricardo succeeds in subduing the enemy and seizing the ship. The couple return home in triumph and are married with the general approval of all.[70]

The passion of Halima for Ricardo has counterparts in the passion of Manto for Habrocomes in the *Ephesiaca*, of Arsace for Theagenes in the *Aethiopica*, of Melitte for Clitophon in Achilles Tatius's work, and—much older—of Potiphar's wife for Joseph. The plot to bury at sea a substitute for the heroine so that the heroine—apparently dead—can be ravished without pursuit, is similar to an incident in *Clitophon and Leucippe:* Clitophon is kept from pursuing Leucippe's abductors when a young woman dressed in Leucippe's clothes is beheaded within the sight of the hero and the body cast into the sea. The romance was known in Spanish by 1617, four years after the publication of *Novelas exemplares*, but available in complete form in Italian as early as 1550. By 1613 the Italian translation had been published at least ten times.

It is interesting to realize that two giants of Renaissance fiction, Boccaccio and Cervantes, should both choose to imitate Greek novels in their assays at long romantic narrative, *Il Filocolo* and *Persiles y Sigismunda*,[71] and that there should be further parallel in their choice of materials for some of their more widely read novellas. Nine tales from the *Decameron* embody Greek romance motifs, six of the twelve *Novelas exemplares*. The aura of Greek romance in "La gitanilla," "La ilustre fregona," "La Señora Cornelia," and "Las dos doncellas" may mean no more specific a relationship with the tradition than the general interest in such material reflected by their frequent Renaissance publication, although "La gitanilla" and "La ilustre fregona" do bring to the old materials a new background of realistic detail. In "El amante liberal"—like "Madonna Beritola" of the *Decameron*—the connection seems to be more conscious or direct. Coupled with the traditional separation plot are the same high moral intention, arbitrary characterizations, rhetoric, soliloquy, and harangue that characterize the Greek romance.

The direct relationship of *Persiles y Sigismunda* to Greek romance, however, is attested to by Cervantes himself, when in speaking of his novel he said that it dared to "compete" with Heliodorus. Such implies that he meant the *Persiles* to be popular as the *Aethiopica* was then popular; that he meant it to entertain; and that he meant it to be a prose-poem, a chivalric-heroic epic in prose, as was the *Aethiopica*. It implied accordance with the then-current critical opinions of Pinciano. That *Persiles y Sigismunda* is tedious, its few modern readers agree. The dullness results from wooden characters, too much incident, and the lack of bearing of the episodes on the narrative. Although *Don Quixote* towers above the *Aethiopica*, there is no doubt that the *Aethiopica* is better reading than *Persiles y Sigismunda*, but coming as it did at the beginning of the era of heroic romance, it played an important role in literary history by showing the way to Gomberville, la Calprenède, and Mille. de Scudéry.[72] Difficult as it may be to read with pleasure today, within two years of its publication in 1617 the *Persiles* had been translated into French and into English, and within twelve more years there had been ten editions.[73]

Chapter Three

Shakespeare & the Derived Tradition

THE ELIZABETHAN BACKGROUND

Like Boccaccio and Cervantes, Shakespeare also knew and utilized the materials of Greek romance. It is, however, especially difficult to assess how much he knew at firsthand and how much came to him through secondary or even more remote sources, for the strong continuing Greek romance tradition in Medieval and Renaissance letters was English as well as Continental. By 1572 the influence of these romances seems to have reached the London stage: a play (no longer extant) entitled *Theagines and Chariclea* was performed for the Christmas celebration at the Court of Elizabeth I. This has been identified as the same play as the lost *Queen of Etheiopia*, acted by Lord Howard's men at Bristol in September 1578.[1] One suspects that Heliodorus is the source, for Sanford's (1567) and Underdowne's (1558–1569) translations of the *Aethiopica* were in circulation in time to inspire the composition.[2] In the plays *Common Conditions* (*c.* 1576) and *Clyomon and Cla-*

mydes (1599) the general structural scheme as well as the conventional separation plot motifs of Greek romance are present.[3]

Probably the first Elizabethan work of fiction to bear clear and extended marks of the Hellenistic novel was Barnaby Riche's collection of tales, *Farewell to Military Profession* (1581).[4] Besides the Greek romance apparatus of "Apolonius and Silla," the story of "Sappho, Duke of Mantona" probably drew some of its wording as well as its narrative materials (a separation plot and a final trial scene modeled on the *Aethiopica*) from Underdowne's Heliodorus.[5] In 1584 William Warner published *Albion's England: Pan and His Syrinx*,[6] a suite of stories in the style of the *Aethiopica*, which it resembles in framework, structure, locale, moral atmosphere, and in the opening scenes of foreboding gloom. The story of "Argentile and Curran" is a variant of the stock pastoral plot. In John Dickenson's *Arisbas* (London, 1594) lovers flee parental opposition. Pretending in Greek romance fashion to be brother and sister, they take a sea voyage, experience kidnapping, lust, shipwreck, and pirates before they are united at a religious ceremony.[7]

Although the publication of Sidney's *Arcadia* was delayed until 1590,[8] its composition probably took place between 1578 and 1580. Probably it circulated among the London literati during the decade of the 1580s.[9] Its actual publication was marked by such decided success that six editions had appeared by 1605, and during the course of the seventeenth century there were ten more editions, two French translations, and one each in German and Dutch. Such a record has great significance in tracing the literary afterlife of Greek romance, for Heliodoran influence strongly marks the work. This influence seems to have been noticed first by Thomas Wharton in *The History of English Poetry* (London, 1774–1781), where in a discussion of Underdowne's Eng-

lish version of Ovid's *Ibis* he said casually that Heliodorus "seems partly to have suggested Sir Philip Sidney's
Arcadia."[10] Later scholars have confirmed Wharton's
opinion, but expanded it to include the idea that the
Aethiopica was a structural model for the revised *Arcadia* as well as (along with *Clitophon and Leucippe*) a
source for narrative materials, stock incidents, and
some aspects of the elaborate style.[11] Samuel Wolff's
opinion that Sidney "learned to write Greek romance in
English"[12] has been modified to include pastoral romance under the influence of Sannazaro and Montemayor, and heroic romance according to the dictates of
Minturno.[13] The pastoral elements of the *Arcadia* include,
of course, the stock plot derived from Longus as well as
other pastoral conventions from Longus, Moschus,
Bion, and Vergil. Book VI (1595–1596) of Spenser's *Faerie Queene* also employs the Longus stock plot in more
or less original detail. The entire book is "Arcadian" in
tone, utilizing besides the stock pastoral conventions,
Greek romance motifs which include the separation of
lovers and the mistaken death of the heroine.

Robert Greene made capital of the popularity of Sidney's work even while it circulated informally in manuscript,[14] seizing at once on the idea of turning out Greek
romance in English. We find the first and second tales of
Perimeides (1588) and *Tullies Love* (1589) draw on
Greek romance materials in the *Decameron:* "Madonna
Beritola" (II, 6), "Gostanza . . . [and] Martuccio Gomito" (V, 2), and "Cimone" (V, i).[15] Wolff demonstrates
Greene's primary indebtedness to Achilles Tatius in a
style heavy with antithesis, balance, and conceit, characteristics of *Clitophon and Leucippe*. Greene's concept
of man's subjection to Fortune may also have come
through Achilles Tatius.[16] *Arbasto* (1584) consists of a
"frame tale" about the narrator's shipwreck, and an
inner tale told by Arbasto to the narrator, precisely the

structural framework of *Clitophon and Leucippe.* In both works the narrator of the inner tale is tempest-tossed, reaches Sidon, makes a thank-offering to Astarte, then in sightseeing is moved by a painting to tell a reluctant stranger his tale, the central narrative of the romance.

The pastoral background in which Greene took such delight—*Pandosto* (1588) and *Menaphon* (1589)—and some of the narrative materials are suggestive of Longus. Some of the more important of Greene's borrowings from Greek romance are found in *Menaphon;* for besides the Longus material there is a paradoxical oracle to set off a chain of events, including the exposure of a royal princess, shipwreck of the princess and her husband, quickwitted answers to unwelcome questions (a specialty with Chariclea), disdaining of love before initial sight of the beloved, reference to Fortune, final restoration of a lost princess, imprisonment of lovers together, betrothal with the understanding that an oracle must be fulfilled before marriage, abduction by pirates, and final fulfillment of the oracle. All these motifs can be found in the *Aethiopica.*[17] *Pandosto* borrows heavily from Longus as well as from Heliodorus and Achilles Tatius.[18]

Sometime before 1598 the pseudo-Shakespeare play *Mucedorus,* almost certainly inspired by the *Arcadia,* was written. It is another example of the stock pastoral plot descended from Longus: A prince disguised as a shepherd rescues a princess from the clutches of a bear and later from a wild man. Also descended from Longus is *The Thracian Wonder* (*c.* 1600), attributed variously to John Webster, William Rowley, and Thomas Heywood. This play was drawn directly from Greene's *Menaphon,* and the pastoral background of the novel which Greene seems to have imitated directly from *Daphnis and Chloe* is also present.

The brooding scholar George Chapman was evidently inoculated with the same infection: Thomas Parrott believes that his *Blind Beggar of Alexandria* (composed *c.* 1595) had a source in Greek romance. He takes into account the Greek names of leading characters and Greek place names as well as the adulterous passion of Aegiale for Cleanthes, her false denunciation of him to the king, the magic of the sorceress, all motifs from the *Aethiopica.*[19] The strange story of St. Anne and his dead wife (the grieving husband refuses to bury her body and devotes his life to worship of the corpse) in Chapman's *Monsieur D'Olive* (composed *c.* 1601) can probably be traced ultimately to the episode of Aegialus and Thelixinoe in the *Ephesiaca.*[20]

THE COMEDY OF ERRORS

In view of this welter of suggestion one expects to find elements of the Greek romances in Shakespeare as well, and they are indeed overwhelmingly easy to identify. In several of the early plays motifs from the Hellenistic romances appear, although no strong evidence shows that they derive from direct sources. Almost any of the examples of such use which one would cite could be matched on the London stage or in popular fiction. In the late romantic plays some conscious imitation of the Greek materials seems likely, in part direct, in part derived from the Greek romances as they filtered through contemporary literature which had imitated them. The early *Comedy of Errors* is a clear example of the use of Greek romance traditions already in the general literary domain; at the same time the use of ancient materials for a separation and reconciliation plot foreshadows the use that would be made of the same material in the late plays. To an anglicized Roman comedy based on the *Menaechmi* of Plautus, Shakespeare has added the apparatus of a Hellenistic separation plot, specifically a sequence which more or less parallels *Apollonius of Tyre*, a romance which had been part of English literary history since Anglo-Saxon times,[21] and was well known through John Gower's *Confessio Amantis*,[22] a work which was later to furnish the substance of *Pericles, Prince of Tyre*.

Shakespeare deviates very little from the *Menaechmi* in the main plot of *The Comedy of Errors*, although the idea of a double set of twins is usually traced to the *Amphitruo* (the *Menaechmi* deals with a single set). But the addition of what one might call the Apollonian framework alters the entire tone of the play and effects our view of the farcical scenes. *The Comedy of Errors* opens with a father of twins on trial for his life because he is a Syracusan driven by misfortune to the city of Ephesus. A feud exists between the two cities. At the trial Aegeon recites the story of his tragic past, how during a storm at sea shipwreck and pirates separated him from his wife, one of his twin infant sons, and one of twin infant slaves; and how after eighteen years the son and slave remaining to him set out in search of their missing brothers. Since five years passed without their return, the old Aegeon is seeking them. In spite of moving the Duke to sympathy, Aegeon is condemned to die unless his ransom can be raised by evening. The Plautine material interrupts, but in the last act the tale of Aegeon is picked up again: As the old father is being led to execution, the party stops to investigate confusion outside an abbey where one of the twins has taken refuge. The other twin appears, and the situation is clarified by the abbess, who recognizes her husband and sons. She had been separated by force from the son and the slave which she had protected, and had lived out her life in the chaste seclusion of the abbey. The family reunion is followed by a general pardon and a banquet.[23]

The parallels with *Apollonius of Tyre* are obvious in the storm at sea which separates husband, wife, and infants;[24] the wife's taking refuge in the religious life; the long years of journey by the father; and the final recognition of the husband and children by the wife— all details of the plot of *Apollonius of Tyre* (except that in the Greek romance only one infant, a girl, is lost),[25] and all details which do not appear in the Plautine sources. Further, *Apollonius of Tyre* concludes at Ephesus, where in a dream the father-hero had been directed to go, and where he found his wife in the service of Diana. *The Comedy of Errors* takes place entirely at Ephesus; the *Menaechmi* takes place at Epidamnus, although Shakespeare maintains the link with the Plautine material by having Aegeon say that he and his family had sailed out of "Epidamnum" just before the shipwreck.

Structurally, the addition of the Apollonian material is only a device for resolving the mistaken identity farce of the Roman material. Actually, it is much more important, for it alters the entire tone of the play, giving it a romantic cast, lending weight to a Christian coloring, and altering our view of the farcical scenes. At the opening in Aegeon's speech about his family, their shipwreck, and loss, a tragic note is struck that reverberates throughout the farcical scenes. "Hapless Aegeon, whom the fates have mark'd" (I, i, 140)[26] elicits not only the Duke's sympathy, but ours, and we view the comic action against anxiety for Aegeon on his way to execution.

The hilarious middle scenes include also a troubled awareness of something amiss at Ephesus: witchcraft and sorcery, loss of identity, family disorder, disorder between master and servant. A Christian coloring—albeit not a very deep one—unsuggested by the Plautine sources results from the coupling of the tragic plight of Aegeon and allusions recalling St. Paul's association of

Ephesus in Acts 19 with sorcery and magic, and his exhortations on the marital relationship and relationships between master and servant in the Epistle to the Ephesians (5:22–23 and 6:5–9). The transference of the locale of the play from Epidamnum to Ephesus thus contributes to the Christian coloring through the Pauline allusions.[27] The transference of the wife from priestess of Diana to a holy abbess retains the idea of faith throughout to a deeply tried marriage vow, and helps to develop the Christian associations. Further, the abbess becomes the instrument for upbraiding Adriana's shrewishness and jealousy.

The central themes of *The Comedy of Errors* are restoration and reconciliation and the crisis of identity. These accord well with the romantic Aegeon-Aemilia plot, which appeals to sentiment in showing us Aegeon's wretched loneliness, his pathetic lack of money and friends, his welcoming the thought that at evening he will die, and his final joy when his family is restored and his death sentence is lifted. The identity theme occurs repeatedly in *Apollonius of Tyre*, when Apollonius and his daughter go in disguise through numerous adventures and when the wife assumes a new identity at the temple of Diana. Both reconciliation and concern for personal identity in the Roman material agree well with the Christian tone created by the Pauline allusions, and the somber note set in Act I by Aegeon's sad history is maintained as an undercurrent in the identity crisis, the breakdown of family, personal, and social relationships, and suggestions of sorcery in the farcical plot. The conclusion of it all at the Priory lends a redeeming quality to the Greek romance theme of reunion and reconciliation that was to be more fully developed in the late plays; for although an undertone of tragedy and a Christian coloring are undoubtedly present in *The Comedy of Errors*, they often go unobserved in the rollicking bustle and play of the mistaken identity farce.

There is a kind of logic in Shakespeare's blending the Apollonian material with a farce dealing with the breakdown of marriage and loss of identity. The broken marriage bonds of Aegeon and Aemilia due to outside forces that they cannot control contrast with the broken marriage of Antipholus of Ephesus and Adriana, a breakdown caused by internal forces—temperamental misbehavior on the part of both marriage partners. The projected marriage of Luciana and Antipholus of Syracuse—a Shakespearian addition to the Roman plot—adds to the note of romantic love and provides a decent chaperone for the wife through some of the sexually suggestive scenes of the farce. The conclusion of the Aegeon-Aemilia affair in fulfillment of romantic desire after long separation, the anticipated marital happiness of Antipholus of Syracuse and Luciana, and the temporarily repaired marriage bonds of Antipholus of Ephesus and Adriana give an added perspective to the old play and enrich the plot with undertones of love and restored order.[28] A further logic in the blend rests in traces of romantic ancestry buried in the *Menaechmi*. E. M. W. Tillyard points out that its motif of recognition of lost children, its closeness to the sea, and its allusions to shipwreck and pirates connect it remotely with the Greek novel, which he believes had a common origin with Latin comedy.[29] L. G. Salinger calls it "romance in the Euripidean tradition" which carries on "the tradition of exemplary romance, too."[30]

In 1911 Joseph de Perrot published an essay outlining details of the correspondence between the events which conclude *The Comedy of Errors* and *Clitophon and Leucippe*.[31] Ephesus is the locale in both instances, although the temple of Artemis in the pagan romance becomes an abbey in the Renaissance play. In both works the end occurs just before an execution, which is prevented by unforeseen circumstances. One of the twins in *The Comedy of Errors* finds refuge in an abbey; Leucippe of the romance finds refuge in a temple. The duke presiding over the final act of the play assumes a role somewhat similar to that of the judge who presides over the trial-like conclusion of *Clitophon and Leucippe*. After stories are exchanged and all are saved from condemnation, a banquet is held. The similarity is slight, although these details do not appear in the Plautine sources nor in *Apollonius of Tyre*. *The Comedy of Errors* is usually dated *c.* 1590, with 1594 as the ultimate limit suggested as possible.[32] The first English translation of Achilles Tatius was not published until 1597, although there were versions in Italian by 1544, French by 1545, and Latin by 1552. Thus a bibliographic possibility exists that Achilles Tatius is a source, although a rereading of both texts does not persuade one of any significant relationship.

TWELFTH NIGHT, OR, WHAT YOU WILL

The mistaken identity comedy of Viola and her brother Sebastian is obviously a variation on the mistaken twin theme of the Plautine plays. The shipwreck that accounts for Viola's believing her brother dead and for her assuming the dress of a man reminds us slightly of almost any Greek romance, though it is a common enough motif in literature. It is a simple alternate of the separation and mistaken death plot, in this case arranged to involve brother and sister rather than a pair of lovers. Further, following the pattern established in *The Comedy of Errors*, de Perrot has recognized the "Olivia" sequence as having strong links with the Melitte episode of *Clitophon and Leucippe*.[33] That the links are direct cannot, however, be substantiated. The motifs that de Perrot cites are to be found in Barnaby Riche's story of "Apolonius and Silla," derived from a novella of Cinthio, although the motifs are less clearly developed than by Shakespeare and are not suggested by related dramatic versions of the plot. In both *Twelfth-Night* and *Clitophon and Leucippe* we find hero and heroine confronted with a beautiful, rich, powerful woman, mistress of a great house. In Achilles Tatius, Melitte, who believes her husband dead at sea, marries Clitophon, who believes Leucippe (his beloved as well as his cousin) dead at sea. Melitte's love is sudden and rather foolish in view of Clitophon's relative youth and his blatant declaration that he still loves another. The steward of Melitte's household, Sosthenes, plays a major role in his cruelty to Leucippe, who has just been returned from the sea and disguised as a slave is also a member of Melitte's household. At the conclusion of the episode, Leucippe's identity has been revealed and Melitte's husband has returned to furnish a solution to the difficulties.

In *Twelfth-Night* Olivia's social position parallels Melitte's. She mourns a dead brother rather than a husband, then falls violently and foolishly in love with the youthful Viola disguised as the page boy Cesario. Viola-Cesario gives no more encouragement to Olivia's desires than does Clitophon to Melitte's. The steward Malvolio plays a major comic role in the play, and the restoration of the lost Sebastian—presumed dead at sea—resolves the difficulties at the conclusion.

In the Melitte episode as well as in *Twelfth-Night* the imprisonment motif occurs: Clitophon is jailed in the Greek romance and Leucippe is confined for a while in a little cabin. In the play Malvolio is held. In each work the major heroines appear in disguise: Leucippe as a slave, Viola as a page boy. In both works the great lady is a sympathetic character, but only the secondary heroine. The primary heroines play the roles of servants. Letters further the plots of both works.

As to dates, Burton's English translation of Achilles

Tatius had appeared in 1597, preceded by the Italian, French, and Latin translations. *Twelfth-Night* was probably written between 1599 and 1602, so direct or indirect influence of *Clitophon and Leucippe* is bibliographically possible, but as with the reported link with *The Comedy of Errors,* it is unconvincing as a direct source when both texts are examined.

Examination of early analogues of *Twelfth-Night,* however, does suggest remote ties between the play and Greek romance and may throw some light on the question of a very indirect link with *Clitophon and Leucippe.* The specific variation of the Plautine plot in which a female twin is disguised as a male can be found in the Italian play *Gl'Ingannati* (Venice, 1537), a product of the Academia degli Intronati at Siena;[34] *Les Abusés* (Lyons, 1543) of Charles Etienne,[35] a French translation of *Gl'Ingannati;* another Italian play, *Gl'Inganni* (Florence, 1562) of Nicolo Secchi;[36] *Los Engaños* (Valencia, 1567) of Lope de Rueda,[37] a Spanish version of *Gl'Ingannati;* another Italian play, *Gl'Inganni* (Venice, 1592) of Curzio Gonzaga;[38] and *Laelia,* a Latin version of *Les Abusés,*[39] performed at Queen's College, Cambridge, probably in 1595, but unpublished until 1910. Prose versions are Matteo Bandello's tale of Nicuola, XXXVI of Volume II of the *Novelle* (Lucca, 1554),[40] derived from the Sienese play; a version of Giraldi Cinthio in the *Hecatommithi* (Monte-Regale, 1562);[41] a translation of Bandello by François de Belleforest, story LIX of Volume IV of the *Histoires Tragiques* (Paris, 1570);[42] and Barnaby Riche's story of "Apolonius and Silla" in *Riche's Farewell to Militarie Profession* (London, 1581),[43] which in turn was derived from the Cinthio version. With such an extended and interrelated list of earlier analogues, scholars have found it difficult to rank one above the other as a source. Riche's "Apolonius and Silla," *Gl'Ingannati,* and *Laelia* usually outrank the others, but Sir Arthur Quiller-Couch's conclusion seems the truly valid one: "that the primal source dates back beyond Boccaccio, beyond Plautus . . . and is in fact as old as the hills."[44] In short, it is likely that Shakespeare derived *Twelfth-Night* as much from a literary tradition as from one or two works, and further it is possible that the tradition coupled the *Menaechmi* plot with Greek romance, the combination perhaps suggested by the Roman play.[45]

In the *Menaechmi,* which is probably older than any extant Greek romance (Plautus lived *c.* 250 B.C. to 184 B.C.), to account for the separation of the twins which makes possible their being strangers to each other, and thus the comic confusion of identity, we are told in a sentence or two in the prologue that a merchant of Syracuse left his wife and one seven-year-old twin son at home and took the other on a sea journey to Tarentum. In a crowd the son and father were separated and a merchant from Epidamnus carried away the child. The father died of grief. Such a situation is, of course, a primitive separation plot, stark and unadorned, which was later to be elaborated into such complexities as the involutions of the *Aethiopica.* Since the Plautine source itself suggests a Greek romance plot, it would be a simple step for later writers to elaborate on the suggestion from the tissue of Greek romance.

In *Gl'Ingannati* the separation motif is slightly more developed than in the *Menaechmi,* the background information being worked into the dialogue: Virginio has lost his son in the sack of Rome of 1527. He and his daughter have escaped, but only after imprisonment. The son and his tutor are at last freed and return to create the comedy situation revolving around the complications of lovers when the sister Lelia (who much resembles her brother) disguises herself as a boy in order to be near her beloved. The action is a variation of the Plautine material. The Bandello version also credits the sack of Rome with the separation of brother and sister, developing the theme with more details of imprisonment and lost ransom letters. The telling, however, extends into two fairly long paragraphs, an expansion of the few lines of dialogue in *Gl'Ingannati*.

It is in *Gl'Inganni* of Nicolo Secchi that the real elaboration begins: Anselmo, a merchant, loved his wife and children so much that he took them when he sailed abroad, dressing both son and daughter as boys for comfort aboard the ship. Pirates attacked, and Anselmo was held fourteen years in slavery. The little son was sold to a courtesan of Naples. The mother and daughter (who continued to pass as a boy to protect her virginity) were also sold in Naples. The mother died, but not before the children learned of their relationship. The plot complications hang on the sister's close resemblance to her brother, her continued disguise as a boy, and the mistaken identity motif. The return of the father resolves the problems and clarifies the identities. But before the love plot begins, in one paragraph of the prologue the audience is treated to most of the stock situations of a Greek romance: sea journey, separation of married lovers, loss of children, attack by pirates, slavery, disguise, kidnapping, preservation of chastity, reunion. Thus, the background and situation for the mistaken identity plot, a family separated at sea and brought toegether years later when a much-traveled father finds his children is reminiscent of *Apollonius of Tyre*, in which an infant and wife are lost at sea and a father travels many years before reuninon and identification resolves all the difficulties.

In the Cinthio version twins separated by shipwreck are reared apart. In "Apolonius and Silla" of Riche a young duke is tossed up in a sea tempest on the island of Cyprus and received by the governor whose daughter

Silla was so much attracted to the hero that "she used so greate familiaritie with hym as her honour might . . . permitte. . . . But Apolonius . . . minde ranne more to heare . . . newes of a merie winde to serve his turne to Constantinople."[46]

One could be reading *Apollonius of Tyre* in which the hero is washed up on an island after a storm at sea, graciously received by the local king, entertained at court, and loved by the princess. Apollonius is slow to perceive her love, but when he does, they are married and set sail for Tyre. At this point Riche departs from *Apollonius of Tyre* and turns to other sources: Riche's Apolonius sets sail without knowing that Silla loves him and Silla sets sail secretly with her servant (calling themselves brother and sister) in pursuit. At sea, the captain appreciates Silla's beauty and offers her a share of his bed. To escape his attentions, Silla draws her knife, planning suicide, but just then a tempest leaves her victim of shipwreck, alone on a strange shore, with only the captain's sea chest to comfort her. To protect her honor, she dresses in man's apparel found in the chest.

The sea journey, shipwreck, and disguise episode remind one of almost any Greek romance except *Daphnis and Chloe.* At Constantinople Silla—now Silvio—takes a post as servant to her beloved Apolonius, and the Plautine comedy picks up with the mistaken identity plot. Silla's brother Silvio suddenly turns up, back from the wars, just in time to confuse the issue. At this point the mistaken identity plot merges with details similar to those of the Melitte episode of *Clitophon and Leucippe,* a similarity possibly governed and explained by a tradition of coupling the Plautine "twin plot" with Greek romance, a tradition which also could account for the similar fusion in *The Comedy of Errors.*[47]

ROMEO AND JULIET

Romeo and Juliet also has a pedigree distinguished in antiquity as well as in complexity. It has been related to such ancient love stories as Hero and Leander, Pyramus and Thisbe, Tristan and Isolde, Troilus and Cressida, Floris and Blancheflor, and ultimately to the separation-potion plot of the *Ephesiaca*.[48] The combination of all the important plot elements of the legend[49] as we know it with the names "Romeo" and "Juliet" probably began in Renaissance Italy. The earliest printed version is that of Masuccio de Salernitano, "Mariotto Mignanelli and Gianozza Saracini" (1474). It seems likely that the names of the hero and heroine were first supplied by Luigi Da Porto's *Historia novellamente* (*c.* 1530).[50] The Masuccio version contains almost all the plot motifs of the later Shakespeare version: Secretly married lovers are separated, and an attempt is made to force the heroine to marry another. Rather than comply, she begs a sleeping potion, drinks it, and apparently dies. She is buried, but awakens in her tomb. The husband receives a false report of her death. (In some later versions she is taken from the tomb by an accomplice before she revives.) After she is rescued from live burial, Gianozza—Masuccio's Juliet—voyages to Alexandria in search of her husband. The husband, meanwhile, having heard a false report of her death, returns with the intention of dying on her tomb. He is taken as a grave robber and is executed. Gianozza returns too late. Learning her husband's fate, she enters a convent and shortly thereafter dies.

The parallel to an episode of the *Ephesiaca* is interesting. Anthia, separated from her husband Habrocomes and forced into an unwelcome and illegal second marriage, begs poison from a physician. He secretly substitutes a sleeping potion which she drinks on her wedding night. Mistaken for dead, she is given a sumptuous burial, but awakens in the tomb, is rescued, and taken to Alexandria by robbers. Receiving a report that Anthia has died and that her body has been carried to Alexandria, Habrocomes journeys to that city, determined to claim the corpse and die on it. The desire to die on or near the body of the dead beloved is common to the later versions of the legend, but the journey to Alexandria, a hallmark of Alexandrian romance, is preserved only by Masuccio.

What may be an even older version of this situation is found in the *Babylonica* of Iamblichus. Certainly the plot materials preserved in the epitome of Photius seem more primitive than those of Xenophon of Ephesus: Rhodanes and Sinonis are married lovers. Garmus, King of Babylon, wishes to marry Sinonis. She refuses him. To escape prison, the lovers flee, experiencing many adventures typical of Greek romance. Finally the couple hide and sleep in an open grave. Later they are captured and take poison rather than be returned to the king. A slave had secretly substituted a sleeping draught, and falling only into a deep sleep, they are placed in a vehicle to be taken to the king. When Rhodanes, frightened by a dream, cries out, Sinonis wakens, and realizing that they are alive, stabs herself. The officer learns their history and, sympathizing, sets the lovers at liberty where they can go to a temple of Aphrodite and Sinonis can be healed of her wound.

If Iamblichus's tale is not a source for Xenophon's, it is surely a very early analogue, and further illustrates the antiquity of the Romeo and Juliet legend. The links are clear: A young married woman is being forced into a second, illegal marriage. To escape the situation she takes a sleeping draught. Unlike Juliet, Anthia and Sinonis both think they are killing themselves. (Juliet, however, worries about death, fearing that Friar Laurence might have tricked her.) Like Juliet, Anthia is buried alive and awakens in the tomb. Sinonis sleeps in an open grave with her husband before the sleeping draught motif occurs, but, like Juliet, she awakens to find her husband beside her and stabs herself.[51]

Except for one thirteenth-century manuscript in the library of the Benedictines at Florence, no direct bibliographic link can at present be made between the Hellenistic versions of the legend and the Renaissance versions. The *Ephesiaca* was not printed before 1726. The first printing of Photius's epitome of Iamblichus was a Greek edition of 1601. *Romeo and Juliet* is dated between 1591 and 1597. I tentatively suggest that Masuccio's contacts with the humanist circles may have led him to a reading of the La Badia codex, thus establishing the Greek romance potion plot firmly in the domain of Renaissance letters.

MUCH ADO ABOUT NOTHING

In its relationship to Greek romance *Much Ado About Nothing* presents a situation almost exactly duplicating *Romeo and Juliet,* for the main plot, the story of Hero and Claudio, closely resembles parts of *Chaereas and Callirhoe* of Chariton, and the story was retold frequently enough throughout the Renaissance to take on some of the legendary overtones which surround *Romeo and Juliet.* Similarly, the link between Chariton and the Italian Renaissance could have been the same codex which provided the link with Xenophon of Ephesus, for like Xenophon's work, Chariton's romance was not printed in any form before the eighteenth century and is apparently preserved in its entirety only in the manuscript which also preserves the *Ephesiaca.*

The primary source of Shakespeare's Hero-Claudio plot is probably "Signor Timbreo . . . [and] Fenicia

Lionata," tale XXII of the *Novelle* (Lucca, 1554) of Matteo Bandello. Sir John Harrington's translation (London, 1591) of Ludovico Ariosto's *Orlando Furioso* (Ferrara, 1516)[52] may have furnished some significant material in the story of Genevra and Ariodante of Canto V. Both works embody a similar plot situation, the oldest known version of which is to be found in Chariton: A young man is tricked by a rival through the connivance of his lady's servant into thinking he sees a "lover" secretly enter her chamber. As a result the lady is falsely accused and a disastrous situation results. Eventually the lady is cleared. The main outlines of this plot are recognized in an early Spanish novel of Johan Martorell, *Tirante el blanco* (Valencia, 1490).[53] An English version in verse by Peter Beverly, *Ariodanto and Ieneura* (London, 1565–1566), and the story of Phedon and Claribell in Book II, canto iv, of Edmund Spenser's *Faerie Queene* (London, 1590)[54] follow the Ariosto version in retelling the story. The story of Gianetta in Giraldi Cinthio's *Hecatommithi* imitated the version in *Tirante el blanco*. In 1576 George Whetstone adapted the Genevra story as "The Discourse of Rinaldo and Giletta" in *The Rocke of Regard* (London), adding to it many typical Renaissance love conventions. The Bandello version was retold by François de Belleforest in the third volume of the *Histoires Tragiques* (Turin, 1569).[55]

As Bandello tells the tale: Shortly after the Sicilian Vesper massacre Timbreo and his sworn brother, Girondo, fall in love with Fenicia, daughter of Lionato. Timbreo arranges a marriage. Girondo, hoping to break it off and claim the lady, asks a friend to tell Timbreo that Fenicia unchastely receives a lover. Through connivance with a servant of Fenicia, Timbreo is made to witness the "lover" entering Fenicia's quarters and to overhear talk of previous visits. He is thus convinced of Fenicia's guilt and breaks off the marriage. Stunned,

Fenicia falls into a deep swoon and is reported dead. She recovers, but to protect her honor, her parents feign her death and conduct a funeral with great pomp. Girondo repents, confesses before Fenicia's tomb, and begs Timbreo for death. Timbreo forgives him and laments. All is made clear to Lionato, who forgives Timbreo when he promises to marry a wife of Lionato's choosing. After a year Fenicia appears and a double wedding is celebrated between Timbreo and Fenicia and Girondo and Fenicia's sister.

The Ariosto version, the tale of Genevra, embodies the same motif of the slandered lady through the connivance of a rival lover and the servant's tricking the "hero" into believing he sees a "lover" enter the heroine's chambers. He accuses his lady, but the apparent death motif is replaced with a plot line in which the lady's life is in jeopardy unless a champion defends her within a brief period of time.

That the Bandello version of the slandered bride tale is a primary source of *Much Ado About Nothing* is generally undisputed, although Shakespeare might have drawn material for the masquerade deception of Hero's waiting woman from the Ariosto version or from one of its adaptations or translations. But whatever was Shakespeare's immediate source, the oldest known version of the plot has been recognized since 1898 as Chariton's *Chaereas and Callirhoe.*[56]

The correspondence is with Books I and VIII of Chariton: (Book I) Almost immediately after Chaereas and Callirhoe are married, unsuccessful suitors of Callirhoe deceive Chaereas into believing that he sees his wife admit a "foppish lover" into her quarters. Chaereas, enraged, rushes into the house and kicks his wife. She drops apparently dead. Chaereas learns of the deception and in remorse begs for death. When the treachery is revealed he is publicly forgiven by Callirhoe's father. Callirhoe is buried with much state, but awakens in the tomb, only to be kidnapped by grave robbers. Chaereas tries to kill himself on her empty tomb, but is saved by a friend, Polycharmes. (Books II through VII) After a series of adventures—the typical Greek romance separation plot—against a background of the Persian-Egyptian war (Book VIII) Chaereas and Callirhoe are reunited and received with public rejoicing and ceremony. A marriage is then celebrated between Polycharmes and Chaereas's sister.

The similarities between the Bandello and the Chariton plots are several: Both have a genuine historical background in Sicily to lend credibility. Bandello set his novel in the time of the Sicilian Vesper massacre, 1282; Chariton makes his heroine the daughter of the historical Hermocrates and sets the adventures against the background of the Persian-Egyptian wars of the fourth century B.C., the fairly distant past to a writer of the second century of the Christian era. In both cases the apparent death of the heroine is caused by the hero's false accusation of adultery. In both the hero is deceived by a rival with the cooperation of a servant of the heroine into thinking that he has witnessed a "lover" enter his lady's apartments. Both Fenicia's and Callirhoe's funerals are conducted by grieving parents. Both heroes are readily forgiven by the fathers of the innocent ladies when the deceptions are made known and when the heroes and friends go to the tombs of the "dead" heroines to lament. In Chariton the hero is prevented from suicide by his friend. In Bandello the guilty friend is prevented from suicide by the hero. Both versions of the legend end with the celebration of the wedding of the hero's friend and the happy reunion of the separated lovers. In Chariton the bride of the friend is the hero's sister; in Bandello the second bride is the heroine's sister. Both reunions meet with public approval and celebration.

The differences between the Italian and the Greek

versions are several, although less significant than the similarities: In Bandello the heroine is engaged to marry the hero; in Chariton she is newly married to him. In Bandello the hero and the intriguer are comrades, sworn brothers; in Chariton no personal contact occurs between them, but the hero is furnished with a close friend and confidant. In Bandello the "death" of the heroine results from a psychic blow. In the older version it results from a physical blow—an interesting cultural transformation, or perhaps a change made necessary by the change from the marriage of passion in Chariton to the marriage of convenience in Bandello, which is all that the Renaissance version of the affair can be called.

The Ariosto version and its descendants relate to Chariton and to Shakespeare's *Much Ado About Nothing* primarily in the similarity of the deception and accusation motif. It is Bandello's novella that must be recognized as the possible connecting link between Shakespeare and the Chariton romance: Claudio is deceived into thinking that his promised wife Hero secretly receives a lover. His brutal accusation causes her apparent death. After the mock burial comes Claudio's repentance at the tomb, forgiveness by the injured lady's father, the reappearance of the supposedly dead lady, and a triumphant conclusion in the double union of the protagonists and their friends, Beatrice and Benedict.

Bandello was a competent Greek scholar, the translator of the *Hecuba* of Euripides, the friend and correspondent of Julius Caesar Scaliger, and the tutor of the renowned Lucrezia Gonzaga. It is not impossible that he read the manuscript of Chariton's work. The portion of it by Xenophon of Ephesus had been advertised to the humanist public in 1489 by Poliziano, and the portion by Achilles Tatius had appeared in Cruceio's Latin translation in 1544 and in the Italian of Ludovico Dolce (1546) and Francesco Angelo Coccio (1550). In 1559—just five years after Bandello's publication—the world would see the Longus portion in a French translation by Jacques Amyot.

This said, one must consider the older versions of the tale related to the deception plot: *Tirante el blanco* of Martorell and the episode of Genevra and Ariodante in *Orlando Furioso* of Ariosto, a poet learned in Latin, but apparently without knowledge of Greek. One might conjecture oral tradition, lost manuscripts of Chariton, or say simply that they illustrate the pervasive influence of the Greek romance motifs throughout the course of Medieval and Renaissance literary history, a force so pervasive that when one reads such a play as *The Merchant of Venice* one is tantalized by a Greek romance aura—specifically a Heliodoran aura—in several details and situations: A "Moor"—to the Elizabethan usually a black man or an Ethiopian—is one of the princely suitors of Portia. Disguises are employed, both in the elopement of a pair of young lovers, Jessica and Lorenzo, and in the trial scene by Portia and Nerissa. The heroine is a richer, stronger, more intelligent and resourceful character than her husband, who indeed seems to be willing simply to love while his lady leads, as in the case of Theagenes in his relationship with Chariclea. Further, the climax, like the climax of the *Aethiopica,* comes in a great trial scene at which the heroine is the central and guiding character, as Chariclea is the focus of the trial scene of the *Aethiopica.* Coupled with all these details, there is a kind of contracted separation plot of married lovers: Shortly after Portia and Bassanio are married, he must leave her to help his friend Antonio in his problem with Shylock. His lady sets out in disguise to assist him. All this suggests that both *Much Ado About Nothing* and *The Merchant of Venice* were based on stories widely current in the Renaissance, stories which at some early stage, possibly through oral tradition or folk versions, took on features which are to be found in some of the Greek romances.

OTHELLO

A similar aura surrounds *Othello*, for not only is its story line a modification of the slandered bride plot of Chariton, but it also contains some aspects that recall Heliodorus. For example: In the *Aethiopica* Theagenes the Greek marries a Negress, Chariclea, the crown princess of Ethiopia. She was born "white" accidentally, for at the moment of her conception her mother happened to look upon a picture of the white Andromeda (anything can happen in the *Aethiopica*). But Chariclea has Negro parents and she carries on her arm a black birthmark to attest to her "black blood." *Othello* deals with a white woman married to a "Moor," to the Elizabethan an Arab or a Negro.[57] The role, however, has traditionally been interpreted as for a Negro, and elements of the characterization indicate that Othello was also thought of as an Ethiopian. Fernand Baldensperger thinks that both his race and his nation were suggested by Heliodorus.[58]

First, Othello is characterized as a Christian.[59] Ethiopia had long been a stronghold of the faith. If he is to be interpreted as an Arab, he would have been characterized as a Muslim, a pagan to the Elizabethan. Very little characterization of Othello can be found in the Cinthio source, the seventh tale of the third decade of the *Hecatommithi* (Venice, 1566). He is called a "Moor" and a powerful general in the service of Venice, but he is not noble or high minded, nor is he specifically Christian as in Shakespeare. The murder of the wife in the novella is cold conspiracy, not the crime of passion that it becomes in the play.

Although Cinthio furnished the name "Disdemona," which Shakespeare transformed to "Desdemona," "Iago" (a form of "Jacob" common in Ethiopian documents) and "Othello" are furnished by Shakespeare. According to Baldensperger, the name "Othello" may derive from "Oxello," a word found in Jesuit reports of Ethiopia, and the names "Iago" and "Othello" carry an Ethiopian coloring.[60]

In the novella the fatal handkerchief is only a wedding gift. Entirely absent are the qualities of magic—a talisman offering protection against evil, a mother's gift dipped in the "mummy of Egypt"—which it assumes in the play. Yet these qualities are aspects of the magical "Pantarbe" of the *Aethiopica*, Chariclea's talisman, her mother's gift, a powerful agent against evil, which she carried all through her adventures in Egypt and Ethiopia.

It was tales of the marvelous, descriptions of strange animals, "travel's history," "And of the Cannibals that each other eat,/ The Anthropophagi, and men whose heads/ Do grow beneath their shoulders" (I, iii, 143–45) that won Desdemona for Othello. No such tales appear in Cinthio. The *Aethiopica* abounds in them. Neither is Desdemona's lack of interest in other suitors suggested by Cinthio: "[Brabantio] So opposite to marriage that she shunn'd/ The wealthy curled darlings of our nation" (I, ii, 67–68). But Chariclea of the *Aethiopica* was a priestess of Diana before Theagenes came into her life: "Shee hath bidden mariage farewell, and determineth to live a maiden."[61]

Further, the elopement of Desdemona and Othello is not suggested by the novella. Cinthio's Disdemona and her Moor had "lived in . . . harmony and peace in Venice"[62] for some time before they went to the island of Cyprus and treachery. But the lovers of the *Aethiopica* elope, and the grief of Chariclea's foster father is emphasized,[63] as is the fatal grief of Brabantio, Desdemona's father.

It is probably unwise to assert strongly that the *Aethiopica* furnished materials for *Othello*, for there is considerable evidence of interest in things African in sixteenth-century England,[64] and *Othello* is not the only literary treatment of a Negro character besides that of Heliodorus. On the other hand, in view of the publication record of the *Aethiopica* in relation to the date of *Othello* (1604), it would be unwise not to take it into consideration:[65]

AETHIOPICA

1534	A Greek text; 1551, a Greek text of Book I
1547–1596	Seventeen issuings of Amyot's French translation
1551–1601	Six issuings of Stanislaus Warschewiczki's Latin translation
c. 1554–1597	Six issuings of Johann Zschorn's German translation
1554–1581	Three issuings of a Spanish translation by *"por un segreto amigo"*
1566–1588	Eight issuings of Leon Ghini's Italian translation
1557, 1559, 1567	Versions in Italian, French, and English by Hieronymus Bossi, Claude Colet, and James Sanford, respectively
c. 1569–1587	Three issuings of Thomas Underdowne's English translation
1584, 1587, 1591	Versions in Latin, Spanish, and English by Martini Crusii, Ferñado de Mena, and Abraham Fraunce, respectively.

Interesting also is the fact that *Othello* is clearly a sophisticated variant of the slandered bride plot of *Chaereas and Callirhoe*, of which an earlier Shakespeare parallel is *Much Ado About Nothing:* Treachery, aided by the wife's servant, causes Chaereas to believe falsely that his wife entertains a lover. He strikes her brutally and she apparently dies. Waking to life later, she continues to love her husband. Never does she blame him for his cruelty, although she does not understand its motivation. Othello, similarly, is falsely led to believe his wife guilty. He is deliberately deceived, as is Chaereas, and the deception is furthered (in this case unwittingly) by his wife's attendant, Emilia, when she gives the handkerchief to Iago. In Act IV, scene i, Othello in anger and rage strikes Desdemona in the face. She does not understand the reason for the blow, but she is not angered by it and continues to love him. When Othello finally kills her, Desdemona's dying words are indicative of love and forgiveness, although she never knows the reason for the attack.

The hero's striking the heroine in rage is a common Greek romance motif, although in Cinthio it has become a cold-blooded plot which leads to real death rather than the traditional apparent death. Othello's preliminary blow and Desdemona's touching, innocent forgiveness are developments by Shakespeare which help to lift the sordid old tale into a level of tragic power it had not before known. The old versions had incorporated a fantastic element: the trickery of seeming death and restoration. There is little genuine psychological motivation for the blow, and the stories concentrate mostly on the aftermath of seeming death, repentance, and glorious resurrection. Shakespeare has shifted the emphasis from the maudlin repentance, attempted suicide, and the titillating return from the dead to a realistic display

—a step-by-step development—of the psychological pressures and tensions in a shattering of faith which leads an admirable character from love and trust through suspicion, corruption, rage, disintegration, and the murder of his beloved. The psychological movement leading to the fatal blow left no room for any aftermath but the real death of the slandered bride and the real suicide of a husband overwhelmed by grief and guilt in learning how he he had been duped.

Though much of *Othello*'s tragic power is due to a shift in emphasis in the narrative, much also is due to the development of the character of the husband from a hot-tempered, pretty youth in Chariton; a cold conspirator in Cinthio; rather ordinary young men in search of good matches in Bandello and in Claudio of *Much Ado;* to the admirable, noble Othello, a great Negro warrior and leader, a descendant of an ancient line, an aristocrat high in the councils of a foreign state, a man carrying with him a deep religious consciousness and a capacity for great and dignified love. Shakespeare did not make Othello a young "lover." From the first act he is a "husband." His love is dignified, calm, serene, protective. Only when it is made wretched by the charge of dishonor against Desdemona does it turn to the blind passion of anger. Then ironically she is sacrificed for honor: "An honorable murderer, if you will" (V, ii, 293). Mistaken as such honor may seem in the cold light of reason, it is far higher in tragic power than the rage of injured ego and revenge in the earlier versions.

Similarly, Desdemona's character is lifted from the ladylike blandness of her predecessors to that of a young woman, still almost girlish in her innocence and purity, but capable of risking all to make a socially undesirable love match, to leave behind family and friends, to stand bravely and continue loving in the face of a public blow she neither understands nor deserves, and finally to die with forgiveness on her lips. The power of the characterizations in *Othello* is so great that the vestige of the old Greek romance plot has been buried almost beyond recognition in the emotional intensity engendered by the tragedy.

Othello and *Much Ado About Nothing* are a good illustration of the old knowledge that the materials of tragedy and comedy are one. It is the treatment that makes the difference. A cruel and unfair psychic blow fells Hero in *Much Ado*. We are sorry, but not deeply touched. Claudio is too shallow to be taken very seriously, and Hero has too much about her of convention and propriety for us to be very moved, especially since she is surrounded by such sparkling associates as Beatrice and Benedict, and such unforgettable police protection as Dogberry, Verges, and the watch. In such a world, all must and will end in a peal of merry wedding bells and silver laughter. The very absence in *Othello* of a second plot not only helps to deepen its intensity but also darkens the solitary center and brings on its inevitable doom.

AS YOU LIKE IT

As You Like It illustrates in quite another manner the pervasive influence of Greek romance on Renaissance letters by drawing at secondhand on the stock pastoral plot derived from *Daphnis and Chloe,* utilized by Shakespeare with varying modifications in *The Winter's Tale, Cymbeline,* and *The Tempest,* as well as by Sir Philip Sidney in the *Arcadia* (1590), by Edmund Spenser in the episode of Meliboe and Pastorella (Book VI) in the *Faerie Queene* (1596), and by Thomas Lodge in *Rosalynde: Euphues Golden Legacie* (London, 1590).[66] It is from Lodge that Shakespeare derived most of the narrative materials for *As You Like It:* Lodge's heroine Rosalynde, banished from her rightful place at court, lives disguised as a shepherd boy near the forest of Arden. Thus is fulfilled the first requirement of the stock plot: A heroine of unknown parentage lives in a pastoral setting. Rosalynde's companion Alinda (Shakespeare's Celia), a shepherdess who is really another exile from the court, doubles the motif. Rosader (Shakespeare's Orlando), the hero, is the abused younger brother of a wealthy landowner. By hiding out as a forester he satisfies the second article of the stock plot: The highborn lover of the heroine lives and labors in lowly estate. The third point, the complications of the situation and the comic relief supplied by a country bumpkin suitor for the heroine, is modified from the tradition by having the humble, though comic shepherdess Phoebe fall in love with Rosalynde (a woman diguised as a boy). Rosader's slaying the lion which comes to devour his brother furnishes the melodramatic incident which proves the hero's muscle, although it had earlier been demonstrated in the wrestling match. The captivity episode appears only in vestigial form in the unsuccessful attempt to kidnap Alinda, the secondary heroine. The revelation that Rosalynde and Alinda are duke's daughters satisfies the final stock requirement: the disclosure of the heroine's true identity and high birth in order to make it possible for her to marry the highborn hero. It might be added that the restoration of the lost child to the parent, an important motif in Greek romance, and especially in *Daphnis and Chloe*, is here repeated in the reunion of Rosalynde and her father, the rightful duke living in exile.[67]

The action of Shakespeare's *As You Like It* differs from Lodge's novel by the enlargement of the comic elements through the introduction of Jaques, Touchstone, William, and Audrey, and by the omission of the vestigial captivity motif retained by Lodge. The melodrama of the hero's slaying a lion is softened to a mere report that he slew a lion and a snake, but the final scene of revelation, recognition, and reunion of parents, children, and lovers is delightfully and fully developed in the true Greek romance manner.

Two traditional pastoral motifs of *As You Like It* do not derive from Lodge: the comic relief supplied by the rustics William and Audrey and the melancholy, malcontent Jaques, a stock character derived from the Italian and Spanish pastorals. The tradition of introducing a lonely observer and commentator into pastoral romance can probably be traced to the old philosophic shepherd Philetas of *Daphnis and Chloe*. His function is observation and instruction. He teaches the lovers to understand themselves and he comments on the life and love he sees about him with the understanding of a man who once knew "true love" himself. But great age and mutations of time have turned him into the cynical Jaques, who, as the exiled duke says, was once "a libertine,/ As sensual as the brutish sting itself" (II, vii, 65–66). And thereby came the difference.

The golden world of Shakespeare's forest of Arden clearly reflects the tradition of Theocritus, the eclogues of Vergil, and their descent through the Italian and Spanish pastorals and through Sidney and Spenser. Within them all in varying degrees is the stock plot derived from Longus, but there seems to be no evidence that in *As You Like It* the plot was derived in any way except through the tradition as it was handled by Lodge. It seems likely that Lodge's source for the story of Rosader (Orlando) and his brothers and the woodland life of the dispossessed duke was the fourteenth-century *Tale of Gamelyn*[68] (unknown in print before 1721) with assistance from the Robin Hood legend. This old romance has no love interest. Lodge's heroine and the love plot were superimposed on its completely masculine world, possibly through the suggestion of Day's version of *Daphnis and Chloe*, newly published in 1587, or from the French of Amyot, circulating since 1559, but just as likely from the tradition which had slowly evolved through the Renaissance from the Greek source.[69]

Shakespeare treats the hackneyed, old plot with refreshing originality, turning it in upon itself, demanding that it look critically at its own conventions. Longus had viewed his incredibly innocent country lovers with the amused cynicism of adult city eyes. The Spanish and Italian pastorals usually turned them into porcelain figurines—milkmaids in Dior ginghams, swains in slacks by Brooks Brothers—mouthing unreal feelings in an elaborate, mannered style. Lodge's creatures are more convincing, and he treats them with humor, but often their humanity is smothered under the Euphuisms of the style, especially in the love speeches. Shakespeare examines the pastoral conventions through the kind of combat of wit that had proved to be so effective in *Much Ado About Nothing*. Rosalind is the center, a real young woman, a Beatrice more poetically conceived, more delicately reared. The others are foils for her wit, even her lover Orlando, but none of them are bisque mantel ornaments as their predecessors often are.

Rosalind is deeply in love—as convention demands—and she knows it. But she knows also the difference between the love and the conventions of its expression. She laughs at Orlando's love poems:

> *Cel.*[*ia*]   Didst thou hear these verses?
> *Ros.*[*alind*]   O, yes, I heard them all, . . . some of them had . . . more feet than the verses would bear.
> *Cel.*   That's no matter: the feet might bear the verses.
> *Ros.*   Ay, but the feet were lame, and could not bear themselves.
>
> (III, ii, 173–80)

She laughs at his declaration that he will die of love: "men have died from time to time, and worms have eaten them, but not for love" (IV, i, 110ff). Yet she loves, and at the same time she knows that love is folly. She is full of play, full of unexpected sincerity: "O coz, coz, coz, my pretty little coz, that thou didst know how many fathoms deep I am in love!" (IV, i, 217ff). But her laughter is not satire, though often satire is present in Jaques's attacks on the duke, Orlando, and Touchstone. Touchstone laughs too, laughs everyone back from romance to reality. Withal, however, there is more of humor than of satire or parody in the treatment of the pastoral conventions, and more of wit and play than of humor. The various features of the pastoral tradition are held up, brought into focus, examined one against the other: the eclogue, the stock plot, the lovers in disguise (Rosalind and Orlando), the artificial lovers (Silvius and Phoebe), the casual—even crude—country courtship of the lowborn (Touchstone and Audrey), even the note of Hardyan realism (old Corin who earns what he eats and takes his greatest pride in seeing his "ewes graze" and his "lambs suck" [III, ii, 82]).

Chapter Four

Shakespeare's Greek Romances [1]

THE CRITICAL TRADITION

On reading Shakespeare's dramatic romances that marked the last years of his career—*Pericles, Prince of Tyre; Cymbeline; The Winter's Tale;* and *The Tempest* —one is immediately conscious of an artistic and philosophic unity binding them together. All four make use of traditional romantic conventions, and all four conclude on the same note of forgiveness, reconciliation, and hope, Shakespeare's peace with the world after the *Sturm und Drang* of *Hamlet,* the hopeless tragic irony of *Othello* and *King Lear,* the onrushing doom of *Julius Caesar* and *Macbeth.* Even in the fury of Leontes's unreasoned jealousy, the ugly cynicism of Iachimo's treachery, the ghoulish horror of Imogen's awakening in her grave, there is a note of unreality to the evil and an assurance of only temporal agony, a legacy, perhaps, from the romantic components of their structures, episodes, and plots.

Most critics of the four late plays have recognized this unity in tone, theme, and incident; and although they also see romance elements in other Shakespeare plays, they have made of them an almost separate genre—a kind of special academic discipline within the Shakespeare canon, a romance genre which frequently disregards narrative or psychological reality and moves its way with sweeping metrical freedom from states of prosperity through tragic upheaval, loss, and destruction, to restored order and tranquillity. During the last thirty years the romances have been very fashionable in the Shakespeare industry, and larger claims than can always be substantiated have sometimes been made for them.

When academic interest in Shakespeare was fired by a need to define his personality and to search out the facts of his biography, the late romances were thought to be reflections of the poet's old age: his mature acceptance of life, coupled with a mood of repentance, reconciliation, and peace. When styles changed and Shakespeare became a dramatist sensitive to popular moods and tastes, the plays were linked with the Beaumont and Fletcher romances, especially *Philaster*. Later they were seen as theatrical adaptations to the tastes of a courtly, sophisticated audience which frequented the Blackfriars Theater. Recently influential criticism has described them as instruments for allegory, symbol, and myth, and as existing simultaneously on multiple levels. Since these plays do deal with themes of loss and restoration, disaster and recovery, death and rebirth, they are readily open to such interpretation. More recently it has been suggested that the late plays describe a new vision beyond the scope of tragedy, a vision which accepts the tragic and evil elements in life, but refuses to admit them as final, sees such negative elements as no more than a transient stage in the everlasting cycle of birth, death, and rebirth, a movement in the human condition clearly analogous to the annual vegetative cycles, its majestic, formal interpretation projected in the procession of the liturgical year from Advent through Christmas, Good Friday, and Easter. It has been suggested that the idea of redemption through tragedy may have come to Shakespeare as he observed the workings of *King Lear,* seeing in the restorative force which Cordelia becomes to the wretched, bewildered king the factor giving to both their deaths a quality of the tranquil inevitable, a force lifting tragedy into the rebirth of hope, a force whose very seeds were sown before the winter solstice of the soul, as though some wise preparator had laid them down against the darkness of the gathering storm.

The most recent critics admit aspects of the romance tradition in the early and middle Shakespeare plays: the Aegeon-Aemilia plot of *The Comedy of Errors,* the romantic elements in *Much Ado, Twelfth-Night,* and *As You Like It,* and they recognize that romance is essentially oriented to move through travail and vicissitude toward a world of golden perfection: prelapsarian Eden, the Forest of Arden, the literary Arcadia. More importantly, the critics now recognize that the late romances exist not only on the mythic and allegorical level, not only to illustrate that life is a mystery through which we feel our ways to beauty and peace, to reality behind deceptive appearances; but also they recognize that the romances exist simply as entertainment, as a means to delight through the spectacle of wish-fulfillment patterns of tragedy resolved, of error revealed, of restoration and new birth. Since such themes are universals of human desire and experience, valid allegory and myth can, indeed, be woven from them and can be read into these plays that embody them.[1]

This separate subdivision of the Shakespeare canon —*Pericles, Cymbeline, The Winter's Tale,* and *The Tempest*—belongs to the tradition of the Greek romances, a fact long recognized about *Pericles,* and more or less understood about *Cymbeline, The Winter's Tale,* and *The Tempest.* That Greek romances have a curious affinity to drama is old knowledge. The ninth-century critic Photius called them dramatic narratives, and their own authors, especially Chariton, Heliodorus, and Achilles Tatius, often refer to parts of their work in terms of drama and dramatic convention.[2] By the time these plays were being written, all the extant Greek romances except Chariton's and Xenophon's were easily available in English and had behind them long histories of Continental publication. True, Burton's Achilles Tatius and Day's Longus were available in only one edition each, but *Apollonius of Tyre* could be had in at least three contemporary versions, seven editions in all. James Sanford's and Abraham Fraunce's versions of Heliodorus had each been issued only once, but Underdowne's translation had appeared five times by 1607. Jacques Amyot's French Heliodorus had been issued eighteen times by that year, and his Longus had gone through three editions. As to Greek and Latin editions, modern scholarship has quietly closed the books on romantic Victorian opinion that Shakespeare was either an untutored genius singing native woodnotes wild, or a well-lettered neurotic preserving his name modestly in cryptic anagram. T. W. Baldwin's research in the curricula of the Elizabethan grammar schools reveals a wealth of classical exposure even for the average student.[3] Whatever his Greek may have been, it is likely that Shakespeare's Latin scholarship was rather deep; especially is this true if he read William Lambarde's *Archaionomia,* a copy of which bearing his supposed signature is preserved in the Folger Library.[4] *Archaionomia* prints Anglo-Saxon laws on one side of a page with Latin translations on the other. The Latin style is difficult and the vocabulary well outside the usual schoolroom lists. Had Shakespeare wished to dispense with the convenience of

English translations, available as they were, it seems likely that he could have read the Greek romances in Latin.

PERICLES, PRINCE OF TYRE

The history of the criticism of *Pericles, Prince of Tyre* would, however, seem to deny that affinity to the stage, for although the play was popular in the seventeenth century, after the Restoration it was seldom produced until the mid-twentieth century, when it has had a slow revival.[5] The lack of critical regard has been due in part to a corrupt text and in part to the prevailing opinion that Shakespeare did not write the first two acts, although most critics admit the poetic power of the last three as his. Further, critical belittlement has been due to the romance narrative structure, until recently out of fashion as something to be admired. Nevertheless, when we consider Shakespeare's use of the Greek romance tradition, Exhibit A must be *Pericles*, and for the sake of discussion we must assume his hand in the entire play, whatever the truth may be.

Pericles (*c.* 1607–1608) is the earliest of the four dramatic romances. In adapting the narrative of *Apollonius of Tyre* to the stage, Shakespeare and his collaborator are completely faithful to the durable old plot, indeed, far more faithful than Shakespeare usually is to his sources. The chief deviation from the old Latin version is in the names of the characters: The hero Apollonius becomes Pericles; Athenagorus, suitor to Apollonius's daughter, becomes Lysimachus; Archistrates, father of Apollonius's wife, turns into Simonides; Hellenicus, a Tyrian friend of the hero, is slightly disguised as Helicanus and transformed from a humble messenger to a "grave Counsellor." The new Helicanus governs Tyre during the king's absence and seems to be modeled after

Castiglione's ideal of the courtier who advises honestly and without flattery.[6] The pair of villains who reared and wronged the daughter change from Stranguillo and Dionysias to Cleon and Dionyza. The wife, nameless in most versions, is called Thaisa. The daughter Tharsia, born at sea, becomes most appropriately Marina. In three names Shakespeare differs from the usage of all authorities—Pericles, his wife Thaisa, and Marina—although most of the changes were suggested by one version or another.[7] Actually Shakespeare had a kind of remote authority even for the change from Apollonius to Pericles in a French version (MS 3428, Wiener Hofbibliothek) in which Apollonius calls himself "Perillie."[8] Thaisa may be derived from Tharsia, the traditional name for the daughter. Since Antiochus retains in *Pericles* the ancient name he bore in history and in the Apollonius romance, the play bears a significant hallmark of the early Greek novel in having about it a vaguely historical background achieved by the suggestive influence of famous names. The wide derivation of the names from "Apollonian" sources is interesting and suggestive of conscious research and wide reading as a practice preliminary to composition.

Aside from changing the names of the leading characters, the startling difference between the Shakespeare version and the traditional recital of the romance is the addition of the dumb shows and of the poet John Gower in the role of chorus. The plot is not altered and both additions can be explained by dramatic exigency. In turning the loosely constructed, slowly developed romance into a play, the authors were faced with the major problem of condensation. Thus Gower, who had earlier told the same story, is introduced to fill in the background material, comment on the situation, and carry forward by recitation, often imitative of his own Medieval style, incidents of the plot which dramatic compression could omit as cumbersome or superfluous. From Gower we learn of the incest episode, the shipwreck, the marriage of Pericles and Thaisa, the death of Antiochus and the inheritance of Pericles, the life of Marina at Tarsus, Pericles's travel to reclaim his daughter, his learning of her apparent death, and Marina's career after escaping from the brothel—all incidents which parallel the narrative of *Apollonius of Tyre*. Finally, in the epilogue Gower comments on the poetic justice which has been measured out. The dumb shows illustrate Gower's tale and a great mass of necessary material is thus economically presented. The device of the chorus and the dumb shows was a happy one in that it enabled Shakespeare to preserve in its entirety the venerable story and at the same time spread a graceful air of antiquity over the play. Although no chorus is present in the Greek romance from which the play derives, such a device is conventional in Greek drama and was transmitted to the Renaissance stage through Seneca. F. David Hoeniger, however, finds the origins of the chorus in Medieval religious drama, which, he thinks, also furnished the episodic structure and the pageant-like quality of *Pericles*.[9]

While preserving intact the ancient plot, Shakespeare also maintained the motifs of father-daughter relationships so important in *Apollonius of Tyre*. The strong contrast between the depravity of the relationship of Antiochus and his daughter and the ideal relationship of Archestrates and the princess is repeated, as well as the careless love of Apollonius for his daughter in the Pericles-Marina situation. Shakespeare also maintained the ancient characterizations. Marina is as virtuous and as learned as Tharsia of the earlier versions. Resisting all temptations in the brothel, she declares that she can earn her own way honestly (IV, vi, 199–201). Pericles is as clever at riddles as was Apollonius, but again for the sake of dramatic compression, Shakespeare omitted ten proposed by Tharsia to her father, which in the older accounts did much to establish him as a learned and serious prince. Coupled with the description of the hero as "music's master" (II, v, 30), the riddle serves, however, to maintain his traditional characterization as learned. This comment is especially interesting, for it is made at the banquet scene, where Pericles (unlike Apollonius) does not perform. It would seem to indicate either a lack of revision or a subconscious echoing of the sources. Thaisa's lecture on the knight's devices is an addition of Shakespeare, but it continues her traditional characterization as an intellectual. Medieval knights in a Greek romance are surely anachronistic, but hardly more here than in the curious combination of classical antiquity and feudalism in Chaucer's "Knight's Tale," shortly afterwards enacted in *The Two Noble Kinsmen* (*c.* 1613).

Shakespeare did make one other fairly interesting change. The traditional blow which Apollonius gives his as yet unidentified daughter is modified to a vague request of Marina that Pericles do no "violence" on her (V, i, 100f). There are no stage directions to clarify the statement, but Shakespeare has excised at last the ugly tradition reaching all the way back to Chariton that a Greek romance hero should strike the heroine, having failed to recognize her because of disguise, or for some other mistake.

Other changes are in the addition of characters. The single fisherman who helps Apollonius after the shipwreck becomes three fishermen when Pericles needs help, giving Shakespeare opportunity to write a comic scene for the clowns of his troop (II, i). The two bawds who trouble Tharsia are three when Marina is thrust into the brothel, again giving Shakespeare opportunity to write more flexible and realistic comedy (IV, iv).

Shakespeare's introduction of Gower is the obvious clue to one of the immediate sources, *Confessio Amantis,* Book VIII. Gower declares his source to be: "Of a cronique in daies gon,/ The which is cleped Panteon,"[10] which is to say the popular account of *Apollonius* by Godfrey of Viterbo in the *Pantheon.* The descent of the Gower version can be traced in four steps: (1) A conjectured Greek romance of the second or third centuries A.D.; (2) A Latin translation of the conjectured romance, *c.* fifth century A.D.; (3) Godfrey of Viterbo's *Pantheon,* twelfth century; and (4) John Gower's Book VIII of the *Confessio Amantis,* 1390.[11] Evidence exists that Shakespeare also used the Twine version,[12] which does not differ much from Gower's narrative, but derives from the version of *Apollonius* in the Latin *Gesta Romanorum* of the thirteenth and fourteenth centuries rather than from the account in the *Pantheon.* The *Gesta* version is, of course, directly descended from the same conjectured Greek romance and its fifth-century Latin translation from which developed Godfrey of Viterbo's *Apollonius.* Thus, *Pericles,* drawing upon both Gower and Twine, unites the two versions of the romance which during the Middle Ages developed independently, probably from the same classical source.[13]

Shakespeare's achievement in *Pericles* is totally different from that of his earlier work and, indeed, quite different from that of the old *Apollonius* romance. By use of the archaic romance materials with their inevitable circular movement from prosperity and well-being through adversity to joy and prosperity again—a stringing out of events which seem to end where they began rather than the development of plot out of character—he has infused the play with an air of oft-repeated ceremony and ritual, giving it the tone of old myth, the quality of pageant and spectacle reenacting the predictable cycles of life. Pericles has been turned from a scholar-prince to a kingly Everyman: Job, who must be tried by loss and adversity, who must bear it patiently, not because he must be purged of evil, but because suffering is an aspect of his human condition. Pericles's submission to fate in his loss, his joy in the recovery of his child and his wife become an enactment of a ritual of wonder at the inevitable. Much of this air of ceremony and ritual is achieved by the addition of music and spectacle to the presentation: the appearance of Antiochus's daughter, the very personification of female evil, to the sound of music:

> Ant.[*iochus*]   Bring in our daughter, clothed like a bride,
> . . . . [*Music.*]
> Per.[*icles*]   See, where she comes apparell'd like the spring,
>
> (I, i, 6, 12)

the chivalric procession of knights who display their shields before Thaisa; the awakening of Thaisa by Cerimon through music, fire, and ceremonial application of unguents and spices:

> Cer.[*imon*]   She is alive! behold,
> Her eyelids, cases to those heavenly jewels . . .
> Begin to part their fringes of bright gold;
>
> (III, ii, 98–101)

Pericles's recognition of Marina:

> Per.[*icles*]   O! come hither,
> Thou that begett'st him that did thee beget;
>
> (V, i, 196f)

the vision of Diana; the restoration of Thaisa before the high altar of chastity. We are not touched by the ritual of events, by presentation of life, but we are suffused with a sense of miracle and transcendental wonder. We are left satisfied by a playing out of the human ritual of prosperity, loss, despair, restoration, joy. In short, the triumph of time, some fifteen years rolling before us in stately processional in the course of a few hours' pageant. G. Wilson Knight says of it: "*Pericles* is the result of no sudden vision: it is Shakespeare's total poetry on the brink of self-knowledge."[14] The knowledge of the transcendant human development that is achieved through tragedy becomes poetically fulfilled in *Cymbeline, The Winter's Tale,* and *The Tempest.*

CYMBELINE

Cymbeline continues in the pattern established by *Pericles,* although it is a complex embodiment of classic Greek romance properties rather than an adaptation of a specific Greek romance. This said, one must note that E. C. Pettet's study *Shakespeare and the Romance Tradition*[15] shows clearly that the final plays embody also aspects of the romantic mode that are to be found in *Guy of Warwick, Sir Bevis,* the *Morte d'Arthur,* and in the works of Ariosto, Tasso, Sidney, and Spenser. This tradition couples ideas of love as a sublime and ennobling experience with the chivalric ideals and the romance plot compounded of journey, intrigue, mistaken identity, royal children, and happy endings. In *Cymbeline* the mixture is made of pseudohistory and pastoral romance tied together with an Italian novella plot, resulting in a play that has not always had high critical regard,[16] although Knight argues in its favor convincingly.[17] When the composition is viewed generically as dramatized Greek romance its disturbing elements can often be explained, even though they might not always find psychological or artistic justification.

Each of *Cymbeline*'s three story threads is characteristic of the Greek romance genre: the wager story and Imogen's travels, the loss and restoration of Cymbeline's heirs, and Cymbeline's war with Rome. The wager story supplies motifs of a separation plot: separation and travels of married lovers, suspicion of the heroine's chastity, mistaken identity, mistaken death, triallike conclusion at which all is explained and all are united. The loss and restoration of Cymbeline's two sons, and later of Imogen, is also a development, perhaps in part suggested by the popularity of the Greek novel, and the background of Cymbeline's war with Rome was an almost necessary addition if Shakespeare was to give the historical aura expected in Greek romance. That the materials from it were derived from Holinshed does not lessen its connection in *Cymbeline* with the Greek genre, since it is to be expected that Shakespeare would nationalize the background of a play where he could. Indeed, Knight finds in *Cymbeline*'s military thread its primary purpose: a symbolical interweaving of England's two central historical foundations, Britain and Rome, the union of which at the conclusion transfers to England "the heritage of ancient Rome . . . the Roman power . . . [to a] Britain destined to prove worthy of her Roman tutelage."[18] The combination of the pastoral and Italian elements with the historical material makes possible the final scene of recognition and reunion. Peace is made; heirs are restored; lovers are reunited; the heroine's chastity is proved; mistaken death is explained, a conclusion conventional in Greek romance, and usually taking the form of a public triallike occasion as in *Cymbeline*.

The wager story which forms an important action of the play Shakespeare probably derived from Boccaccio's "Bernabo da Genoa" (II, 9) of the *Decameron*, though he possibly also used English versions, *Frederyke of Jennen* (Antwerp, 1518, *c.* 1520, *c.* 1560) and a

tale in *Westward for Smelts* (London, 1603?, 1620) by
Kitt of Kingstone. The story was widely known in
French throughout the Middle Ages; the metrical version of Gibert Montreuil, *Roman de la Violette ou de
Gérard de Nevers* (c. 1225) is perhaps the most familiar
today. Somehow the late fourteenth-century play *Ostes,
Roy d'Espaigne*, one of the surviving *Miracles de Nostre
Dame* is remarkably like *Cymbeline* in plot details,
"emotional movement and final effect," the link perhaps
in the miracle play tradition from which Robert G.
Hunter thinks the late romances descend.[19] There are
also analogues in German, Swedish, Danish, and Icelan-
dic.[20] The wager story is a variation of the slandered
bride plot which had already done service for Shakespeare in *Much Ado* and *Othello:* A husband makes a
foolish wager that his wife cannot be seduced. A villain,
trying her virtue and finding it inviolate, tricks the husband into believing that the wife has lain with him. (In
many versions, including Boccaccio's, the villain is
aided in the deception by the wife's servant, as is the
case in *Chaereas and Callirhoe* and the version of the
slandered bride plot upon which *Much Ado* is based.)
The enraged husband orders a servant to kill his wife,
but the servant is merciful and permits her to escape,
reporting to the husband that she is dead. The wife
travels far and wide in disguise (in the Boccaccio version to Alexandria, often a focal point in the Greek
novel) until various circumstances make possible a
proof of her chastity.

That the plot closely parallels Chariton's is obvious,
although the details of the wife's seeming death are
different and the wager motif is added. Shakespeare's
version is even closer to *Chaereas and Callirhoe* than are
his sources; for like Callirhoe, Imogen is led to believe
that her husband is dead and like Chaereas, Posthumus
regrets his hasty action, laments, and meditates suicide

—motifs missing from Boccaccio. Although no biblio-graphic connection has, to my knowledge, been estab-lished between the wager cycle and the Chariton ro-mance, they have such a family resemblance as to make them seem variant developments from a single more ancient parent, or the wager story a descendant of *Chaer-eas and Callirhoe,* modified by the natural mutations which time and successive generations bring about.

In his discussions of *Romeo and Juliet* in its relation to the *Ephesiaca,* Francis Douce remarked that the sleeping draught which Imogen takes and her awaking in the cave duplicate the similar situation in *Romeo and Juliet,* and parallel the Greek romance. He also likened Pisanio's sparing of Imogen to another episode of the *Ephesiaca:* Anthia, held in slavery, is ordered to be killed when her mistress Manto becomes jealous of her. A servant helps her to escape and reports her dead.[21] Imogen's story is much like Juliet's: Although she is already married, her parents try to force her into an-other marriage. A sleeping draught makes her appear dead; she is buried, and awakens in a grave beside the dead body of one who seems to be her husband. Edwin Greenlaw asserts that Shakespeare's source for this por-tion of the *Cymbeline* plot is Shakespeare himself, in his earlier *Romeo and Juliet.*[22] Ultimately, of course, it is Da Porto or Masuccio and the Xenophon of Ephesus ro-mance. The sparing of Imogen by Pisanio, however, does not have a parallel in the sources of *Romeo and Juliet,* but is an indispensable motif in the wager cycle, and appears in *Apollonius of Tyre* as an adventure of Thar-sia. Except for that incident, the wager story has no other especially close parallel to the *Ephesiaca.*

The stock pastoral plot derived from Longus is modi-fied in the Guiderius-Arviragus thread of *Cymbeline:* The infant sons of King Cymbeline are stolen by a banished courtier and reared in the wilderness in ignorance of their parentage, a variant from the common situation in which the lost or disguised heir is a girl. (The reversal has ancient authority in the situation of Daphnis in Longus's romance.) Princess Imogen, disguised as a boy, is introduced in place of the usual lover. Probably because the princes and Imogen are brothers and sister, Shakespeare did not admit the erotic love motif, but he permits her charms to be sensed. The unworthy suitor appears in the person of Cloten, a comic character, a variant from the "rude, bumbling country swain" to the rude, bumbling courtly swain. Cloten is foiled by the highborn foresters. The potion scene, the trance, and the burial take the place of traditional melodrama and country activity. The funeral of Imogen is entirely pastoral, of course. The captivity motif is supplied by Imogen's joining the Roman soldiers and their capture by Cymbeline's forces. The heroine and the two lost princes are restored to their parent and their birthrights are proclaimed. The heroine is also restored to her lover, albeit he was not involved in the pastoral interlude.[23]

Thus Shakespeare's story is essentially that of the traditional pastoral plot derived from Longus, although it deviates in the all-important aspect of *not* having the heroine in disguise love the highborn hero in country habit. The reasons for the deviation are obvious: Imogen was already provided with a lover before her pastoral life began, and for Arviragus or Guiderius to have loved her erotically would have been doubly unnatural, since she was not only their unknown sister, but also disguised as a boy. The young men are provided by Shakespeare only with awareness of her charm and a desire to make a "brother" of her. In short, Shakespeare chose to avoid the sensational and abnormal which could have been a mine of opportunity for a Ford or a Webster.

The Greek romance motifs in *Cymbeline* which are linked with Chariton, Xenophon of Ephesus, and Longus are surely secondhand, derived from other sources, and generally part of Shakespeare's literary heritage. But such is less obviously the case when we consider the materials which seem analogous to Achilles Tatius and Heliodorus. Interesting in this connection is the dramatic theme of mistaken death which occurs three times in *Clitophon and Leucippe:* Once Leucippe is apparently eviscerated by robbers; once she is apparently beheaded by pirates; and once a false report of her death is made. In *Cymbeline* the motif of mistaken death occurs at least four times: Imogen is poisoned and a deathlike trance results; Posthumus is apparently decapitated; Imogen is falsely reported dead; the lost sons of Cymbeline are for many years thought to be dead. The decapitation incident has several parallels with the similar situation in Achilles Tatius.

In the romance Leucippe is kidnapped by pirates and carried aboard their ship. Clitophon pursues them in another ship, but he suddenly sees Leucippe on the deck of the pirates' ship, her hands bound behind her. She is then decapitated and her body is cast into the sea. The pirates escape with the head, taking it further out to sea. Clitophon recovers the body, laments, and buries it. At the end it develops that a harlot had been dressed in Leucippe's clothes, killed, and the head carried off so that Clitophon would believe Leucippe dead and give up the pursuit.

In *Cymbeline,* Cloten, the unwelcome suitor of Imogen, is dressed in Posthumus's clothes when he insults Guiderius. In a hand-to-hand fight, Guiderius decapitates him and casts the head in a stream which will carry it to sea. With the help of Belarius and Arviragus, he places the body in a cave near the supposedly dead Imogen. Imogen awakens, and recognizing her husband's cloth-

ing, believes the body that of Posthumus. She laments
and buries it. Not until the last act is the confusion
resolved.

The parallel is obvious: In both cases a lover mistakes a headless body dressed in the beloved's clothing
for the body of the beloved. In both cases the head is
disposed of in the sea to make identification impossible
or less likely. Interesting is the fact that the sea figures
in Shakespeare's inland decapitation as well as in
Achilles Tatius's waterfront horror, and for the same
reason. To avoid identification of Cloten's body, Guiderius says: "I'll throw't into the creek/ Behind our rock,
and let it to the sea" (IV, ii, 151f). In Imogen's lament
over the body nautical imagery occurs: "damn'd Pisanio,/ From this most bravest vessel of the world/
Struck the main-top!" (IV, ii, 318–20). In Clitophon's
lament over the body, he cries: "the least part of thy
shape is left to mee."[24] In both cases the greater importance of the lost head over the rest of the body is emphasized in the lament by the bereaved.

Another passage which suggests Achilles Tatius occurs in the bedroom scene of *Cymbeline*. Iachimo steals
from the trunk and looks down upon the sleeping Imogen. As material for his treacherous report he notes:
"She hath been reading late/ The tale of Tereus; here
the leaf's turn'd down/ Where Philomel gave up" (II, ii,
44–46). Imogen has been reading the hideous tragedy of
Philomel and Tereus just before she sleeps, while Iachimo lurks secretly in the trunk waiting to wreak his
treachery against her. The tale is a portent of evil and
symbolizes the suffering and sorrow to follow for Imogen.

Similarly, just before Leucippe, as a result of a
friend's treachery, falls into the hands of the pirates and
suffers her most agonizing tribulations, she and Clitophon are given a sign of trouble ahead: "I did beholde a

table, wherein was drawn the mishap of *Progne*, the violence of *Tereus*, the cutting out of the tongue of Philomela."[25]

In both instances the tale of Tereus is an omen of evil which precedes treachery on the part of a friend, separation of lovers, the apparent death of the heroine, and much sorrow and unhappiness for the protagonists of the tales. Taken alone this would not necessarily suggest Achilles Tatius, but coupled with the similarities which occur in the decapitation incident, it becomes more significant. A few other parallels between Achilles Tatius and *Cymbeline* are interesting: As the novel opens Clitophon is being forced by his father into an unwelcome marriage with his half sister, the child of his father's second wife. Similarly, Imogen is out of favor as the play opens because she has chosen against the will of her father to marry Posthumus rather than the son of the father's second wife. The baleful effects of Imogen's precious compound, which she swallows innocently as medicine, has a kind of parallel in the double-strength love potion, innocently downed, which drives Leucippe to madness.

In the play when Iachimo gives false evidence of having lain with Imogen, he begins with a fairly extended description of her bedchamber:

> [*Iachimo*] . . . it was hang'd
> With tapestry of silk and silver; the story
> Proud Cleopatra, when she met her Roman,
> And Cydnus swell'd above the banks, or for
> The press of boats or pride;
>
> . . . .
> . . . The chimney
> Is south the chamber, and the chimney-piece
> Chaste Dian bathing; never saw I figures
> So likely to report themselves;
>
> . . . .

> The roof o' the chamber
> With golden cherubins is fretted; her andirons—
> I had forgot them—were two winking Cupids
> Of silver, each on one foot standing, nicely
> Depending on their brands.
>
> (II, iv, 68–91 passim)

The description is in the tradition of a formal ekphrasis of a work of art, a commonplace of the elaborate Hellenistic style and frequent in Achilles Tatius, which, indeed, begins with an ekphrasis of a painting, as does *Daphnis and Chloe*.[26] In the Greek works the ekphrases which begin the novels in both cases symbolize the stories to follow. Those within the body of the work sometimes have symbolic relationship to the content. In *Cymbeline*, however, the description of Imogen's bedroom becomes a facet of the plot. If there is symbolic purpose it may be chaste romantic love, but certainly it is used psychologically to help convince Posthumus that Iachimo has, indeed, been in Imogen's private chamber.

Close examination reveals that *Cymbeline* was probably influenced by the *Aethiopica* and was perhaps even a conscious imitation of that romance. If so, the idea of an imitation, of a new Heliodoran romance, could have been suggested by Sidney's imitation, *The Countess of Pembroke's Arcadia*, with which it has much in common; although the *Aethiopica* was popular enough to have been its own suggestive force. Whichever was so, there seems to be evidence that Shakespeare gathered ideas and materials directly from the *Aethiopica* in writing *Cymbeline*, and it is logical to conclude that he derived them from the very widely read translation of Thomas Underdowne.

First, *Cymbeline* is clearly an example of the Heliodoran structural concept, of beginning *in medias res* and then filling in the necessary information about earlier action by means of the "tale-within-the-tale" or the "flashback," episodic passages which serve to advance the plot and further its complications. The plot finally becomes deeply entangled by three distinct threads of action, all of which are unraveled together in the final scenes. In the involved chronology of the *Aethiopica* many important events have occurred before the story opens. These are explained episodically in careful stages as the story proceeds by various characters who were more or less directly involved in them. Most important is the gradual revelation of the birth, abandonment, and education of Chariclea, the heroine. In *Cymbeline*, two important actions occur before the play opens: the story of Posthumus—his unhappy birth, education, marriage, and subsequent loss of favor at court—and the kidnapping of Cymbeline's two sons. We learn the details of Posthumus's history early in the play as one courtier tells another. We learn of the missing princes at the same time, but, as with Chariclea, further details of their story are later revealed, and the mystery is not really resolved until the final scene.

The narration of the past action and the withholding of details to create suspense is one of the oldest and commonest of literary devices, and Shakespeare did not have to learn it from Heliodorus. Indeed, he had used it countless times before *Cymbeline*, but if he were consciously modeling a play into a Heliodoran romance, it was a necessary structural element.

Second, the plot of *Cymbeline*, like the plot of the *Aethiopica*, is a complicated arrangement of three separate threads. Their mutual cohesion is not felt until near the conclusion of novel and play:

AETHIOPICA	CYMBELINE
1. Elopement of Theagenes and Chariclea—leads to apparent death,	1. Marriage of Imogen and Posthumus—leads to separation of couple,

separation of couple, un-fortunate adventures occasioned by travel, suspicion of heroine's chastity.	unfortunate chastity wager, apparent death, travel.
2. King Hydaspes's lost heir—the birth, abandonment, and education of Chariclea.	2. King Cymbeline's lost heirs—the kidnapping and education of Guiderius and Arviragus.
3. King Hydaspes's victorious war with Egypt —leads to recovery of lost heir; peace brings about the denouement.	3. King Cymbeline's victorious war with Rome —leads to recovery of lost heirs; peace brings about the denouement.

These three plot threads in the *Aethiopica* and *Cymbeline* parallel each other, and all are being unfolded more or less concurrently as the novel and the play proceed. The lost-heir stories and the victorious wars of the kings are obviously similar themes, but the stories of the pairs of lovers also reveal a connection. Theagenes and Chariclea are forced to elope because Chariclea's foster father wishes to marry her to his nephew. Their travels occasion many unfortunate adventures, including the apparent death of the heroine and separation of the couple, but finally result in approval of the union. Similarly, Imogen and Posthumus marry secretly because Imogen's father wishes to marry her to his stepson. Posthumus is banished because of the marriage; thus the couple are separated. Now the wager story intervenes and makes less clear the parallel with the *Aethiopica*. Actually, it leads to the supposed death of the heroine, adventures occasioned by travel, and, ultimately, to the approval of the union. Even if Shakespeare deliberately imitated the *Aethiopica*, he was far too fine an artist to imitate slavishly and not to improve on his models when he saw room for improvement. The wager

story certainly furnishes better motivation for the supposed death and adventures of Imogen than the casual
depredations of robbers and brigands who do all the
mischief-making in the romance.

Third, both in the *Aethiopica* and in *Cymbeline* the
action takes place against a background of war and
empire. The recovery of heirs to the throne and the
business of state are central themes. The love affairs of
the chief protagonists are conducted in a field of inter-
national tension and concluded in a great public gathering on a note of popular approval. As the *Aethiopica*
can be called a historical romance, so *Cymbeline* can be
called a historical play; not a history play like those of
the Lancastrian tetralogy, but one such as Sir Walter
Scott might have written—a historical novel dramatized
—the background vaguely true, the lovers pure fiction.
Like Cymbeline, Hydaspes is victorious in war, but he
surrenders his rights as a conqueror and moves his
troops back inside the borders of Ethiopia. Magnan-
imously, he restores to power the conquered ruler of
Egypt, Oroondates, and there is a gracious aura of reconciliation throughout the last book of the romance.
Cymbeline, too, seems to have preferred the status quo.
After he wins a victory against Rome—in a war ostensibly fought because Britain was too proud to pay tribute
—he proclaims the victory to all and announces to the
conquered:

> My peace we will begin. And, Caius Lucius,
> Although the victor, we submit to Caesar,
> And to the Roman empire; promising
> To pay our wonted tribute.
>
> (V, v, 460–63)

And to the critics baffled by Cymbeline's failure to take
advantage of his victory and cast off the bonds of Rome,
I suggest that Shakespeare could have been mindful of

Hydaspes's example and wished to end the play on the same harmonious note that concludes the romance.

Fourth, the protagonists of the *Aethiopica* and *Cymbeline* are strikingly similar in their characterizations and in their marriage relationships. Both pairs are married, but in each case the consummation of their union has been withheld. Before their elopement, Chariclea and Theagenes make an oath to preserve their virginity until Chariclea is restored to her parents;[27] but they are obviously recognized as married, although Heliodorus makes no reference to the ceremony, for in the denouement Chariclea declares Theagenes to be her husband, and the queen tells King Hydaspes: "this yong Greke [Theagenes] is your daughter's husband."[28]

The bond that unites Imogen and Posthumus seems to have been a handfasting, an old form of irregular or probationary marriage contracted by the parties' joining hands and agreeing to live as man and wife. Obviously, in Imogen's case it was not considered irrevocable, or Cymbeline could not have continued to press Cloten on her; and in no instance does Imogen refuse Cloten for that best of all reasons, a previous marriage. Yet she refers to Posthumus as "husband":

> A father cruel, and a step-dame false;
> A foolish suitor to a wedded lady,
> That hath her husband banish'd: O! that husband,
> My supreme crown of grief!
>
> (I, vi, 1–4)

And Posthumus calls her "wife," at the same time making clear that the marriage is not yet a legal finality:

> . . . my mother seem'd
> The Dian of that time; so doth my wife
> The nonpareil of this. O! vengeance, vengeance;
> Me of my lawful pleasure she restrain'd
> And pray'd me oft forbearance; . . .
>
> (II, v, 6–10)

Besides this similarity in their marriage relationship, there is marked agreement in the characterizations of the couples. Both heroines are princesses and heirs to the crown. Imogen loses her right of succession when her brothers are restored, but during most of the action she holds it. Both girls are supremely beautiful and faultlessly chaste, although in each case their chastity is called into question. Chariclea, like other Greek romance heroines, is often mistaken for a divinity: When Belarius first sees Imogen in the cave he cries:

> By Jupiter, an angel! or, if not,
> An earthly paragon! Behold divineness
> No elder than a boy!
> (III, vi, 42–44)

Chariclea is the first among all the Greek-romance heroines for ready wit and quick, inventive intelligence in time of danger. By evasion or clever thinking she worms her way out of every scrape that arises. She handles pirates and enemies with duplicity, and her nimble wit turns every occasion to advantage. Stronger than her lover, she prevents Theagenes from suicide when he thinks their situation beyond hope. It is she who thinks of traveling in disguise, and it is Chariclea who whispers to her lover, "remember [I am] your sister," when they are being led into a difficult situation with another woman.[29] Imogen is no less clever. Roman soldiers find her lying stunned on the headless body of Cloten and rouse her. They demand her story, and she who has just come through the devastating experience of waking from a poison-induced trance to find the headless trunk of her "husband" lying beside her has the presence of mind to make up a new identity and a good story on the spot and without a moment's hesitation:

> *Imo.*[*gen*]:   I am nothing; or if not,
> Nothing to be were better. This was my master,

A very valiant Briton and a good,
That here by mountaineers lies slain. Alas!
. . . .
Luc.[ius]:   . . . Say his name, good friend.
Imo: Richard du Champ.—[*Aside.*] If I do lie and do
No harm by it, though the gods hear, I hope
They'll pardon it.—Say you, sir?
Luc: Thy name?
Imo: Fidele, sir.

(IV, ii, 367–70, 376–79)

Chariclea and Imogen are equally capable and single-minded in the handling of their affairs in the triallike denouement. At the conclusion of the *Aethiopica*, Chariclea becomes mistress of the entire proceeding, and by her clever management of the situation she establishes proof of her chastity, saves both Theagenes and herself from death, manages an official recognition of herself as the child of Hydaspes and heir to the crown of Ethiopia, and wins parental and public approval of union with Theagenes.[30] Imogen handles her business with equal capacity. Disguised as a boy and serving as a page to the captive Roman leader, she is led before Cymbeline. He is pleased with her and grants her a boon. Her master, Lucius, who has just begged her life, says:

I do not bid thee beg my life, good lad;
And yet I know thou wilt.

(V, v, 102–103)

But Imogen has just discovered Iachimo wearing her diamond, and all sentimental considerations are brushed aside for the heart of the matter:

Imo.[gen]:   No, no; alack!
There's other work in hand.

(V, v, 103–104)

And from there she manages to wring a full confession of guilt from Iachimo, dispel all doubts of her chastity, and claim her husband. Sentiment is also brushed aside when she first sees Posthumus after she had been led to think him dead. Still dressed as a boy, she calls to him. Failing to recognize her, he strikes her in anger and she falls unconscious. Waking, she finds Pisanio bending over her. Instead of calling for her husband as one would expect, she sets about at once to settle the score for the poison Pisanio had ostensibly given to her. This businesslike attitude, which duplicates that of Chariclea in Book X, eventually solves all problems of poison and identity and wins her the blessing of her father on her marriage with Posthumus.

Despite their ready wit and single-minded determination in business matters, these heroines occasionally refuse to speak out frankly. Chariclea cannot bring herself to tell her father the truth of her relationship with Theagenes: "But what fellow is this [Theagenes], that was taken with thee . . . Cariclea blushed, and cast down her eyes. . . . what he is in deede, he can tel you better then I: for he is a man, and therefore wil not be afraid to speak more boldly then I that am a woman."[31] But sent aside to a private tent with her mother, after much hesitation she makes clear her marriage.[32]

Imogen blushes even with her husband:

> [*Posthumus*] . . . [Imogen]   pray'd me oft forbearance; did it with
> A pudency so rosy the sweet view on't
> Might well have warm'd old Saturn.
>
> (II, v, 10–12)

Sometimes she, too, prefers to talk in private. When she sights Iachimo and the king sees her eyes fix on him, he questions their relationship. She replies:

I'll tell you, sir, in private, if you please
To give me hearing.

(V, v, 116–17)

As with the heroines, there is a similarity in the characterizations of the heroes. Both are personally attractive, successful soldiers, and much is made of their descent from military heroes. Of Theagenes one is informed in more than one full page of text that "he fetched his petigree from Achilles . . . who doth deeme no lesse by his tall stature, and comely personage, which manifestly confirme Achilles bloud, Saving that he is not so arrogant, and proude as he was, but doth moderate, and asswage . . . with commendable courtesie."[33] Posthumus was the son of the noble Sicilius who fought against the Romans and "So gain'd the sur-addition Leonatus" (I, i, 33). Of Posthumus a courtier says:

[*First Gentleman*]   . . . I do not think
So fair an outward and such stuff within
Endows a man but he.

(I, i, 22–24)

Yet each hero is outranked by his lady, the crown princess, and each is less capable of good judgment. Theagenes depends on Chariclea to extract him from difficult situations: she thinks of traveling in disguise; she thinks of acting as his sister when he is being pursued by a powerful and wicked woman; she finds means to save him from suicide; and it is Chariclea who engineers the conclusion of their adventures in such a way that his life is saved, he is recognized as her husband, and he is granted a kind of official priestly status in the kingdom.[34] Posthumus makes the incredible mistake of getting involved in the wager about his wife's chastity. He doubles his foolishness by setting Iachimo's word above his wife's known virtue. And as suicide seems the escape for Theagenes, so suicide is Posthumus's plan when he begins to repent the supposed death he had brought to his wife:

> [*Posthumus*] . . . Well, I will find him; [death]
>
> · · · · · · · · · · · · · · · · · · ·
>
> . . . fight I will no more,
> But yield me to the veriest hind that shall
> Once touch my shoulder.
>
> (V, iii, 73 and 76–78)

Yet both are cheerful in prison. Theagenes jokes about his golden chains when he is made a captive: "Good lorde, whence commeth this trimme chaunge? Truly fortune flattereth us wonderfully, we chaunge yron for gold and in prison we are inriched, so that wee bee more worth in our bandes."[35] In *Cymbeline*, much of Act V, scene iv, is comic repartee between Posthumus and his jailers.

Further characterization of Posthumus is provided through the use of a motif typical in Greek romance: the hero strikes the heroine. Such a blow occurs in *Chaereas and Callirhoe, Apollonius of Tyre*, and the *Aethiopica*. In the *Aethiopica* the situation is as follows: Unfortunately separated from Theagenes, Chariclea is disguised and is traveling as a female beggar. After much suffering and searching she reaches Memphis during a public triallike combat. Recognizing Theagenes in the crowd of spectators she "ranne to him like a mad woman, and hanging by her armes about his necke . . . saluted him with certaine pittifull lamentations. He . . . supposing her to be one of the makeshifts of the Citie, . . . cast her off, . . . and at length gave her a blow on the eare, for that she troubled him."[36] In *Cymbeline* there is a similar situation: After long separation and travel, Posthumus and Imogen, unknown to each other, are present in the triallike scene when Cymbeline makes peace with Rome. Imogen recognizes Iachimo and he is forced to tell the story of his guilt. Posthumus hears his lady exonerated, and in agony confesses his responsibility for her death. Imogen recognizes him and runs to make herself known. He fails to recognize her, and thinking she scorns his agony, strikes her so that she falls (V, v). After her identity is made clear, Imogen embraces him and Posthumus says, "Hang there like fruit, my soul/ Till the tree die" (V, v, 263–64).

Posthumus's rage is better motivated than Theagenes's, and although it was not necessary to the plot, it is a fine bit of characterization. Yet, such action is bound to lessen the appeal of the hero, even if the one he struck were only the page he thought her to be. Theagenes's blow was a Greek romance motif, typical of the genre and expected by the reader. Posthumus's blow seems to be a rather self-conscious duplication of it, for in both instances the blow occurs at a triallike public occasion after long separation of the lovers. In both instances the heroines are disguised and thus recognize the heroes first. In both instances the heroes cast aside their wives in temper, but since they act before the ladies are recognized, censure is uncalled for. In neither case does the blow advance the plot.

Finally, the triallike denouement, which ends both romance and play, probably affords the most conclusive evidence that Shakespeare was influenced by Heliodorus. Both denouements take the form of a great public assembly presided over by a king who has just recently been the leader of a victorious army. Hydaspes of the *Aethiopica* has drawn his people together for a public sacrifice of the prisoners of war to celebrate the victory in Egypt. Cymbeline's gathering seems to be to announce the victory over Rome and to make disposition of the prisoners of war. In each case the king has a lost daughter and suffers the loss of the heir to his crown.

During the proceedings, the lost daughter is present, but the relationship is at first unknown to the father. In the *Aethiopica* Chariclea has been appointed, since she is a prisoner of war, as a sacrifice to the moon goddess. When she is led in, her mother is moved to think of her lost daughter and begs the king to release Chariclea to her service. Hydaspes's reply is: "Yet am I moved somewhat too with the maide, and have compassion uppon her."[37] Likewise when Imogen is brought in a prisoner of war—she has been serving the Roman leader as a page —her father says:

> *Cym.*[*beline*]:   I have surely seen him;
> His favor is familiar to me. Boy,
> Thou hast look'd thyself into my grace.
>   (V, v, 93–95)

After Chariclea has been led in as a sacrifice, proof of her chastity is established in a trial by fire. Shortly after Imogen has been presented to her father, her chastity is attested by Iachimo's confession, an interesting cultural transformation. The kings who conduct the gatherings each condemn their lost heirs to death unknowingly. Chariclea is ordained a state sacrifice, despite the queen's pleading and Hydaspes's own contrary inclinations, for he puts public duty above private preference. Guiderius, the lost son and heir of Cymbeline, confesses his slaying of Cloten. The king reluctantly condemns him to death; he too putting public duty above private feelings, for Guiderius has just helped him to win the victory against Rome:

> *Cym.*[*beline*]:   Marry, the gods forfend!
> I would not thy good deeds should from my lips
> Pluck a hard sentence: prithee, valiant youth,
> Deny't again.
>   (V, v, 288–91)

But Guiderius does not deny it and, like Chariclea, is saved from the death sentence only when his identity as the king's heir is finally revealed. In each case, before the identities are proved, the kings disdain the suggestion that the veins of Chariclea and Guiderius contain the blood royal:

> *Aethiopica*
> "Soft (quoth Cariclea) you woonder at small things, there be greater matters then this, for I am not onely one of this countrey borne, but of the bloud royall. Hydaspes despised her words, and turned away as though they had beene to no purpose. . . . Therewith the king not onely despised her, but waxed very wroth."[38]

> *Cymbeline*
> Bel.[*arius*]:   Stay, sir king:
> This man is better than the man he slew,
> As well descended as thy self;
> . . . .
> Cym.[*beline*]:   Why, old soldier,
> Wilt thou undo the worth thou art unpaid for,
> By tasting of our wrath? How of descent
> As good as we?
> Arv.[*iragus*]:   In that he spake too far.
> Cym: And thou shalt die for't.
>   (V, v, 302–304, 307–11)

Finally, of course, the heirs are identified. Chariclea has a royal robe, various jewels and tokens, and a fascia —work of her royal mother—as well as a black birthmark to attest to her paternity. Belarius declares that Arviragus

> . . . was lapp'd
> In a most curious mantle, wrought by the hand
> Of his queen mother,
>   (V, v, 361–63)

and Cymbeline recalls that

> Guiderius had
> Upon his neck a mole, a sanguine star;
> It was a mark of wonder.
>   (V, v, 364–66)

In each case the lost heirs are identified by an intellectual who has been responsible for their rearing and education. Sisimithres, a gymnosophist, found Chariclea as an infant and reared her for seven years. He is present at the denouement and identifies her tokens and admits his part in her history. Charicles, a Neo-Pythagorean priest of Delphi and a follower of the philosophy of Apollonius of Tyana, reared Chariclea from the age of seven years to adulthood. He, too, is present at the conclusion and clarifies details of her history which are unknown to Sisimithres.

In a similar manner, Belarius, who kidnapped, reared, and educated both Guiderius and Arviragus, identifies those heirs and is characterized as an intellectual, a kind of philosopher escaped from court to the woodlands. In this sense he reflects the traditional philosophic shepherd found in most pastoral plots, including the parent plot, *Daphnis and Chloe*. Belarius constantly philosophizes in dialogue and soliloquy, presenting ideas which reflect a robust love of nature and the hardy life which seem to have been the key principles in the education which he provided for the young princes.[39]

In both novel and play the symbolism of birth is concurrent with the restoration of the heirs. Before Chariclea is restored to her parents, her mother says that she dreamed "I was with childe, and brought foorth a daughter which was marriageable presently."[40] And when Cymbeline is surrounded at long last by his three children he says:

> . . . O! what, am I
> A mother to the birth of three? Ne'er mother
> Rejoic'd deliverance more.
>
> **(V, v, 369–71)**

But to leave the heirs for the heroes: Both Theagenes
and Posthumus are prepared to be executed during the
denouement. Theagenes as a prisoner of war is ordained
a sacrifice to the sun god, but is saved on account of his
relationship to Chariclea. Posthumus, also condemned
as a prisoner of war, is saved by his relationship to
Imogen.

The heroines in each case are the especial concern of
the leaders of the defeated armies. Oroondates, whom
Hydaspes had restored to power after victory over him,
writes a letter requesting Chariclea's return. It is read
during the denouement: "There was a certaine maid
who in carriage from Memphis, happened to fall into
your handes by chaunce of warre, . . . this wench I
desire you to sende me, both for her owne sake, but
most for her fathers [Charicles, the foster father]."[41]
Lucius, the noble leader of the defeated Roman army,
pleads for Imogen—this before she is recognized—

> . . . This one thing only
> I will entreat; my boy, a Briton born,
> Let him be ransom'd; never master had
> A page so kind, so duteous, diligent.
>
> **(V, v, 83–86)**

Before the conclusion of the denouements oracles are
unraveled. In the *Aethiopica* the priest, Charicles "re-
membered him selfe of the Oracles answere at Delphi,
and sawe that fulfilled in deede, which was promised
before of the Goddes."[42] In *Cymbeline*, Posthumus's
dream-delivered oracle is unraveled by the soothsayer,
Philarmonous, and the conditions are declared fulfilled

in the restoration of the two lost princes and the reunion of Imogen and Posthumus.

The ends of both novel and play ring a similar note:

> *Aethiopica*
> Hydaspes then came to the altars, . . . ready to be-
> ginne sacrifice[43]

> *Cymbeline*
> Cym.[*beline*]:   Laud we the gods;
> And let our crooked smokes climb to their nostrils
> From our bless'd altars.
>
> (V, v, 477–79)[44]

On this body of evidence is based the conclusion that
Cymbeline was meant to be a kind of dramatized Greek
romance and was probably modeled after the *Aethiopica* of Heliodorus. Such a conclusion does not displace
the long-recognized sources, but explains the combination and arrangement of the Boccaccio and Holinshed
materials and makes clear the need for the Guiderius-Arviragus subplot. In short, it seems likely that Heliodorus
is the source of the structural elements and some of the
plot materials which make *Cymbeline* a modern example of Greek romance.

If we accept the conclusion that *Cymbeline* was
meant to be a Heliodoran romance, we can account for
several details which have occasioned unfavorable criticism. Foremost among these is the fourth scene of the
fifth act, which contains the comic banter of Posthumus
with his jailers and his subsequent oracular dream. The
clumsy oracle[45] and the comedy have both been called
out of place, unnecessary, and unworthy of Shakespeare's genius. They have been labeled the work of
another, an interpolation.[46] But if Shakespeare were deliberately creating a Heliodoran romance the scene can
be understood as duplicating motifs in the source mate-

rial, and although it is not thus artistically commended, such an interpretation is evidence against the contention that the scene is not from Shakespeare's pen. The Heliodoran concept of *Cymbeline* accounts for Posthumus's unfortunate behavior, for it makes appropriate the wager plot requiring a test of the heroine's virtue and leads to several Greek romance essentials: travel and separation of married lovers, seeming death of the heroine, triumphant vindication of the heroine's chastity, and final recognition and reunion. The wager plot also was capable of being engineered to include that other Greek romance motif, the striking of the heroine by the hero. The conclusion that *Cymbeline* is a Heliodoran romance also partly accounts for King Cymbeline's mysterious surrender of his rights of victory to Rome, and it explains a seeming flaw in Imogen's characterization: her first settling with Pisanio about her own poisoning, while Posthumus, whom she had long thought dead, stands by waiting to speak with her. Imogen simply duplicates here some of the elements in the characterization of Chariclea.

In connection with the suggestion that *Cymbeline* is Heliodoran romance, it is interesting to note that where Shakespeare selects materials unrelated to the *Aethiopica,* his genius for recognizing and seizing the appropriate led him unerringly to materials which evolved from, or have an affinity to other Greek romances. The wager plot seems to be a Renaissance development of Chariton's *Chaereas and Callirhoe;* the lost-heir motif can be linked with *Daphnis and Chloe* of Longus; the apparent death of Imogen seems to go back to the *Ephesiaca* of Xenophon of Ephesus; and the mistaken death of Posthumus parallels an incident in *Clitophon and Leucippe* of Achilles Tatius. Only the Holinshed materials cannot be called Greek romance.[47]

But Greek romance generally, and Heliodorus in particular, demanded a shadowy historical background to the love story, and Shakespeare met the demand nationalistically, satisfying both the public and Heliodorus by his choice.[48]

Chapter Five

Shakespeare's
Greek Romances [2]

THE WINTER'S TALE

Like *Cymbeline* and *Pericles, The Winter's Tale* appears
to be a conscious adaptation of Greek romance to the
stage. On first reading, the exposure of Perdita and the
pastoral fourth act suggest Longus as the major Hellenistic influence. Reflection, however, leads inevitably to
recognition of Heliodorus as the central romance inspi-
ration, perceptibly shadowed by the ever-elusive Chariton. A second or third reading makes clear to the initiated that almost all the stock Greek romance plot
motifs in *Pericles* and *Cymbeline* fall, as with the turn of
the kaleidoscope, into new positions in *The Winter's
Tale.* Indeed, although there is some evidence that
Shakespeare drew directly from Angel Day's Longus
(1587), and most certainly reaped the major portion of
his plot from Robert Greene's *Pandosto: The Triumph
of Time* (London, 1588),[1] he might just as easily have
gathered his materials from his two earlier romantic
plays.

Most obvious in the Greek romance tradition is the
stock pastoral plot of Longus, which Shakespeare had

used already in *As You Like It* and *Cymbeline*. Greenlaw recognized only two features of this plot in *The Winter's Tale*, both derived by Shakespeare from his source in Greene's *Pandosto*, or as it is often called, *Dorastus and Fawnia*: Perdita, a child of unknown parentage, is reared by shepherds. A highborn lover, Prince Florizel, dresses as a shepherd to woo her. The genetic mutation can be easily traced, for other points of the stock pastoral plot are in the play and might be called recessive genes in the source. Greene's heroine, like the heroines of the *Arcadia*, is besieged by the traditional rude country lovers, although Shakespeare permits no clowns to trouble Perdita. Instead he substitutes her foster brother (who could not conventionally be expected to pursue her) and Mopsa and Dorcas to supply the comic country incidents expected by the audience of a pastoral play. The usual melodrama of an attack by a lion or a bear was introduced when poor Antigonus cried "This is the chase: I am gone for ever." And the stage directions say so bluntly: *"Exit, pursued by a bear"* (III, iii, 56–57). A further substitute can be found in the threat by Polixenes to have Perdita's "beauty scratch'd with briars" (IV, iii, 437) and his wrath which leads to the elopement of the lovers. The traditional captivity motif occurs in *Pandosto*, but is omitted from *The Winter's Tale*. The fifth act revelation of the heroine's high birth, smoothing the path to marriage, Shakespeare sets in the aristocratic atmosphere of the court, following Greene's lead and paralleling Longus, who took his cast to a great banquet in the city for the revelation of Chloe's high birth.

Samuel Lee Wolff's study of *Pandosto* suggests Longus as an immediate source of *The Winter's Tale* as well as an indirect source dependent on an evolved tradition which included Theocritus, Vergil, Tasso, Sidney, Greene, and Lodge.[2] The particulars of Perdita's expo-

sure, rearing, love affair, and restoration seem to derive
from the similar story of Chloe, through Fawnia's experience in Greene's novel.³ Wolff thinks, however, that
Shakespeare might have gone directly to Day's translation for some of the materials, since a detail of *The
Winter's Tale* agrees with Day, but has no parallel in
Greene: In *Daphnis and Chloe* a hunting party of young
Methymnaean gentlemen make such noise that sheep
and goats, frightened from their highland pasture, run
to the shore. Shakespeare borrows the detail of the hunt
and uses it economically to provide for the bear to
devour Antigonus and to send the old shepherd, seeking
after his herd, to the shore where he will find the child.⁴
The storm which destroys the ship may have been suggested to Shakespeare by Day's Longus, for such a
storm occurs there in connection with the hunt and has
no parallel in Greene: "This great afraie [storm] continued . . . all the night long, . . . in . . . [a] terrible
manner"⁵ and in the old Greek romance tradition did its
work in providing a turn for the plot.

The fourth act of *The Winter's Tale* is filled with the
general pastoral conventions to be found in both Greene
and Longus and in almost every other Renaissance pastoral. The rude shepherd of Longus is the clown in Shakespeare. The lists of flowers and country frolic at the
sheepshearing festival are traditional and pervasive in
pastoral literature, although Longus was one of the earlier writers to employ them. The visit of the king and
Camillo in *The Winter's Tale* parallels the visit of the
lord of the manor and his train in *Daphnis and Chloe*.
The visitation in each case leads to the recognition and
recovery of lost heirs. This may be another instance of
Shakespeare's turning directly to Longus, for in *Pandosto* the king and his train do not visit the heroine's
pastures until after the couple have eloped; thus, they
are not present at the country frolic. Interesting is one
minor point: Daphnis's, Dorastus's, and Florizel's par-

entage is revealed in the country setting; Chloe's, Fawnia's, and Perdita's parentage is revealed in a setting of high life—the city and the court.

In his study of *Pandosto,* however, Wolff attaches even more importance to the model of Heliodorus than to that of Longus. He concludes that the general scope of the plot, in its dependence on the association of a shipwreck with the oracle and with the exposure and restoration of a child, is Heliodoran in concept, and especially as "Fortune" is everywhere recognized as the instrument to create the peripeties and to work out the destined ends of the protagonists. The grand ensemble scene in which occurs the vindication of the queen's chastity at public trial by the oracle, the sudden deaths of Garinter and the queen, and the great three-day swoon of the king, Wolff considers reminiscent of the final ensemble scene of the *Aethiopica,* and he points to the fact that the double death at this gathering is called a "tragical discourse of fortune."[6]

As in the *Aethiopica,* the entire moving force of the plot is a king's jealousy. Fear of being accused of adultery caused Persina to abandon the infant Chariclea, and so began the chain of events which made up the plot of the romance. The jealousy of Pandosto causes him to suspect his queen of adultery. This leads to the exposure of the infant Fawnia and the subsequent details of the plot. As Chariclea was delivered over to Fortune: "I determined [says her mother] to ridde my selfe of shamefull death (counting it certaine that thy coulor woulde procure me to be accused of adulterie . . .) . . . and to commit thee to . . . fortune."[7] So was the infant Fawnia: "And shalt thou, sweet babe, be committed to fortune, [says her mother] when thou art already spited by fortune? . . . Let me . . . put this chain about thy little neck, that if fortune save thee, it may help to succour thee."[8]

The betrothal, elopement, sea journey, and shipwreck

of Dorastus and Fawnia parallel the unconsummated marriage, elopement, sea journey, and shipwreck of Theagenes and Chariclea, although the motif is a common one in the tradition. Finally, at the denouement of *Pandosto*, the moment of last suspense, the king unknowingly condemns his lost daughter and only heir to death, as does Hydaspes near the conclusion of the *Aethiopica*. In both cases the sentence is dismissed by the revelation of identity made by the foster parent and substantiated by tokens provided by the child's mother at the time of abandonment.

The same Heliodoran elements that occur in the source are reflected in Shakespeare. A shipwreck, perhaps inspired by the storm in Longus, but in the whole romance tradition, removes Antigonus's crew after Perdita has been abandoned and he has been devoured by a bear. An oracle at a public trial proclaims the queen's innocence and the necessity for the recovery of the child. In the last act it is said that the oracle had provided hope to the injured queen during her years of seclusion. The exposure and restoration of Perdita agree in general with the Heliodoran pattern in Greene. The tokens of the mother and the public revelation by the foster parents agree, but the motif of the father's unknowingly condemning his child to death is not in *The Winter's Tale*. Perhaps this is because Shakespeare had already used it in *Cymbeline*, but more likely it is because the character of Leontes needed softening.

Shakespeare, too, recognizes the hand of Fortune in the affairs of men. When Perdita is condemned by her father, he says:

> This female bastard hence; . . .
>
> . . . .
>   As by strange fortune
> It came to us, I do in justice charge thee,
>
> . . . .

That thou commend it strangely to some place,
Where chance may nurse or end it.
(II, iii, 174–82 passim)

And when Antigonus abandons the infant he says:

There lie; and there thy character; there these;
Which may, if fortune please, both breed thee,
    pretty . . .
(III, iii, 46–47)

Fortune is recognized by characters in other situations too:

Per.[*dita*]   O lady Fortune,
Stand you auspicious!
(IV, iii, 51–52)

[*Florizel to Perdita*]   Though Fortune, visible an
    enemy,
Should chase us with my father, power no jot
Hath she to change our loves.
(V, i, 216–18)

But Shakespeare does not make his characters slaves to chance; he employs natural causation frequently where Greene, like Heliodorus, explains an occurrence by a simple attribute to Fortune. For example: Antigonus dreams that Hermione has commanded him to leave the children in Bohemia; whereas in Greene the child, placed in a little boat, is through the agency of Fortune washed upon a friendly shore. Shakespeare provided a hunt to send a shepherd to the shore after his sheep and, thus, to find the child. In Greene, the shepherd goes by chance to the shore in seeking the sheep. Further, when Florizel and Perdita elope they are directed by Camillo to the court of Leontes where they expect to receive a friendly reception. Dorastus and Fawnia arrive at Pandosto's court simply because they are blown by the wind and washed ashore by the sea.[9]

Nevertheless, it would seem that Heliodorus may be an important secondary source of *The Winter's Tale*, for in several instances where Greene has perhaps borrowed Heliodoran materials and concepts for the working out of the plot, Shakespeare has absorbed them into his play. Although the Heliodoran elements are in no case so positively suggested as the pastoral portions suggest Longus, they are numerous enough and visible enough to make one say that the play as a whole is more Heliodoran in character than it is pastoral. Since there is clear evidence that Shakespeare had studied the *Aethiopica* before writing *Cymbeline*, it seems possible that he recognized the Greek romance in the background of *Pandosto*, and thus selected it for the foundation of his play, consciously continuing the tradition established and popularized in *Pericles* and *Cymbeline*. This conclusion is substantiated in part by an examination of Shakespeare's major deviation from *Pandosto*— his permitting the heroine to suffer seeming death rather than real death, the fate of Greene's Bellaria. This one change not only lifts the significance of *The Winter's Tale* to the level of a resurrection myth or allegory, but it brings Shakespeare even closer to Greek romance than his source, for seeming death of the heroine is a standard motif of the genre, and appears in each of the romances under consideration except *Daphnis and Chloe*.

For the deathlike swoon of Hermione and her dramatic return to life, it has been convincingly suggested that Shakespeare looked again to the twenty-second tale of the first part of Bandello, "Signor Timbreo di Cardona and Fenicia Lionata," the same tale from which he had drawn materials for *Much Ado About Nothing*. The parallel in the situation is striking: King Leontes accuses Queen Hermione of unchastity. She falls into a deathlike swoon, and although Leontes believes her dead and buried, she is revived and lives secluded from him. The king does penance at her tomb and finally surrenders judgment as to whom he shall marry to Paulina, the person responsible for the queen's seclusion. A "living likeness" of the "dead" queen is produced by Hermione's posing as her own statue. The reconciliation is quickly effected and is followed by a marriage of the king's friend Camillo with the queen's friend Paulina.[10]

It is obvious that the situation in *The Winter's Tale* closely resembles the Hero-Claudio plot of *Much Ado*, even to the marriage of the secondary characters at the conclusion. The living statue motif might have been suggested by the description of Fenicia in her deathlike swoon: "si lasciò andare come morta, e perdendo subito il natiuo colore, più àvna statua di marmo che à creatura rassembraua."[11] The possible tie with Bandello links *The Winter's Tale* with the romance of *Chaereas and Callirhoe* of Chariton, which is probably the ultimate source of Bandello's novella. So again it would seem that in selecting plot materials for his play, Shakespeare turned to a source that was as much like Greek romance in its fundamental nature as was *Pandosto*.

Unlike *Pericles* and *Cymbeline*, which draw firsthand on the Greek romances, *The Winter's Tale* seems thus to be a composite of several romances through secondary sources. Heliodorus and Longus are present where Shakespeare followed Greene; Chariton may appear at the conclusion. It is also possible that the romance of *Amadis of Gaul* furnished Prince Florizel with a name and suggested the idea of the statue.[12] But the significant fact is that in almost every case there is some evidence that Shakespeare developed *The Winter's Tale* out of Greek romance materials, and where he deviated from his major source, *Pandosto*, he deviated in the direction of other Greek romances.

Coupled with the splendor and supple beauty of the

poetry, it is the great deviation from *Pandosto* back to Greek romance in the restoration of the supposedly dead queen to her husband that lifts *The Winter's Tale* into what may be both the intellectual and artistic culmination of the ancient narrative and thematic materials. In part they are to appear once more in *The Tempest*, a play written about a year after *The Winter's Tale*, embodied there in almost perfect form, but carrying a note of epilogue—the *nunc dimittis* of a poetic career if we may call *The Winter's Tale* the *benedicite omnia opera*—rather than the climax of definition. The deeply moving themes of loss and recovery, reunion, forgiveness, and reconciliation that lift the hackneyed story of *Pericles* into a ritual of wonder and turn the aged plot involutions of *Cymbeline* into a kind of prophecy of British national destiny are restated in *The Winter's Tale* in terms of deeper understanding of the human condition and of "great creating nature" (IV, iv, 88). By restoring the queen Shakespeare made it possible to read the play concurrently as drama of the human experience of repentance and forgiveness; as allegory of the Christian redemption theology; and as a restatement of the Ceres-Persephone myth,[13] the ancient explanation of the seasonal cycles of dearth and fertility; of growth, decay, and regrowth; and by extension, as symbolic of human life cycles. The miracle of *The Winter's Tale* is partly in its poetry, partly in its revelation that as evil— often as illogical and as unreasoned as Leontes's jealousy—is an aspect of the total human condition, so also is good (in Hermione, Paulina, Camillo, Perdita); and so also are the very seeds of regeneration and reconciliation planted and dormant (the conception of Perdita) before the winter of death falls on the land. Further, *The Winter's Tale* demonstrates regenerative factors surviving within us (Leontes's repentance) even in the midst of self-inflicted tragedy, in our human powers of self-knowledge and contrition. As aspects of "great creating nature" work for the universe in cycles and measures diurnal, annual, millennial (the great sixteen-year gap in time between the events of the first three acts and the hymn to creative fertility that forms the fourth act), so do they work in man (a creature of nature) in human life cycles of marriage, birth, and death, the creation and dissolution and reformation of families, and by philosophic extension of nations and races of people. But there is realism in the romance. If the cycles of nature mend and restore what evil has ravished, yet all is not restored. Often the innocent are swallowed up. Hermione lives and is returned to a contrite husband, but her little son is still dead of his father's wrath, she has missed the natural pleasure of nurturing and rearing her daughter, and sixteen years of isolation and suffering have left her "so much wrinkled . . . / So aged as this seems" (V, iii, 28–29).

THE TEMPEST

Even more than *The Winter's Tale, The Tempest* is an amalgam of materials from various sources, part literary, part folk belief, part perhaps the tissue of human dreams. Although only one Greek romance, *Daphnis and Chloe*, is obviously indicated, it is a major thread in the complicated fabric of the play. The problem of the source of *The Tempest* has long intrigued scholars, because a single entirely satisfactory work has never been uncovered to account for its origin. Many significant contributions to the solution of the problem have, however, been offered. In 1817 Ludwig Tieck pointed to *Die schöne Sidea*, a play by Jacob Ayrer, as a source or close analogue. Its plot parallels *The Tempest* in that it centers on a prince-magician, served by a spirit, father of a daughter whose hand is won when the son of an enemy carries logs. *Die schöne Sidea* was surely written before 1605, the date of Ayrer's death, but since it went unpublished until 1618, seven years after the composition of *The Tempest,* a common ancestor is conjectured for the two, and most scholars are left unconvinced of a primary relationship.[14] The Italian *commedia dell' arte,* a form of entertainment very popular in Shakespeare's England, is also thought to have been a suggestive force for *The Tempest.* Several of the comedies dealt with the theme of men shipwrecked on an island ruled by a "Mago." Love intrigues between the crew and the natives formed the plot materials, and often the greed of the sailors provided the comic situation.[15] A possible source for the political intrigue which resulted in Prospero's banishment has been found in William Thomas's *History of Italy* (Pamplona, 1609).[16] The play has also been linked to the Spanish *Noches des Invierno* of Antonio Eslava, in which a dethroned king raises a magic castle in mid-ocean, where he lives with his daughter until, also by magic, he brings about a marriage between her and the son of an enemy.[17] The *Aeneid* of Vergil is credited with inspiring the storm and the meeting of the lovers[18] as well as the vanishing banquet. In Book III Harpies devour food set before Aeneas and his company. In Act III, scene iii, of *The Tempest,* Ariel in guise of a Harpy manages the disappearing meal.[19] Many contemporary accounts of storms and shipwrecks have also been offered as sources for the storm of the first act, and in many there can be found a few similarities to the storm of the play.[20] Montaigne's essay "Of the Caniballes," published in 1603 in a translation by John Florio, takes credit for suggesting the nature of Caliban, and Golding's translation of Ovid's *Metamorphoses,* VII, probably suggested characteristics of Sycorax and Prospero's valedictory address (V, i, 33–50).[21] Even after careful study of all these works it is clear that the marvelous composite quality of *The Tempest* is not entirely traced to its sources, and it is without questioning the value of these recognized materials, nor assuming that one more suggestion will make for a final explanation, that Longus's romance of *Daphnis and Chloe* is named as another important influence on the genesis of the play.

First, *The Tempest* is primarily a pastoral play, having some affinity to Italian pastoral drama.[22] The plot easily fits into the framework of the stock Renaissance pastoral derived from Longus:

(1) Miranda, unaware that she is the daughter of the rightful duke of Milan, is reared in pastoral seclusion on a desert island.

(2) Ferdinand appears in the role of her lover and undertakes pastoral labors to win her (carries logs).

(3) Caliban replaces the blundering shepherd. Before the play opens he has made an attempt against Miranda's honor:

> [*Prospero to Caliban*] . . . I have us'd thee,
> Filth as thou art, with human care; and lodg'd thee
> In mine own cell, till thou didst seek to violate
> The honor of my child.
>
> (I, ii, 345–48)

The comedy scenes between Caliban and the crewmembers, Trinculo and Stephano, provide humor and reveal Caliban as a bumbling coward. He is, however, the foil to Ariel rather than to the hero.

(4) The traditional melodramatic elements supplied by an attack of a lion or a bear are omitted, unless the storm be designated melodrama.

(5) The captivity episode is represented by the plot of Caliban, Trinculo, and Stephano to kidnap Miranda. The plot is not successful, but the captivity motif is thus present.

(6) At the conclusion the identity of Miranda and her father is revealed to the strangers, a reconciliation is effected, and the lovers make plans for marriage.

The seventh element of the stock pastoral plot, the melancholic or philosophic shepherd—represented by Jaques in *As You Like It*, Philisides in Sidney's *Arcadia* —is not obviously present; for this Renaissance tradition of melancholy and discontent has been passed over and the thoughtful character, represented in *The Tempest* by Prospero, reverts to the earlier purely philosophic type as represented by the shepherd Philetas in *Daphnis and Chloe*. But significantly present in *The Tempest* is another feature which was not in the stock pastoral as it developed during the Renaissance: supernatural direction. In *Daphnis and Chloe*, Pan and the nymphs handle the problem of motivation and preside over the peripeties, while Eros personally conducts the love story. In *The Tempest* the supernatural control is in the hands of Prospero, but is executed by Ariel.

If it is agreed that *The Tempest* embodies elements of the Longus romance which were the typical pastoral material of the Renaissance, the problem now becomes one of determining just how direct the influence of Longus is on the play. The stock features as outlined could have been derived from almost any pastoral composition of the period. The omission of any melancholy or malcontent element in Prospero's characterization—the so-called Italian or Spanish feature of the stock plot— and the addition of the supernatural machinery point directly to Longus rather than to an intermediary source, except that omission cannot be a conclusive argument, and supernatural direction abounds in classical literature. Other close parallels with Longus do, however, exist, and these, coupled with the Greek features of the plot, lead one to suggest that Shakespeare was familiar with *Daphnis and Chloe* before he wrote

The Tempest, an idea bolstered by recognition of *Daphnis and Chloe* as a primary source of the pastoral sections of *The Winter's Tale.*

To turn to an examination of the romance and the play: First, there is a general parallel in theme, setting, and structure. Both *Daphnis and Chloe* and *The Tempest* take as a central topic the idea of celebrating the innocence of youth. Miranda and Ferdinand, Daphnis and Chloe are blessed innocents as lovers. Both works are island stories: in each the locale of the action is a sea-surrounded paradise. Nature plays a significant part in the background and becomes an important aspect of the intangible atmosphere of both novel and play. The characters in both refer frequently to nature and seem to be aware of it as a kind of presence.[23] Structurally, both works are tightly unified. Unlike the other Greek romances which roam all over the Mediterranean world, *Daphnis and Chloe* takes place in one location, the island of Lesbos, except for a few short paragraphs at the conclusion when Chloe goes to a nearby city to establish her identity. Although time in other Greek romances is vague and impossible to account for, in *Daphnis and Chloe* all the action occurs during the course of a year and an additional summer, except for a page or two of introductory matter which explains the nurture and rescue of the abandoned children. There are no subsidiary story lines in *Daphnis and Chloe* as in other Greek romances. All attention is focused on the central situation of the lovers. *The Tempest* has a similar unity. The action is all tightly bound to a sea island location and to the course of three hours' duration, a practice not frequent in Shakespeare, although he had followed it earlier in *The Comedy of Errors.* Shakespeare's romances based on *Apollonius of Tyre* and Heliodorus follow the structures of those works rather closely. Attention in *The Tempest* is centered so clearly on the brief conclusion of an action going back some twelve years in time that one could accurately describe the play as an extended fifth act. From the start all seem to be ready to come together for explanations, pardons, reconciliation, and farewell.

Second, there is a general correspondence in the characters. Daphnis and Ferdinand are both pretty youths who engage in pastoral labors, and, although Daphnis is country bred and Ferdinand court bred, both approach the heroines with innocent and reverent love. There is no more trivial sophistication in the love of Ferdinand for Miranda than in the pasture-bred love of Daphnis for Chloe. Further, Daphnis is led to Chloe by the supernatural agency of Eros: "So nowe haue I [Eros] . . . in . . . charge . . . Daphnis and Chloe, . . . this morning [I] brought them together vnto the downes."[24] And Ferdinand is led to Miranda by the supernatural agency of Ariel: "*Re-enter* ARIEL *invisible, playing and singing;* FERDINAND *following*" (I, ii, following line 374). Ariel literally sings Ferdinand to his bride.

Chloe and Miranda are both reared in pastoral seclusion, ignorant of their high births. Both are characterized as innocent of the world and of love—Miranda has seen no man but her father and the semi-man Caliban before she beholds Ferdinand. Chloe does not understand her emotions which are aroused by the sight of Daphnis. Chloe helps with Daphnis's herds; Miranda begs to carry logs for Ferdinand. Both have a high regard for their pastoral rearing. At the end of the novel, Chloe's city-born aristocratic background has been established; nevertheless, she and Daphnis return to the country for their wedding and settle there for a long life of pastoral delights. When Miranda hears of her former high estate, she says to her father: "What foul play had we that we came from thence?/ Or blessed was't we did? (I, ii, 60–61).

Philetas of the novel and Prospero of the play generally coincide. Philetas is a philosophic shepherd who
supervises the love affair of Daphnis and Chloe and acts
as a judge when Daphnis is tried for trouble created by
city gallants. He is generally respected and is a kind of
presiding patriarch of his island home. Prospero is also
a philosopher, although he combines the philosophy
with magic. By magic he instigates the love affair of
Miranda and Ferdinand. At the end of the play he serves
in a judgelike capacity when all identities are revealed
and the knots of the plot are untied. He, like Philetas, is
the deeply respected patriarch of an island.

Eros is the supernatural instigator and director of the
loves of Daphnis and Chloe; Philetas only supervises
and instructs. Invisible to the lovers, Eros leads them
together. He is associated with gardens, sunlight, laughter. He is birdlike in movement and in song: "some
preatie flieng partridge. . . . hee tendred vnto my hearing a sound so sweete, amiable, and well pleasing, as
there is no nightingale, thrush, or other kinde of bird
whatsoeuer, that haunteth either woods or hedge-rowes,
that euer gaue foorth . . . so delightfull a melodie . . .
fluttering . . . no otherwise then if it had bin some
pretie plesant redbrest."[25]

In the novel Eros is a semi-allegorical character. His
presence is felt; his work is recognized; but he is invisible to all except Philetas. Matching him in *The Tempest*
is Ariel, the supernatural spirit who leads Miranda and
Ferdinand together. Prospero instigates the plans for
this love, but Ariel executes them. Thus, the roles are
reversed. Like Eros, Ariel is associated with the pleasant
and sunny aspects of nature. His coming seems to create
music. He sings some of the loveliest songs in Shakespeare. Prospero refers to him as "my bird" (IV, i, 184).
He is at will invisible to all but Prospero, but others feel
his presence and seem to be aware of his influence. The

actual derivation of his name is from the Hebrew Ca-
bala, where he is the Prince of the Angels,[26] yet the
verbal correspondence between *Ariel* and *Eros* is
suggestive.

An incidental correspondence between *Daphnis and
Chloe* and *The Tempest* may rest in Prospero's command to Ariel: "Go make thyself like a nymph of the
sea" (I, ii, 301). The reason for the command has been
questioned, since there is no obvious advantage presented in the play by the proposed transformation.[27] But
nymphs figure in *Daphnis and Chloe* as the guardians of
the heroine, and they play an important role in the
supernatural machinery of the novel. On the supposition
that Shakespeare was familiar with the pastoral traditions established by Longus, it is here suggested that
Ariel in the role of a nymph simply suggested itself,
since he was to be the supernatural agent to accomplish
in *The Tempest* something of what the nymphs accomplish in *Daphnis and Chloe*.

Dorco functions in the novel as the rude, bumbling
shepherd, the rival of Daphnis, who supplies the comedy
in his uncouth efforts to win Chloe. As part of his suit he
supplies her with abundance of country gifts: "new
made fresh cheeses, couered wyth a faire white napkin,
and strowed ouer wyth the most sweete and delicate
floures, . . . skimmed creame, spice-cakes, and other
. . . faire tokens."[28] When these fail to win her, he disguises himself in a wolf-skin and attempts rape. Caliban
corresponds closely with Dorco, except that his "wolf-
skin" is part of his nature. He is kind of half-man,
half-beast, frequently represented on the stage dressed
in an animal skin. In the play he is referred to variously
as a cat, puppy-head, fish, or tortoise. Thus, he can be
interpreted as any animallike man-monster, or as a very
uncouth man. Before the play opens he has tried to rape
Miranda; he functions in the comic scenes with Trin-

culo and Stephano, and to win their friendship offers them a profusion of country gifts:

> Cal.[*iban*]   I'll shew thee the best springs; I'll pluck
>   thee berries;
> I'll fish for thee, and get thee wood enough.
> . . . .
> I prithee, let me bring thee where crabs grow;
> And I with my long nails will dig thee pig-nuts;
> Show thee a jay's nest and instruct thee how
> To snare the nimble marmozet; I'll bring thee
> To clust'ring filberts, and sometimes I'll get thee
> Young scamels from the rock.
>   (II, ii, 173–74, 180–85)

There are a few incidental correspondences between novel and play which suggest that the pastoral influence on *The Tempest* might have had its source in Longus. An incursion of foreigners takes place in both, and in both instances is associated with a great storm at sea. In *Daphnis and Chloe*, gallants of Mytilene come to the island to hunt. They make trouble, are punished, and in revenge kidnap Chloe. At this, Pan deliberately creates a fearful storm and commotion at sea. Angel Day translates the storm passage thus:

> it seemed *at night in the middest of their banqueting*, that *all the land about them was on fire*, and a sodaine *noise arose in their hearing as of a great fleete, and armed nauie for the seas, approaching towardes them*. The sound whereof and dreadfull sight, made some of thē to crie *Arme Arme*, and others to gather together their companies & weapons. One thought his fellowe next him was hurt, an other feared the shot that he heard ratling in his eares, this man thought his companion slaine hard by his side, an other seemed to *stumble on dead carcasses*. In brief, the *hurrie and tumult was so wonderfull and*

straunge, as they almost were at their wittes endes.
. . . *A dreadful noise was heard from the rocks,* not
as the sound of any naturall trumpets, but far more
shril and hideous, . . . about the middest of the day,
. . . Pan himself in a vision stoode right before him,
and beeing as he was in the shape vnder the *Pine* before described, [orders him to return Chloe] . . . .
The Captaine . . . caused present serch to be made
for Chloe . . . and shee being found with a chaplet
of the *Pine* tree leaues vppon her head, hee declared
vnto them the expresse commaundement and direction of the god: . . . Chloe was no sooner parted out of
the vessel where shee was, but they heard from the
hie rockes a sound againe, but nothing dreadfull as
the other, but rather *much sweete, melodious, and
pleasing, such as the most cunning sheepheards vse*
before their flockes and heards.[29]

In *The Tempest,* Neapolitan and Milanese noblemen
and their retainers come ashore on the island as a result
of a great storm created by the supernatural direction
of Prospero and executed by the supernatural agency of
Ariel. The storm is described as follows:

[*Miranda*]   The sky, it seems, would pour down
stinking pitch,
But that the sea, mounting to th' welkin's cheek,
Dashes the *fire* out.

(I, ii, 3–5)

[*Ariel*]   I boarded the king's ship; now on the beak,.
Now in the waist, the deck, in every cabin,
I flam'd amazement: sometime I'd divide
And *burn in many places;* on the topmast,
The yards, and boresprit, would I *flame distinctly*
Then meet, and join: *Jove's lightnings,* the precursors
O' the *dreadful thunder-claps,* more momentary
And sight-outrunning were not: the fire and cracks
Of sulphurous roaring the most *mighty Neptune*

Seem to besiege and make his bold waves tremble,
Yea, his dread trident shake . . .

. . . .

        Not a soul
But felt a fever of the mad and play'd
Some tricks of desperation. All but mariners,
Plunged in the foaming brine and quit the vessel,
Then *all a-fire* with me: the king's son, Ferdinand,
With hair up-staring,—then like reeds, not hair,—
Was the first man that leap'd; cried, 'Hell is empty,
And all the devils are here.'
        (I, ii, 196–206, 208–15)

Fer.[*dinand*] Where should *this music* be? i' th' air,
  or th' earth?
It sounds no more;—and sure, it waits upon
Some god o' th' island. Sitting on a bank,
Weeping again the king my father's wrack,
This music crept by me upon the waters,
Allaying both their fury, and my passion,
With its sweet air: thence I have follow'd it,
        (I, ii, 385–91)

[*Prospero*]   *I have bedimm'd*
The noontide sun, call'd forth the mutinous winds,
And 'twixt the green sea and the azur'd vault
Set roaring war: to the dread-rattling thunder
Have I given fire and rifted Jove's stout oak
With his own bolt: the strong-bas'd *promontory*
Have I made shake; and by the spurs pluck'd up
The *pine* and cedar: *graves at my command*
Have wak'd their sleepers, op'd, and let them forth
By my so potent art.
        (V, i, 41–50)[30]

 Thus do the situations parallel: an incursion of foreigners to a sea island is associated with a supernaturally created storm. The storms are accompanied by
darkness during daylight hours, illusions of fire, super-

natural visions of dead men, and desperate behavior on the part of those trapped in the fray. Both tumults are compared to war, and both end on a strain of sweet music. Ultimately it is found that no harm has occurred to the unfortunates involved in them. The parallels in the descriptions of the storm are indicated by italics, but to assert that the Day version of Longus contributed to Shakespeare's thinking is unsound, for Amyot's French translation is equally suggestive:

> soubdainement advis que toute la terre devint en feu, & entendirent de loing tel que seroit le flot d'une grosse armée de mer, qui fust venuë contre eulx: l'un cryoit à l'arme, l'autre appelloit ses compagnons, l'un pensoit estre jà blessé, l'autre cuydoit veoir un homme mort gisant devant luy; . . . & entendoit-on le son d'une trompe du dessus d'une roche haulte & droicte, estant à la crime de l'escueil, ["promontory" or "cliff"] au pied duquel ilz estoyent à l'abryt; mais ce son n'estoit point plaisant à oüyr, comme seroit le son d'une trompette ordinaire, ains effroyoit ceux qui l'entendoyent, ne plus ne moins que le son d'une tromperte de guerre la nuict: . . . que l'on entendit derechef le son de la trompe dedans le rocher, mais non plus effroyable en maniere de l'alarme, ains tel que les bergers ont accoustumé de sonner quand ilz menent leurs bestes aux champs.[31]

If one accepts these passages as evidence that Shakespeare knew Longus, it would be impossible to decide whether it was Day's or Amyot's. Certainly the French version was the more accessible of the two, for although Day's would be the easier to read, Amyot's had gone through four editions between 1559 and 1609, while the English version appeared once in 1587. The 1578 French translation of "L. L. L." was also buried in one edition.[32] There is, however, evidence in the marriage festivities that if Shakespeare was influenced by *Daphnis and*

Chloe when writing *The Tempest*, he probably had read a version other than Day's, or had read Day's as well as another.

Whatever may have been the contemporary reason for interrupting the action of *The Tempest* with the marriage masque of Act IV, its appropriateness to the play cannot be denied, for the masque was a major attraction at many wedding festivities involving people of royal or noble rank during the Elizabethan period, and it serves in the play to elucidate the pastoral nature of the love of Miranda and Ferdinand and to give a kind of pastoral blessing to their projected union. First Ceres, "most bounteous lady . . . Of wheat, rye, barley, vetches, oats, and peas" (IV, i, 60–61) is called in by Iris, "Who with . . . saffron wings . . . Diffusest honey-drops, refreshing showers" (IV, i, 78–79) to Ceres's "bosky acres" (IV, i, 81). Then Juno enters and with Ceres sings a wedding song to Miranda and Ferdinand.[33] Next the nymphs "of the windring brooks" (IV, i, 128) are called. They enter, followed by "sun-burn'd sickle-men, of August weary" (IV, i, 134). The nymphs and reapers join together in a dance just before the masque vanishes.

Nothing else in the play proclaims its essential pastoral nature so positively as does the masque. The structure of the stock pastoral plot is nearly perfect, but it is hidden from the unobservant behind the conventional romance of the situation and the elements of magic in Prospero's characterization. The same air of magic tends to conceal the pastoral quality of the island setting. It is as though Shakespeare saw this and would loudly and clearly proclaim the play pastoral by the device of the masque.

The pastoral blessing on the marriage of Miranda and Ferdinand may have been suggested by the country wedding of Daphnis and Chloe: "Her father gave Chloe

away in the presence of the Nymphs, . . . and regaled
[the villagers] . . . luxuriously. . . . the entertainment
was all of a rustic and pastoral kind. One sang the song
the reapers sing, another cracked the jokes the vinta-
gers crack."[34] Day, perhaps tired when he reached the
final page, omits the wedding from his translation, but
Amyot follows his source more closely: "& Megaclès
derechef devoüa sa fille Chloé aux Nymphes, & oultre
plusieurs autres offrandes, . . . & là comme entre villa-
geois, tout s'y disoit & faisoit à la villageoise: l'un chan-
toit les chansons que chantent les moissonneurs au
temps des moissons; l'autre disoit des brocards; que
l'on a accoustumé de dire en foulant la vendange."[35]

Thus it can be seen that if the nymphs and the reapers
dancing in Shakespeare's bucolic marriage masque were
suggested by the nymphs and the reapers of Daphnis
and Chloe's wedding, they probably derive from Amyot,
not from Day. Of course the Greek editions would not
have been beyond Shakespeare's reach, but they are less
obvious considerations.

The conclusion that Longus is an ultimate influence
on *The Tempest* is based on the presence of the elements of the stock pastoral plot, from which it deviates
in only one instance. The conclusion that Longus is a
direct influence is not so surely established, but coincidences in the storms and in the chief characters, and the
similarities of the wedding festivities suggest that
Shakespeare was familiar with Longus. In connection
with this it is well to recall Wolff's conclusion that
Longus is a primary source of *The Winter's Tale*, a play
written probably no more than a year before the composition of *The Tempest*.[36] One might also recall other
classical elements in the play: materials from Vergil
and Ovid, and obedience to the classical structural cri-
teria in the use of the four unities, the beginning of the
action *in medias res*, and the supernatural machinery
provided by both Ariel and Prospero.

It is naive, however, to think of Longus as having contributed more than a web for the weaving of a tapestry as complexly beautiful as *The Tempest*. The pages of *Daphnis and Chloe* abound with appreciation of natural beauty and fertility in the land and in the lovers, but not with the air of transcendental supernaturalism and magic that invests Prospero's island. There is no hint in Longus of the arcane knowledge and philosophy of Prospero that tantalizes and raises in the thoughtful questions about the meanings of the play. Is one to read *The Tempest* as allegory of nature and nurture (Miranda and Caliban)? of the vegetative, sensitive, and rational aspects of the soul[37] (Caliban, Ariel, Prospero)? Is the "brave new world" (V, i, 183) that has such creatures in it as the primitive Caliban, the falsely sophisticated Sebastian and Antonio, the wise and learned Prospero, the natural Utopia of the Americas ready for exploitation or for spiritual exploration? the creation of an ideal society where cruelty and shabby intrigue give way to mercy, repentance, spiritual regeneration, and magnanimity? As a poem of "sea-sorrow" (I, ii, 170) and "sea-change" (I, ii, 403) do we read allegory of everlasting birth? of the ocean which threatens, overwhelms, cleanses, regenerates, and essentially provides for immortality? If Prospero's magic is good (and he never misuses it), if it comes from real knowledge and self-control, why does he renounce it?[38] Questions about *The Tempest* go on forever and the really important answers will not go back to Greek romance, except to recognize that Longus has helped to provide a vehicle that carries such a complex freight.

CONCLUSIONS

The final estimate of the significance of any literary influence must be based on intellectual and artistic factors rather than on enumeration of details, however necessary a consideration of details may be in assembling the data from which the assessment is made. As to the real presence of Greek romances in Renaissance literature, there is enough factual evidence to declare the genre an important aspect of the classical tradition which was a major intellectual force of the age. Three of the greatest Renaissance writers—Boccaccio, Cervantes, and Shakespeare—drew on Greek romance deliberately for major works. A multitude of lesser men embodied in their writings Greek romance, either at firsthand or through a persistent derived tradition.[39] It is in Shakespeare's last plays, however, that the final test of the importance of the genre seems to rest. Boccaccio's *Il Filocolo* and Cervantes's *Persiles y Sigismunda* seldom lift their ancient materials above the sources. Shakespeare's earlier works which embody Greek romance motifs and patterns have not utilized them with obvious or direct intention, but simply as convenient vehicles to carry forward other purposes. It is in *Pericles, Cymbeline, The Winter's Tale,* and *The Tempest* that we finally see the ancient genre deliberately utilized and lifted to new dimensions, turned from a rather inconsequential literature of escape to a new vision of reality, a vision created artistically by moving from the world of reality to a world of romance, wherein the compound of the primitive Greek materials and the psychological crudity and immaturity of the genre make possible, when combined with great poetic power of expression, symbolic interpretation of the characters and events.

The four late plays of Shakespeare all carry the Greek romance separation plot through an orderly movement toward poetic justice softened with mercy, forgiveness, and reconciliation. On the way one is offered a profound reading of human experience in the concern with the ever presence of evil, evil which seems almost entirely unmotivated, evil which destroys the innocent as well as the guilty: in *Pericles*, the attempt on Marina's life by her foster parents; in *Cymbeline*, the infamous treachery of Iachimo against Imogen; in *The Winter's Tale*, the unmotivated jealousy of Leontes which ends in the death of his little son and the loss of his wife and daughter; in *The Tempest*, the seizure of Prospero's authority by his brother and the subsequent exile of Prospero and Miranda.

By establishing a dramatic pattern of prosperity and well-being destroyed by evil, and finally re-created through forgiveness and reconciliation (the essential Greek romance plot) Shakespeare takes us through subtle considerations of the human experience and condition. Quickly we perceive that immediate human actions have remote consequences on other lives: Posthumus's foolish wager leads to Imogen's betrayal; Leontes's unmotivated sexual jealousy leads to Antigonus's death in the jaws of a bear—a scene which also demonstrates that the tissue of comedy and tragedy are often one. At the same time, all the conflict is occurring in what Northrup Frye calls "the cyclical movement of nature," the opposite poles of which are the enemy—"winter, darkness, confusion, sterility, moribund life, and old age"—and the hero and heroine—"spring, dawn, order, fertility, vigor, and youth."[40]

In the new vision of reality, especially in the pastoral interludes, the Golden Age is *now*, not long ago and far away in some Arcadian seclusion. Time is relative; the past and present merge: when the ancient Gower, a relic of the Middle Ages, tells us in *Pericles* what will happen now in classical antiquity to an infant who will be full grown in the next act; when Leontes, deep in emotional trauma of his past guilt, finds his lost child—the seed of rebirth and forgiveness which had been germinating in darkness even before his wretchedness began; when Miranda is clearly shocked today by a recital of long past events which will converge in a few hours to her meeting with Prince Ferdinand, the symbol not only of her future, but of her wonder at the "brave new world,/ That has such people in't!" (V, i, 183–84). Yet these people who just a few hours before were reenacting with each other the same treachery which many years ago had resulted in her exile will soon be numbered among her friends.

As time becomes relative, so do levels of reality, truth, and order. Leontes's belief in Hermione's guilt makes him behave as if she were guilty. Her suffering is no less real—Perdita and Mamillius no less lost—because he is mistaken. Posthumus's mistake about his wife's virtue, Cymbeline's false assessment of his wife, lead to suffering and injustice and disorder just as real as if the truth had been apparent.

In the Golden Age of the last plays, which is now, the natural is a vehicle to transmit the supernatural; the sacred is an aspect of the secular; that is, the symbol is embedded in the person, the act, the artifact. Caliban and Ariel are negative and positive aspects of nature and man: the gross and the corrupt, the spiritual and the sublimate. At the same time they exist on a realistic level, have past histories, present duties, and hopes for the future. Marina, Perdita, and Miranda are at once innocent girls who serve to reconcile their broken families and symbols of fertility and regeneration. As within the Christian tradition, the world of symbol in these last plays is ambiguous. The lost Perdita restored is both a vegetation and a fertility symbol—the child of Ceres, Persephone, Queen of Darkness, lost in the underworld, restored to earth with the vernal equinox—and at the same time a symbol of her father's expiation of guilt, the rebirth of her injured mother from "death" to "life," the power of creation and natural virtue which has been growing throughout the course of destruction, death, and decay occasioned by the willful wickedness of her father. Through her the sterile king—heirless, and thus the leader of a bereft nation—is revitalized and a future for his people is assured. Such ambiguity is firmly within the Christian tradition in which the Son is the Father; the bread and the wine, the body and blood of the Son; and at the same time instinct with mystical divinity. Perdita is symbolically the saving victim, as are Marina, Imogen, and Miranda in varying degrees.

In short, the humdrum of the Greek romance has finally in Shakespeare's last plays been lifted into great poetry and makes penetrating observations upon the human condition, taking us all the way from Paulina's:

> . . . A thousand knees
> Ten thousand years together, naked, fasting,
> Upon a barren mountain, and still winter
> In storm perpetual . . .
> (*The Winter's Tale,* III, ii, 211–14)

to Miranda's:

> O, wonder!
> How many goodly creatures are there here!
> How beauteous mankind is! O brave new world,
> That has such people in't!
> (*The Tempest,* V, i, 181–84)

Appendix

A BIBLIOGRAPHIC SURVEY

For the student of English letters *Apollonius of Tyre* is the most interesting of the Greek romances, for it has been part of the living literature during every period of the language. MSS Corpus Christi College, Cambridge, 201, is an eleventh-century fragment of the romance translated into Old English prose.[1] Another fragmentary manuscript is a metrical *Apollonius* in pre-Chaucerian Middle English of Winborne Minster in Dorsetshire, first published by J. C. Halliwell-Phillips in 1850.[2] A later Middle English version is Book VIII of John Gower's *Confessio Amantis*. In 1510 Wynken de Worde published *Kynge Apollyn of Thyre*,[3] Robert Copland's translation of a French metrical version. In 1576 and 1607 the romance appeared as Lawrence Twine's *The Patterne of Painfull Adventures*, a translation of Chapter CLIII in the fourteenth-century Latin *Gesta Romanorum*.[4] The next year Shakespeare dramatized the story as *Pericles, Prince of Tyre*, basing his play partly on Twine's romance and partly on Gower's version. The changes that Shakespeare made were picked up by George Wilkins, who, in the same year, published *The Painful Adventures of Pericles, Prince of Tyre*.[5] With all this persistence in English it is not surprising that versions of the romance exist in Danish, Dutch, French, German, Hungarian, Italian, Neo-Hellenic, Polish, Portuguese, Provençal, Russian, Spanish, and Swedish as well.[6]

Behind all these vulgate versions are at least sixty

Latin manuscripts[7] bearing mute testimony to its charm for centuries of readers. The oldest of these is a Florentine codex of the ninth or tenth century.[8] One of the most important versions is a Latin metrical *Apollonius* of Godfrey of Viterbo (*c.* 1180), the foundation of the Gower text, and through it Shakespeare's *Pericles*.

What may be the earliest printing of any Greek romance is a Latin version of *Apollonius* extant in a unique copy in the Vienna Hofbibliothek. It lacks a title page, but is certainly fifteenth century. In 1471 a German version by Heinrich Steinhöwell was published at Augsburg. This apparently went through nine more editions during the next eighty-five years. Between 1470 and 1642 *Apollonius* was issued in one form or another possibly sixty-four times: fourteen in Italian, eleven in German, nine or ten in English, seven in French, seven in Greek, possibly six in Dutch, five in Latin, three in Spanish, and at least once each in Danish and Hungarian.

The question of the identification of Heliodorus kept the *Aethiopica* well known into the fourteenth century. The fifth-century A.D. Socrates of Constantinople in his *Historia Ecclesiastica* declared that Heliodorus of Emesa in youth wrote the *Aethiopica* and later in life became the Bishop of Tricca in Thessaly.[9] The ninth-century Photius repeated Socrates's identification and summarized the romance, characterizing it as dramatic, simple, sweet in style, and diversified in narrative.[10] In the fourteenth century Nicephorus Callistus again repeated Socrates, adding that the *Aethiopica* created such scandal that the bishop was forced to abandon his office.[11]

Moses Hadas thought the story of the episcopal title attached to Heliodorus was maintained to make the work respectable reading for Byzantine monks, notoriously fond of novels. He saw Heliodorus's book as a glorification of dark-skinned races and an obscure sect, the gymnosophists, and concluded that the author was more likely a gymnosophist—perhaps a dark-skinned one—than a Christian bishop.[12] Since virtue and chastity are central themes of the *Aethiopica*, whatever scandal there may have been was probably created by the pagan pantheon.

The second of the Greek romances to achieve the light of print, the *Aethiopica*,[13] had a history during the Renaissance similar to that of *Apollonius of Tyre*, for in various forms—including five or six dramatizations—it was issued perhaps ninety-six times between 1534 and 1638.

The first edition (1534), prepared by Vincent Obsopoeus, was published at Basle. Obsopoeus had acquired a manuscript of the work from a soldier after the looting of the library of Matthias Corvinus, king of the Magyars, during the battle of Mohacs in 1526.[14] Of the known editions, Greek texts appeared eight times; three different versions in French achieved at least thirty-two issues, twenty-six of these the translation of Jacques Amyot,[15] which remains standard even today. Five English versions were published a total of twelve times; the translation of Thomas Underdowne made from a Latin text prepared by the Polish humanist Stanislaus Warschewiczki[16] accounts for seven. Warschewiczki's text (1552) frequently errs, and where he mistranslates, so does Underdowne.[17] William Lisle's English version (1631) is metrical. Eleven Latin texts appeared, seven accompanied Greek editions. Of these, the 1596 version of Heironimus Commelinus is improved over the *editio princeps* because he made use of manuscripts other than the one known to Obsopoeus.[18] Leon Ghini's Italian version appeared at least twelve times. Besides this, two other Italian versions of the romance were published, as well as one in Spanish, issued at least seven or eight times. An early Spanish version (1545) by Francisco de

Vergara was never printed.[19] A German translation appeared at least eight times by 1624.

With all this it is not surprising that Heliodorus made his presence felt in education. Petrus Olivarius, the teacher of King Edward VI, gave his pupil a method of reading history which included learning chorography from Heliodorus through the study of the pseudohistorical accounts of military campaigns between Egypt and Ethiopia. During the young king's reign the standard curriculum in the fifth form at Harrow included the reading of Heliodorus in Greek. Underdowne's translation was purchased as a textbook for young King James VI of Scotland.[20] The Puritan element, however, did not look with favor on the novel. In that famous invective against the stage, the *Histrio-Mastix* (1633), William Prynne says: "The penning and reading of all amorous Bookes was so execrable in the Primitive times, . . . that *Heliodorus Bishop of Trica was deprived of his Bishopricke by a Provinciall synod, for those wanton amorous Bookes he had written in his youth, his bookes being likewise awarded to the fire to be burnt.*"[21]

During the Byzantine period Achilles Tatius, like Heliodorus, was also identified as having been a Christian bishop. Suidas, the tenth-century lexicographer, so names him in the *Lexicon*, and says also that Achilles Tatius of Alexandria was the author of a treatise on the sphere and works on etymology.[22] The ninth-century Photius, who described and praised his art, but found him inferior to Heliodorus in purity, says nothing of Achilles Tatius having been a bishop. The identification of Suidas was probably a transferral of the Heliodorus story, and a much less credible one, for there is nothing in *Clitophon and Leucippe* to suggest either Christian thought or the higher pagan philosophies. It is a thoroughly profane book. In the eleventh century Michael Psellos wrote a critique of Achilles Tatius, and in the fourteenth century the scholiast Thomas Magister referred to him as an orator,[23] which is to say a rhetorician or a "sophist."

Twenty-three manuscripts of Achilles Tatius were preserved, only twelve giving the romance in full. The oldest, Vaticanus Graecus 1349, is from the twelfth century; most date from the sixteenth. Part of *Clitophon and Leucippe* appears with the manuscript that preserves Chariton and Xenophon of Ephesus.[24] *Clitophon and Leucippe* was the third Greek romance to be published during the Renaissance, and between 1544 and 1640 it was issued about thirty-eight times. The novel was most popular in Italy where a Latin translation by Annibale Cruceio of Books V through VIII appeared in 1544. In 1546 Lodovico Dolce published an Italian translation of the Cruceio material. This was followed in 1550 by Francesco Coccio's Italian translation, the first from a complete text. By 1617 this translation had been published at least fourteen times. In 1552 Cruceio published a full Latin text. Versions of Achilles Tatius in Latin appeared at least eleven times by 1640; versions in Italian at least fifteen. Five different French versions were made, two English translations, and one Spanish. The Greek text prepared from a manuscript in the Palatine Library was first published at Heidelberg in 1601. The finest edition of the Greek text until modern times was made by the scholar Salmasius and published with the Latin translation of Cruceio at Leyden in 1640. This was the first edition to be based on a comparison of readings of the various manuscripts.

No antique tradition supports Longus as the author of *Daphnis and Chloe*, and no mention of his name is known before the Byzantine period. Photius does not notice him.[25] The name may result from a misinterpretation of the Florentine manuscript: Λεσβιακῶν ἐρωτικῶν λόγοι δ'.[26] It appears, however, on the first published edition of *Daphnis and Chloe,* a French translation by Jacques Amyot which appeared in 1559 and continued even to the scholarly edition in Greek with a Latin translation by "Gothofredus Jungermannus" in 1605. The novel, however, shows rather clearly that the author was a sophist of the school of Lucian and the Philostrati. The style and tone link him also with Heliodorus.

At least nine manuscripts of *Daphnis and Chloe* are known, the best text, *codex Laurentianus Conventi Soppressi,* 627, going back only to the thirteenth century. This was more or less unknown until 1809 when it was unearthed by P. L. Courier at Florence. It is the only known extant source for filling in the great lacuna, chapters 12 to 17 of Book I, appearing in the other manuscripts. Unfortunately, after Courier had made a transcription of the lost material, he overturned his ink-pot, obliterating the text, so that scholars must depend on the Courier copy for a complete reading of the romance.[27]

Daphnis and Chloe had a somewhat briefer Renaissance history than *Apollonius,* Heliodorus, and Achilles Tatius. Between 1559 and 1628 it appeared only about fourteen times. The Amyot version was issued at least five times and a French paraphrase was made by Pierre Marcassus. Two offerings were made of an Italian translation of Laurentius Gambara. Angel Daye published an English version in 1587. Greek editions appeared in 1598 and 1605, and a Latin translation in 1601, reissued in 1606. A German version was published in 1615.

The Wonderful Things Beyond Thule and the *Babylonica* of Iamblichus, extant only in the epitome of Photius, left little more than a shadow on Renaissance literature. Greek editions of Photius were published in 1601 and 1611. A Latin translation appeared in 1606 and again with the Greek edition of 1611, but there seem to have been no vulgate translations until modern times. A manuscript of the romance was in the Escorial which burned in 1670. Another copy in the possession of Jungerman, who died early in the seventeenth century, has disappeared.

The *Ephesiaca,* although mentioned by Suidas as a romance in ten books,[28] would appear to have had even less Renaissance history, for the earliest publication was a Greek and Latin text prepared by the Italian scholar-physician Antonio Cocchius and issued at London in 1726; yet the *Ephesiaca* has since 1807 been recognized as the source of the live burial plot of *Romeo and Juliet,*[29] the published sources of which date from at least 1476. Further, it is possible that Boccaccio derived "The Sultan of Babylon" (II, 7) and the episode of the tomb robbery in "Andreuccio da Perugia" (II, 5) of the *Decameron* (1353) from the *Ephesiaca.*[30] The romance is preserved in only one manuscript, the same that preserved the lacuna of Longus and the text of Chariton.

Similarly, *Chaereas and Callirhoe* of Chariton went unpublished until the eighteenth century, when an edition of Jacobus D'Orville was issued at Amsterdam in 1750. Yet the Chariton romance presents a similar bibliographic problem in that it seems to be the source of Matteo Bandello's "Signor Timbreo di Cardona and Fenicia Lionata," since 1898 recognized as the source of the Hero-Claudio plot of *Much Ado About Nothing.*[31] Bandello's novel was published in French in 1582 by François de Belleforest and in English in 1566 by William Painter; thus the elements of the Chariton romance were carried into the sixteenth century. Boccaccio seems also to have known Chariton, for the wager plot of "Bernabo da Genoa" (*Decameron,* II, 9), a source of the wager plot in *Cymbeline,* probably derives from *Chaereas and Callirhoe.* The solution to both bibliographic problems may be found in the thirteenth-century codex containing the *Ephesiaca* and *Chareas and*

Callirhoe along with other Greek erotica and miscellaneous literature. This manuscript was willed by Antonio di Tommaso Corbinelli (d. 1425) to the library of the Benedictine cloister, commonly called La Badia, at Florence, and deposited there by 1439. The manuscript was catalogued under the name "Aesopus,"[32] the most famous author included in its contents. Evidence shows that it was well known during the Renaissance, for in 1489 Angelo Ambrogine Poliziano, the great humanist professor of Greek letters at the University of Florence, quoted the *Ephesiaca* in the *Miscellaneorum Centuria Prima*. Poliziano's work was popular enough to be reissued in 1496 at Brescia, possibly in 1498 and in 1508 at Venice, in 1511 at Paris, and in 1522 at Basle. Uncounted are numerous other publications of the note in the collected works of Poliziano.[33]

Unfortunately, Poliziano's notice and fragmentary excerpt of the *Ephesiaca* are not of the section which links it to the Romeo and Juliet legend. Furthermore, the earliest known printed version of the legend is that of Masuccio de Salernitano, "Mariotto Mignanelli and Gianozza Saracini," published at Naples in 1474, fifteen years before the Poliziano reference. Masuccio's story contains almost all the plot elements of the final version, except the names, finally supplied by Luigi Da Porto in *Historia novellamente ritrovata di due nobili amanti, etc.*[34] The Poliziano note can account for the Da Porto version, for Da Porto seems to have had associations with humanists of his day,[35] but it cannot account for the Masuccio version, which is closer to the *Ephesiaca* story than that of Da Porto, in that Masuccio retains in vestigial form that prime essential of Greek romance, the sea voyage, absent in the Da Porto account. Of course it is reasonable to conjecture that Masuccio[36] and Bandello read the La Badia manuscript —the only extant text—or some other which has since been lost. Bandello may have read it as a result of Poliziano's notice. Boccaccio's apparent knowledge of Xenophon and Chariton probably grew from his active interest in the revival of classical studies.

The Ninus fragment, first published in 1893 by Ulrich Wilcken at Berlin, was an exciting discovery of the nineteenth century. The legendary hero, however, was known to the Renaissance reader, if only through continuing literary and historical tradition. E. K. Chambers lists a lost play, *Ninus and Semiramis, the First Monarchs of the World*, as having been acted in 1595.[37] Further, the "rude mechanicals" of *A Midsummer Night's Dream* enact a parody of the Pyramus and Thisbe story and the lovers die gloriously before "Ninny's tomb."

The pages that follow attempt to list the editions, translations, and adaptations of the Greek romances printed in England and Western Europe from the beginning of the art to 1642. Although this bibliography has been prepared primarily as a chronological chart to demonstrate the accessibility of the Greek romances to the Renaissance reader, it should serve also as a reference guide to accompany the discussion of Greek romance motifs in Renaissance literature. In order to facilitate such dual use, the items are arranged alphabetically by author, and then arranged chronologically. In every case the first known printed edition of the text and the first known English translation of the romances have been included, regardless of the date of their publication. Otherwise the bibliography includes only books printed up to 1642. First editions prepared by a specific editor or translator are listed in full; later issues of the same editions are grouped with the first, but mentioned only by date and place of publication, even though in many instances the title pages differ slightly from the first listing.

Many manuscripts of the romances circulated in the

vernacular and original languages during the Renaissance, but since this list has been prepared primarily to demonstrate the accessibility of the romances to the general reader, these items are not included, even though they may have attained publication after 1642.

Apollonius of Tyre created special difficulties. The romance was frequently included in editions of the *Gesta Romanorum*, and since it would have been impossible to examine all of these individually, only a vernacular *Gesta* which included the romance is cited here. In the case of Angelo Ambrogini Poliziano, possibly the first scholar to take notice of the *Ephesiaca*, the *omnia opera* are omitted, but an attempt has been made to give a complete listing of *Miscellaneorum Centuria prima*, separately published, in which mention of the romance was first made.

ACHILLES TATIUS

1544   *Narrationis amatoriae fragmentum è graeco in latinum conversum*, trans. L. Annibale Cruceio. Lyon [Books V–VIII of *Clitophon and Leucippe*].

1545   *Les deuis amoureaux*, [trans. Claude Colet]. Paris.

1546   *Amorosi Ragionamenti, dialogo, nel quale si racconta un compassion-evole amore di due amanti*, etc., trans. M. Ludovico Dolce. Venice [Books V–VIII of *Clitophon and Leucippe*].

1550   *Achille Tatio Alessandrino Dell' Amore di Leucippe et di Clitophonte*, etc., trans. Francesco Angelo Coccio. Venice.
Reissued: 1551, 1560, 1563, 1568, 1576, 1578, 1600, 1608, 1617, Venice; 1598, 1599, 1617, Florence; 1600, Triviso.

1552   *Achillis Statii Alexandrini de Clitophonis & Leucippes amorib. Libri VIII*, trans. L. Annibale Cruceio. Bergamo.
Reissued: 1554, Basil; 1581, Cologne; 1587, 1589? Cambridge; 1587, Bergamo?

1556   *Les quatre derniers livres des propos amoureux contenans le discours des amours et mariage du Seigneur Clitophant et Damoiselle Leusippe,* etc., trans. Jacques de Rochemaure. Lyon.
Reissued: 1572/3, Lyon.

1568   *Les Amours de Clitophon et de Leucippe, escrits jadis en grec par Achilles Statius Alexandrin,* etc., trans. B. Comingeois [François de Belleforest?]. Paris.
Reissued: 1575, 1586, Lyon; 1575, Paris.

1597   *The most delectable and plesant historye of Clitophon and Leucippe,* etc., trans. W.[illiam] B.[urton]. London.

1601   *De Clitophontis et Leucippes amoribus lib. VIII. Longi Sophistae de Daphnidis & Chlöes amoribus lib. IV,* etc., [trans. A. Cruceio], ed. Juda and Nocolaus Bonnuitius. Heidelberg [Greek and Latin].
Reissued: 1606, Heidelberg.

1617   *Los mas fieles amantes, Leucipe y Clitofonte. Historia griega por Aquiles Tacio Alexandrino,* trans. Diego Agreda y Vargas. Madrid.

1625   *Les Amours de Clitophon et de Leucippe,* trans. A. Remy. Paris.

1635   *Les amours de Clytophon et de Leucippe,* trans. J.[ean] B.[audoin]. Paris [twice].

1638   *The Loves of Clitophon and Leucippe. A most elegant History, written in Greeke by Achilles Tatius:* etc., trans. [Anthony Hodges]. Oxford.

1640   Ἐρωτικῶν Ἀχιλλέως Τατίου, *sive de Clitophontis et Leucippes amoribus libri VIII,* ed. Cl. Salmasius, trans. L. A. Crucejus. Leyden [Greek and Latin].

APOLLONIUS OF TYRE

c. 1470   A unique copy of a Latin text of *Apollonius of Tyre* in the Vienna Hofbibliothek [lacks a title page].

1471   *Die hystory des Küniges Appollonij vō latin zu teutsch gemacht,* trans. Heinrich Steinhöwel. Augsburg.
Reissued: 1476, 1479, 1480, 1516, 1540, 1552, 1556, Augsburg; 1495, 1499, Ulm.

1481   *Die Gesten of gheschienissen van Romen.* Gouda [contains a version of the Apollonius story].
Reissued: 1483, Delft; 1484, Zwolle.

1482?   *Apollin roy de Thire. Cy commence la cronicque et hystoire de Apollin roy de thir . . . et de sa fille,* etc. Geneva.

1483   *tHis [sic] book is intitled confessio amantis, that is to saye in englysshe the confessyon of the louer Maad and compyled by John Gower,* etc., ed. William Caxton. Westminster [Book VIII contains a version of *Apollonius*].

1486   *La Storia di Apollonio di Tiro in ottava rima.* Venice. Reissued: 1489, 1490, 1520, 1535, 1555, 1560, 1598, 1610, 1629, Venice; 1492, Milan; 1580, 1625, Florence.

1493   *Die schoone ende die Suuerlicke historie van Appollonius van Thyro.* Delft.

1495   *Historia de los Siete Sabios y del rey Apolonio.* Seville [apparently no longer extant].

1500/1501   Διήγησις ὡραιοτάτη ἀπολλωνίου τοῦ ἐν τύρω. Ριμάδα, [trans. Gabriel Kontianos or Konstantin Temenos]. Venice. Reissued: 1503, 1534, 1553, 1603, 1624, 1642, Venice.

1510   *Kynge Apollyn of Thyre,* trans. Robert Copland. London. Reissued: 1528, London.

1530   *Plaisant et agréable histoire a' Appollonius prince de thir en Affrique et Roi d'Antioch,* etc., trans. Gilles Corrozet. Paris.

1532   *Jo.[hn] Gower de confessione Amantis.* London [Book VIII contains a version of *Apollonius*].
Reissued: 1554, London.

1559   Godfrey de Viterbo, *Pantheon sive Universitatis Libri qui Chronici appellantur, xx, omnes omnium seculorum et gentium,* etc. Basil [contains a version of *Apollonius*].
Reissued: 1584, 1613, Frankfurt.

1563   *Apollonii Tyrii historia.* Venice.

1576   Juan de Timoneda, *El Patrañuelo.* Valencia [*Patrana* xi
        is a version of *Apollonius*].
        Reissued: 1580, Bilbao.

1576   Laurence Twyne, *The Patterne of painefull Adventures:
        Containing the . . . Historie of . . . Prince Appolonius,*
        etc. London.
        Reissued: 1594?, 1607, 1608, London.

1578   Jacobi à Falchenburgk, *Brittannia Sive de Apollonica
        Humilitatis, Virtutis, et Honoris Porta.* London.

1582   François de Belleforest, *Le Septième tome des Histoires
        tragiques extraites de l'italien,* etc. Paris [contains a
        version of *Apollonius*].
        Reissued: 1583, Paris; 1595, Lyon; 1603, 1604, Rouen.

1591   *Szép jeles Historia egy Apollonius vevü Kiraly Fiurol,
        Miképpen ò egy Mefének,* [trans. Miklos F. Bogáti?].
        Kolozsvar.

1595   *Narratio eorum quae contigerunt Apollonio Tyrio,* etc.,
        ed. Marcus Velser. Augsburg.

1601   *Eine schöne unde kortwylige Historia vam Könige Ap-
        pollonio wo he van Landt unde Lüden vordreven unde
        vorjaget . . . unde doch thom lesten wedder in syn
        Lundt gekamen ys,* trans. Herman Moller. Hamburg.

1607/1608   George Wilkins, *The Painful Adventures of Pericles,
        Prince of Tyre.* London. [A novel based on Shakespeare's
        Pericles. The plot of *Apollonius* is used with different
        names.]

1618   Joach. Bernier de la Brousse, *Les Heureuses Infortunes*
        in *Les Oeuvres Poëtiques.* Poitiers [a play].

1627   *En dejlik og skjön Historie om Kong Apollonio i
        kvilken Lykkens Hjul og Verdens Ustadighed beskrives;
        lystig og fornöjelig at läse og höre.* Copenhagen.

1634   Pieter Bor Christiaensz, *Twee Tragi-comedien in prosa,
        d' Eene van Appollonius, Prince van Tyro, Ende d'ander
        van den selven, onde van Tharsia syn Dochter,* etc. [a
        play].
        [Issued first: 1617, The Hague?]

CHARITON

1750   Χαριτωνος 'Αφροδισιέως τῶυ περὶ Χαιρεαν καὶ Καλλιρροην ἐρωτικων διηγηματων λογοι ἡ *Charitonis . . . de Chaerea et Callirhoe Amatoriarum narrationum libri VIII*, ed. Jacobus D'Orville, trans Joannes Reiskius. Amsterdam. [Greek and Latin].

1764   *The Loves of Chaereas and Callirhoe*, trans. anonymous. London.

HELIODORUS

1534   'Ηλιοδώρου Αἰθιοπικῆς 'Ιστορίας Βιβλία δέκα, *Heliodori Historiae Aethiopicae libri decem*, etc., ed. Vincentius Obsopoeus. Basil [Greek].

1547   *L'Histoire Aethiopique de Heliodorus, contenant dix livres, traitant des loyales et pudiques amours de Théagènes Thessalien, et Chariclea Aethiopiëne*, trans. [Jacques Amyot]. Paris.
Reissued: 1549, 1559, 1560, 1570, 1575, 1583, 1585, 1611, 1613, 1614, 1616, 1626, Paris; 1553, 1596, 1613, Munich; 1559, 1575, 1579, 1584, 1589, Lyon; 1588, 1596, 1607, 1609, 1612, Rouen.

1551   Αἰθιοπικῆς ἱστορίας βιβλία δέκα, *Heliodorus historia aethiopicae liber primus*, etc. Paris [Book I of Greek text].

1551   'Ηλιοδώρου Αἰθιοπικῆς ἱστορίας βίβλία δέκα, *Heliodori historiae aethiopicae liber primus*, etc., trans. Stanislaus Warschewiczki. Paris.
Reissued: 1552, Basil; 1556, Antwerp; 1637, Leyden.

[N.D. 1554?]   *Aethiopica Historia. Ein schöne vnnd liebliche Historie, von . . . Theagenes vnnd . . . Chariclia . . . newlich ins Teutsch bracht*, etc. [trans. Joh. Zschorn]. Strassburg.
Reissued: N.D., Nurnberg; 1562, 1581, Frankfurt; 1580, Bassea; 1597, Leipzig; 1620, 1624, Strassburg.

1554   *Historia Ethiopica . . . Trasladada de Francés en vulgar Castellano por un segreto amigo de su patria y corrigida segun el Griego por el mismo*. Anvers.
Reissued: 1563, Toledo; 1581, Salamanca; 1615, Madrid.

1556   *Historia di Heliodoro delle cose Ethiopiche. Nelle quale fra diversi, compassionevoli avenimenti di due Amanti,* etc., trans. Leon Ghini. Venice.
Reissued: 1559, 1560, 1568, 1586, 1587, 1588, 1611, 1623, 1633, 1636, Venice; 1582, Genoa.

1557   *I primi cinque canti d'Eliodoro in ottava rima* di M. Hieronymus Bossi. Milan.

1559   *L'histoire éthiopique d'Heliodore, parte en dix livres,* etc. [trans. Claude Colet]. Lyon.

1567   *The amorous and tragical Tales of Plutarch, whereunto is annexed the History of Cariclea and Theaginis and the Sayings of the Greeke philosophers,* etc., trans. Ja.[mes] Sanford. London.

[1569?]   *An Aethiopian Historie written in Greeke by Heliodorus: very vvittie and pleasaunt,* etc., trans. Thomas Vnderdoune. London.
Reissued: 1577, 1587, 1605, 1606, 1622, 1627, London.

1584   Martini Crusii, *Aethiopicae Heliodori Historiae Epitome. Cum observationibus ejusdem,* etc. Frankfurt.

1587   *La historia de los dos leales amantes Theagenes y Chariclea. Trasladada agora de nuevo de latin en Romance* por Fernãdo de Mena. Alcalá de Henares.
Reissued: 1614, 1615, Barcelona; 1616, Paris.

1591   Abraham Fraunce, *The Countesse of Pembrokes Yvychurch. Conteining . . . The beginning of Heliodorus his Aethiopical History.* London.

1596   ʾΗλιοδώρου Αἰθιοπικῶν βιβλία δεκα, *Heliodori Aethipicorum libri X. Collatione mss. Bibliotheca Palatinae et aliorum,* ed. Hieronymi Commelini, trans. Stanislaus Warschewiczki. Heidelberg [Greek and Latin].
Reissued: 1601, 1611, Lyon; 1601, Oberursel; 1619, Paris; 1631, Frankfurt.

1605   Wolfgang Waldung, *Aethiopicus amor castus.* Altdorf [a play].

1608   Johannes Scholvin, *Aethiopissa Tragicomoedia nova, ex historia Aethiopica Heliodori Episcopi Tricensis.* Frankfurt on Oder [a play].

1609 Octave César Genetay, *L'Ethiopique Tragicomedie de chastes Amours de Théagène et Chariclée. Rouen* [a play].

1614 Kaspar Brülow, *Chariclia, tragico-comoedia, . . . ex jacunda Heliodori,* etc. Strassburg [a play].

1619 'Ηλιοδώρου Αἰθιοπικῶν βιβλία δεκα, *Heliodori Aethiopicorum Libri X,* ed. J. Bourdelotius, trans. Stanislaus Warschewiczki. Paris [Greek and Latin].

1620 *Les Amours de Théagène et Chariclée, Histoire Ethiopique d'Héliodore,* trans. Jean de Montlyard. Paris. Reissued: 1622, 1623, 1626, 1633, Paris.

1622 *Heliodorus his Aethiopian History done out of Greek* by W. Barret. London.

1623 Alexandre Hardy, *Les chastes et loyalles Amours de Théagène et Cariclée, réduites du Grec de l'Histoire d'Héliodore en huict poèmes dragmatiques, ou théâtres consécutifs,* etc. Paris. Reissued: 1628, Paris.

1631 William Lisle, *The famous Historie of Heliodorus. Amplified, augmented, and delivered paraphrasically in verse,* etc. London [running title: "The Faire Ethiopian"]. Reissued: 1638, London.

1631 M.[athijs] v. Velden, *Calasires Sterfdagh. Ghenomen uyt de Historie van Heliodorus belanghende de kuysche Vryagie van Theagenes ende Cariclea.* Amsterdam [six acts in verse].

1630/1631 'Ηλιοδώρου Αἰθιωπικῶν βιβλία δεκα, *Heliodori Aethiopicorum libri X, collatione mss. Bibliothecae Palatinae et aliorum.* etc., trans. [Stanislaus Warschewiczki], ed. Danielis Parei. Frankfurt [Greek and Latin].

1637 *Heliodorus,* trans. Gulielmo Cantero. Leyden [*Aethiopicorum libri X*].

1637 *Teagene, poem* del cav. Gio. Bat. Basile Napolitano, conte di Torone. Rome.

1640 J.[ohn] G.[ough] *The Strange Discovery: A Tragi-Comedy.* London.

LONGUS

1559   *Les Amours pastorales de Daphnis et de Chloé, escriptes premièrement en grec par Longus*, etc., trans. Jacques Amyot. Paris.
Reissued: 1594, 1596, 1609, Paris.

1569   Laurentius Gambara, *Expositorum ex Longo libri iv. heroico carmine*. Rome.
Reissued: 1581, Rome.

1578   *Histoire et amours pastoralles de Daphnis et Chloé, . . . Ensemble un débat judiciel de Folie et d'amours*, trans. Dame L.[ouise] L.[abé] L.[yonnoise]. Paris.

1587   *Daphnis and Chloe excellently describing the weight of affection, the simplicitie of love, the purport of honest meaning, the resolution of men, and disposition of Fate, finished in Pastorall*, etc., trans. Angell Daye. London.

1598   Λόγγου Ποιμευικῶν τῶν κατά Δάφνιν καί Χλόην βιβλία τέτταρα, *Longi Pastoralium de Daphnide et Chloë libri quatuor*, ed. Raphaelis Columbanius. Florence.

1601   *Achilles Tatius de Clitophontis et Leucippes amoribus lib. viii. Longi sophistae de Daphnidis et Chloes amoribus lib. iv*, ed. Juda and Nicolae Bonnuitius, trans. J. Cornario. Heidelberg.
Reissued: 1606, Heidelberg.

1605   Λόγγου . . . Ποιμενικῶν τῶν κατὰ Δόφυιν καί χλόην βιβλία τέτταρα: *id est Longi Sophistae Pastoralium de Daphnide & Chloe libri quatuor*, ed. and trans. Gothofredus Jungermannus. Hanau.

1615   *Lustgarten der Liebe von steter brennender Liebe zweier Liebhabenden junge Personen Daphnidis und Chloe . . . von Longo*. Frankfurt.

1626/1628   *Les Amours des Daphnis et Chloé*, etc., paraphrased by Pierre Marcassus. Paris.

NINUS

1893   "Ein Neuer Griechischer Roman," *Hermes: Zeitschrift für Classische Philologie*, XXVIII, 161–93, ed. Ulrich Wilcken. Berlin.

1935   *The Love Romances of Parthenius and other Fragments,*
ed. and trans. Stephen Gaselee. London [The Loeb Classical Library Series].

PHOTIUS

1601   βιβλιοφήκη τοῦ Φωτίον· *Librorum quos legit Photius Patriarcha Excerpta et Censurae,* ed. David Hoeschelius. Augsburg.

1606   *Photii Bibliotheca: sive lectorum a Photio librorum recensio, censura atquae excerpta philologorum, oratorum, historicorum, philosophorum, medicorum, theologorum,* trans. Andreas Schottus. Augsburg.

1611/1612/1613   Φωτίον Μυριοβιβλον ἡ βιβλιοθήκη, *Photii Myriobiblon, sive bibliotheca librorum quos Photius Patriarcha Constantinopolitanus legit & censuit,* trans. Andreas Schottus, ed. David Hoeschelius. Geneva.

1920   *The Library of Photius,* trans. John Henry Freese. London [Vol. I of six proposed is published].

XENOPHON OF EPHESUS

1489   Angelo Ambrogini Poliziano, *Miscellaneorum Centuria prima.* Florence [contains a fragment of Book I of the *Ephesiaca* in Latin translation].
Reissued: 1496, Brescia; [1498, Venice?], 1508, Venice; 1511, Paris; 1522, Basil.

1726   Ἐφεσιου των κατα ᾽Ανθιαν και ᾽Αβροκομην Ἐφεσιακων λογοι πεντε, *Xenophontis Ephesii Ephesiacorum libri v. de amoribus Anthiae et Abrocomae nunc primum prodeunt . . . cum Latina interpretatione,* ed. and trans. A. Cocchii. London [Greek and Latin].

1727   *Xenophon's Ephesian History: or the Love-Adventures of Abrocomas and Anthia in Five Books Translated from the Greek,* etc., trans. Mr. Rooke [*sic*]. London.

Notes

CHAPTER ONE

[1] See George Saintsbury, *A History of the French Novel to the Close of the Nineteenth Century* (London, 1917), I, 2.

[2] See Samuel Lee Wolff, *The Greek Romances in Elizabethan Prose Fiction* (New York, 1912).

[3] In 1579 Stephen Gosson in *Plays confuted in five Actions* said: "that *The Palace of Pleasure, The Golden Ass, The Aethiopian History* . . . have been thoroughly ransacked to furnish the play houses of London." Reprinted by John P. Collier, *The History of English Dramatic Poetry to the Time of Shakespeare* (London, 1831), p. 329.

[4] See Erwin Rohde, *Der Griechische Roman und Seine Vorläufer*, ed. Wilhelm Schmid, 3d ed. (Leipzig, 1914). Other important studies of the Greek romances are A. Chassang, *Histoire du Roman . . . dans l'Antiquité Grecque et Latine* (Paris, 1862); Alfred and Maurice Croiset, *Histoire de la Littérature Grecque* (Paris, 1928), V, passim; John Colin Dunlop, *History of Prose Fiction*, ed. Henry Wilson (London, 1911), I, 9–113; Stephen Gaselee, "Appendix on the Greek Novel," *The Love Romances of Parthenius and Other Fragments*, ed. and trans. Stephen Gaselee (London, 1935), pp. 403–14; Elizabeth H. Haight, *Essays on the Greek Romances* (New York, 1943), and *More Essays on the Greek Romances* (New York, 1945); Ben E. Perry, *The Ancient Romances: A Literary-Historical Account of Their Origins* (Berkeley, Calif., 1967); R. M. Rattenbury, "Romance: Traces of Lost Greek Novels," *New Chapters in the History of Greek Literature*, ed. J. U. Powell, 3d ser. (Oxford, 1933), pp. 211–57; F. A. Todd, *Some Ancient Novels* (Oxford, 1940); Wolff, *The Greek Romances.*

[5] Published in *The Love Romances of Parthenius and Other Fragments*, ed. and trans. Stephen Gaselee (London, 1935), pp. 382–99.

[6] See Rattenbury, "Romance," pp. 212–13.

[7] See Bruno Lavagnini, *Le Origini del Romanzo Greco* (Pisa, 1921); Haight, *Essays*, pp. 1–13; Gaselee, "Appendix," pp. 406–10; Perry, *The Ancient Romances*, pp. 33, 37.

[8] See Moses Hadas, "Cultural Survival and the Origin of Fiction," *South Atlantic Quarterly,* LI (1952), 253–60.

[9] See Lavagnini, *Le Origini.*

[10] F. M. Warren (*History of the Novel Previous to the Seventeenth Century* [New York, 1895], pp. 23–24) speculates upon the direct descent of the Greek novel from the Homeric epic tradition.

[11] See Martin Braun, *History and Romance in Graeco-Oriental Literature* (Oxford, 1938), pp. 6–8.

[12] An excellent edition is *Photius, Bibliotèque,* ed. and trans. in French by René Henry (Paris, 1959). See II, 140–49. Dunlop (*History,* I, 13–14) abstracts the story of *The Wonderful Things Beyond Thule.*

[13] In his *Anatomy of Criticism: Four Essays* (Princeton, N.J., 1957), pp. 186–87.

[14] Its most common title. Photius calls it the *Dramaticon.* See *The Library of Photius,* trans. John Henry Freese (London, 1920), I, 168. Only the first volume of the Freese translation has been published.

[15] Photius, *ed. cit.,* II, 34–48, and *Iamblichi Babyloniacorum Reliquiae,* ed. Elmar Habrich (Leipzig, 1960). An English translation is in Photius, trans. Freese, I, 168–77.

[16] The best edition is *Charitonis Aphrodisiensis de Chaereas et Callirhoe Amatoriarum Narrationum Libri Octo,* ed. Warren E. Blake (Oxford, 1938). *Chariton's Chaereas and Callirhoe,* trans. Warren E. Blake (Ann Arbor, Mich., 1939), is scholarly and literary.

[17] See Perry, *The Ancient Romances,* pp. 98–99, and Blake, *Chariton's Chaereas,* p. v.

[18] An excellent edition is Xénophon D'Éphèse, *Les Éphésiaques ou Le Roman D'Habrocomès et D'Anthia,* trans. and ed. George Dalmeyda (Paris, 1926). A recent English translation is "An Ephesian Tale by Xenophon," *Three Greek Romances,* trans. Moses Hadas (New York, 1953), pp. 101–72.

[19] Editions of the Latin and early English texts are *The Old English Apollonius of Tyre* [with a Latin text], ed. Peter Goolden (Oxford, 1958), and *Die alt-und mittelenglischen Apollonius Bruchstücke mit dem Text der Historia Apollonii nach der englischen Handschriftengruppe,* ed. Josef Raith (Munich, 1956). Another scholarly text is the Teubner *Historia Apollonii Regis Tyri,* ed. Alexander Riese (Leipzig, 1893) based on the manuscripts known as "A" and "P." The romance was "gathered into English" by Lawrence Twine in *The Patterne of painefull Adventures* (London, 1607); accessible in *Shakespeare's Library,* ed. John P. Collier and W. C. Hazlitt (London, 1875), IV, 229–334.

[20] See Goolden, *Apollonius,* p. xi. Cf. Perry, *The Ancient Romances,* pp. 320–24. who believes it the creation of a Latin author.

21 Elemar Klebs (*Die Erzählung von Apollonius aus Tyrus* [Berlin, 1899]) is a detailed study of the known manuscripts. See also Albert H. Smyth, *Shakespeare's Pericles and Apollonius of Tyre* (Philadelphia, 1898), pp. 211–17; and Dunlop, *History*, I, 82–83, n. 3.

22 See William Shakespeare, *Pericles, Prince of Tyre*, ed. Alfred Bellinger (New Haven, Conn., 1925), p. 95. Note further that the marriage of half brother and half sister is planned without a hint of scandal in Achilles Tatius's romance. (See *Achilles Tatius*, ed. and trans. Stephen Gaselee [London, 1917], p. 11.)

23 An excellent edition is *Les Éthiopiques* (*Théagène et Chariclée*), ed. R. M. Rattenbury and T. W. Lumb, trans. in French J. Maillon (Paris, 1935, 1938, 1943), 3 vols. *An Aethiopian History written in Greek by Heliodorus, Englished by Thomas Underdowne*, ed. W. E. Henley (London, 1895), is standard. More recent English translations are Moses Hadas, *An Ethiopian Romance* (Ann Arbor, Mich., 1957), and Walter Lamb, *Ethiopian Story* (London, 1961).

24 Philostratus alone among ancient authorities, excepting Heliodorus, located the naked philosophers in Ethiopia. (See Rohde, pp. 469–71.)

25 The best edition is *Longus Pastorales* (*Daphnis et Chloé*), ed. and trans. Georges Dalmeyda (Paris, 1934). *Daphnis and Chloe: The Elizabethan version from Amyot's Translation by Angel Day, Reprinted from the Unique Original*, ed. Joseph Jacobs (London, 1890), first published in 1587, is an adaptation of a translation, both deleting and adding material. Recent English translations are "*Daphnis and Chloe* by Longus," *Three Greek Romances*, trans. Moses Hadas (New York, 1953), pp. 17–98; and *Daphnis and Chloe*, trans. Paul Turner (Harmondsworth, Middlesex, 1956).

26 The *Babylonica* is localized around Babylon, but *all* over and *all* around Babylon in an entangling maze of confusion.

27 A recent text is *Achilles Tatius "Leucippe and Clitophon,"* ed. Ebbe Vilborg (Stockholm, 1955). William Burton's translation is republished as *The Loves of Clitophon and Leucippe . . . Reprinted . . . from a copy . . . printed by Thomas Creede in 1597*, ed. Stephen Gaselee and H. F. B. Brett-Smith (Oxford, 1923).

28 See Donald Durham, "Parody in Achilles Tatius," *Classical Philology*, XXXIII (1938), 1–19.

29 See Haight, *Essays*, p. 12.

30 See Ebbe Vilborg, *Achilles Tatius*, "The Sources of the Text," pp. xvi–xvii.

31 Ibid., "The Transmission," p. lxxiii.

32 *Hysmine and Hysminias* of Eustathius follows Achilles Tatius and Heliodorus rather closely. The central purpose is preser-

vation of virginity, but for no specific reason, religious, moral, or ethical. It utilizes the Heliodoran structure of narrative within narrative and emphasizes the erotic along with the chastity theme. The first edition of 1617 was reissued in 1618, 1634, and 1644. An Italian translation of 1550 was reprinted in 1560 and 1566. Two French translations were published in 1559 (reissued 1582) and 1625, respectively. An anonymous translation appeared at Strassburg in 1573, followed by another in 1594 (reissued, 1610). A third in German appeared in Leipzig in 1663. A Dutch version was published in 1652. (See Ruth Nutt Horne, "Lope de Vega's *Peregrino en su patria* and the Romance of Adventure in Spain before 1604" [Ph.D. diss., Brown University, 1946], pp. 270–71.)

Nicetas Eugenianus's *Charicles and Drusilla* shows the influence of bucolic writers. Filled with erotic digressions, it generally imitates Heliodorus. Theodorus Prodromus, writing in semi-accentual iambics, followed Heliodorus in *Dosicles and Rhodanthe*. Constantinius Manasses's *Aristander and Callithea*, in accentual "political" verse characteristic of modern Greek poetry, is extant only in fragments. (Ibid., p. 413, and Warren, *History*, p. 79.)

CHAPTER TWO

[1] See F. M. Warren, *History of the Novel Previous to the Seventeenth Century* (New York, 1895), p. 56.

[2] See Gaston Paris, "Etudes sur la Littérature du Moyen Age," *Cosmopolis*, XI (1898), 761, 764. Édelstand du Meril ("Introduction," *Floire et Blanceflor: Poèms du XIIIᵉ Siecle*, etc. [Paris, 1856], passim) asserts that the Medieval romances had some roots in Greek romance.

[3] Other interesting examples include Dante's sight of Beatrice in church at Florence, Petrarch's first sight of Laura at a service in Avignon, and Boccaccio's first sight of Fiammetta in church.

[4] John R. Reinhard (*The Old French Romance of Amadas et Ydoine: A Historical Study* [Durham, N.C., 1927], p. 19) lists eleven or more romances that include such symptoms. He thinks that the motif of love-languishment came into European literature through Greek romance as well as Celtic sources (p. 110).

[5] See L. S. Salinger, "Time and Art in Shakespeare's Romances," *Renaissance Drama* (Evanston, Ill., 1966), IX, 7–8.

[6] J. J. Munro ("Introduction," [Arthur] *Brooke's "Romeus and Juliet" Being the Original of Shakespeare's "Romeo and Juliet,"* etc., ed. J. J. Munro [New York, 1908], pp. ix–xx) discusses in detail the separation and potion plots as they relate to *Romeo and Juliet*.

[7] In "Shakespeare's Pastorals," *Studies in Philology,* XIII (1916), 122–54.

[8] See Otto Lohman, *Die Rahmenerzählung des Decameron: Ihre Quellen und Nachwirkungen* (Halle, 1935), p. 48.

[9] See *The Book of the Short Story,* ed. Henry S. Canby and Robeson Bailey, new and enl. edition (New York, 1948), p. 28.

[10] *Il Filocolo* (Venice, 1472) appeared in at least eight editions at Florence, Venice, Milan, and Naples by 1500, and thirteen more by 1600. A French translation by Adrien Sevin (Paris, 1542) appeared five times by 1575. In the fifteenth century Book IV (the episode of the Court of Love) was published separately by Giacomo di Giovanni di Ser Minoccio as *Il Libro di Difinizione.* During the sixteenth century this excerpt appeared in Spanish (1545), French (1530), and in English: *Thirtene most plesant and delectable questions . . . englished by H. G.* [Henry Grantham or Humphrey Gifford?] (London, 1566, 1571, and 1587).

[11] Two early French versions, a rhymed ballad in Italian, and a version in Franco-Venetian are known. (See Thomas C. Chubb, *The Life of Giovanni Boccaccio* [New York, 1930], p. 69.) Édelestand du Meril's discussion (*Floire*) is old but still interesting. John E. Wells (*A Manual of the Writings in Middle English: 1050–1400* [New Haven, Conn., 1926], pp. 139–41) describes two versions of the romance composed *c.* 1250.

[12] See Warren, *History,* p. 80, who thinks that the romances of *Ercale* (*c.* 1169) and *Florimént* (*c.* 1188) have similar backgrounds and that the prototype of the hero in *Ille et Galeron* (*c.* 1168) can be found in the Alexandrine romances (see p. 95). See also B. Zumbini, " 'Il Filocopo' del Boccaccio," *Nuova Antologia di Scienza, Lettere, ed Arte,* XLVIII (1879), 674 (Series 2, No. 18); and Edward Hutton, *Giovanni Boccaccio: A Biographical Study* (New York, 1910), p. 68, n. 1.

[13] See "Les Sources de 'Floire et Blanceflor,' " *Revue de Philologie Française et de Littérature,* XIX (1905). Wilhelm Cloetta, *Abfassung und Ueberlieferung des Poema Moral* (Erlangen, 1884), contains a bibliography of the Apollonius story as it was known to the troubadours. The late thirteenth-century Provençal *Flamenca* contains a story "d'Apolloine com si retene Tyr de Sidoine." A mid-fourteenth-century codex in the Bibliotheca Nazionale of Turin contains a "Tosco-Veneziana" version of *Apollonius.* Albert H. Smyth describes a thirteenth- or fourteenth-century Spanish manuscript of the "Libro de Apolonio" (*Shakespeare's Pericles and Apollonius of Tyre* [Philadelphia, 1898], pp. 38–42).

[14] See Joachim Reinhold, *Floire et Blanceflor: Étude de Littérature Comparée* (Paris, 1906), pp. 119–45.

[15] See Hutton, *Giovanni Boccaccio,* p. 68, n. 1.

[16] Munro (*Brooke's "Romeus,"* pp. xviii–xix, n. 3) sees a rela-

tionship between the *Babylonica* and *Ephesiaca* and the thirteenth question discussed before Fiammetta at the Court of Love: concerning a woman mistakenly buried alive, but rescued when her lover came to kiss her after burial.

¹⁷ Munro (ibid., pp. xiv–xv) considers this a source of the Romeo and Juliet legend: Biancofiore's mother named Giulia (Juliette), the hero banished to Montorio (Mantua), the mention of Alexandria (the earliest printed version of the legend by Massuccio Salernitano includes a journey to Alexandria), the enmity between two families, the incorrect publication of the heroine's death, the hero's lamentations at her tomb.

¹⁸ See "An Ephesian Tale by Xenophon," trans. Hadas, pp. 131–33, 151–52.

¹⁹ "The World of Boccaccio's *Filocolo*," PMLA, LXXVI (1961), 331, on which I have drawn for the discussion of the supernatural elements and the use of "Fortune" in *Il Filocolo*.

²⁰ I have hesitated to write much about the role of Fortune in the Greek romance, since Wolff has treated it fully. I have drawn on his discussion, *The Greek Romances*, pp. 111–20, 123–26, 143, 146, 188.

²¹ Trans. Blake, p. 17.

²² "Boccaccio's *Filocolo*," p. 334.

²³ Xenophon of Ephesus, trans. Hadas, p. 127.

²⁴ "Boccaccio's *Filocolo*," p. 330.

²⁵ The original manuscript of *The Decameron* (c. 1348–1353) is lost; the oldest extant is by Francesco Mannelli, c. 1368. The first printed edition appeared in 1471, and some nine or ten others followed in the fifteenth century. About seventy-seven editions were published in the sixteenth century (see Hutton, *Giovanni Boccaccio*, p. 311). As early as 1414 Laurent de Premierfait translated *The Decameron* into French. The first printing was in 1485, followed by seven editions by 1541. A French translation by Antoine le Maçon appeared in 1545. By 1614 eleven editions had been published at Paris, six at Lyon, and one each at Amsterdam and Rotterdam. In 1429 a Catalan translation was completed. Besides this, a mid-century manuscript of fifty tales of *The Decameron* in Castilian is known. The whole work was published in Catalan at Seville in 1496, followed by four editions by 1550. A German translation by "Arigo" was published in 1473. A second edition in 1490 was followed by four others before 1547. In 1564 Dirck Cornhert published fifty tales of *The Decameron* in Dutch. The other fifty were translated by Gerrit Hendricx van Breugel in 1605. (See Herbert G. Wright, *The First English Translation of the "Decameron": 1620* [Upsala, 1953], pp. 9–11.)

Boccaccio was known in England during the fourteenth century. Franco Sacchetti (1335–1400) in the "Proemio" to his *Novelle* mentions an English translation. If one existed in Sacchetti's time it is now lost, though he might have meant Chaucer's adaptations of Day VIII, tale 1; Day X, tales 5 and 10. The first known English translation, by an unidentified hand, was published in 1620, although translations of separate tales had appeared earlier. The 1620 translation was made indirectly through the French of Antoine le Maçon. (See Harry Carter, "A Note upon the Text," I, vii; and Edward Hutton, "General Introduction," I, xx, in John Boccaccio, *The Decameron . . . Translated into English anno 1620* [New York, 1940], pp. vii, xix–xxi.) The translation of 1620, which may have been made by John Florio, was republished in 1625, 1634, 1657, and 1684. A new English translation of *The Decameron* appeared in 1702, with a second edition in 1712. A third was published in 1741, the author possibly Charles Balguy, and was reissued in 1804, 1820, 1822, 1861, and 1872. In the late nineteenth century Henry Morley edited forty stories of the 1620 translation. John Payne's translation was published in 1886. (See Herbert G. Wright, *Boccaccio in England from Chaucer to Tennyson* [London, 1957], pp. 191, 261–62, 333. See also Wright, *The First English Translation of the Decameron.*)

[26] Marcus Landau (*Die Quellen des Dekameron* [Stuttgart, 1884], p. 296) thinks Boccaccio knew about the romances but had not read them. Arthur J. Tieje ("The Critical Heritage of Fiction in 1579," *Englische Studien*, XLVII [1913–1914], 437, n. 1) says *Fiammetta* parallels the sentimental characteristics of the Greek novel. He notes that Boccaccio could read Greek and that more than one of the *novelle* of *The Decameron* is Greek in origin.

[27] William Painter included the story of Andreuccio (II, 5) in Vol. II of *The Palace of Pleasure* (1566–1567). The tomb scene is utilized in Abraham Fraunce's play *Victoria* (1580). (See Wright, *Boccaccio in England*, pp. 187–88.) Florence N. Jones (*Boccaccio and His Imitators* [Chicago, 1910], pp. 14–15) lists eighteen other versions of the story in German, English, French, Spanish, and Italian, including Hans Sachs, *Schwänke* (1546), Aphra Behn, *The Rover* (1677). Thirteen of those listed date before 1642.

[28] This tale was retold in substantially the same way by Robert Greene in *Perimedes the Blacke-Smith* (1588). (See Samuel L. Wolff, *The Greek Romances in Elizabethan Prose Fiction* [New York, 1912], pp. 370–72.) Jones (*Boccaccio*, p. 15) lists six other versions, including Sachs, *Historia* (1549); Giraldi Cinthio, *Ecatommithi* (1565); Thomas Middleton, *Blurt-Master Constable* (1602); Behn, *The Rover*. Five date before 1642. German, English, French, and Italian versions are known.

[29] Jean de LaFontaine has used this story for his "La Fiancée du Roi de Garbe" (1666). (See John C. Dunlop, *History of Prose Fiction*, ed. Henry Wilson [London, 1911], II, 72.) Landau (*Die*

Quellen, p. 296) relates it to the *Ephesiaca.* Jones (*Boccaccio,* p. 15) cites also a version in Nicolas de Troyes's *Parangon* (1536).

[30] The story appears also in *Westward for Smelts* (1620) by "Kind Kit of Kingston," and in an adaptation of *Cymbeline* by Thomas Durfey, *The Injured Princess, or the Fatal Wager* (1682). It was also retold anonymously in *The Spirit of Boccaccio's Decameron* (1821). (See Wright, *Boccaccio in England,* pp. 250–53, 376.) Jones (*Boccaccio,* p. 16) recognizes versions in Sachs, *Commedia* (1548); Juan de Timoneda, *Patrañuelo* (1566) [who also wrote a version of *Apollonius of Tyre*]; Robert Greene's *Philomela* (1592); Thomas Heywood, *Challenge for Beauty* (1636). Thirteen of Jones's list of twenty-three are earlier than 1642. German, English, French, Spanish, and Italian versions are known.

[31] George Turberville retells the tale in verse in *Tragical Tales* (1576). Jones (*Boccaccio,* p. 22) lists two others, including Sachs, *Historia.* German, English, and Italian versions are known.

[32] Phillipo Beroaldo published a version in 1491. Greene adapted the first part of the story for *Tullies Love* (1589); John Fletcher and Philip Massenger adapted it to the stage as *The Elder Brother* (1637); and John Dryden included a verse translation in his *Fables* (1700) (see Wolff, *The Greek Romances,* pp. 373–75). The tale was translated separately from *The Decameron* in English verse by "T. C." as *A pleasant and delightful History, of Galesus Cymon and Iphigenia* (c. 1556–1560). (See Wright, *Boccaccio in England,* pp. 142–46.) David Garrick's *Cymon* (1766) distorts it thoroughly, as do several nineteenth-century versions (see ibid., pp. 326–28, 455–60). Jones (*Boccaccio,* pp. 23–24) lists nine other versions including Sachs, *Historia.* Eight of Jones's listings date before 1642. Versions in German, English, and Italian are known.

[33] As was pointed out by Wolff, *The Greek Romances,* p. 373; its afterlife is an adaptation in *The Cobler of Caunterburie* (1599) and a tale in Greene's *Perimedes* (see Wright, *Boccaccio in England,* pp. 164–65).

[34] This was retold in *The Spirit of Boccaccio's Decameron.* Jones lists three others; again one is by Sachs, *Petrus floch mit seiner lieben* (1543). Versions in German, English, Italian, and French are known.

[35] *The Greek Romances,* p. 248. Wolff finds a literary history traced to Petrus Alphonsus, *Disciplina Clericalis* (c. 1106); Thomas de Cantimpré, *De Proprietatibus Apum* (after 1251); the *Gesta Romanorum* (c. 1300); Nicolaus Pergamenus, *Dialogus Creaturarum* (13th or 14th century); *El Cavallero Cifar* (early 14th century); *Athis and Prophilias* (c. 1200) (see ibid., pp. 258–59).

[36] See Dunlop, *History,* II, 144.

[37] See Wolff, *The Greek Romances*, pp. 248–61.

[38] William Walter translated this tale in English as *Tytus and Gesyppus*, deriving it from a Latin version of Phillipo Beroaldo, *De Tito Romano Gisippoque Atheniensi* (Bologna, 1491). Wright (*Boccaccio in England*, pp. 132–34) does not know if Walter's preceded Elyot's work. Edward Jenynges turned it into verse as *The Notable Hystory of two faithfull Louers . . . Alfagus and Archelaus* (1574). Thomas Durfey included it as "Titus and Gissippus . . . Done from a Hint out of the Italian, etc." in *Tales Tragical and Comical* (1706) in verse. Charles Lloyd wrote a rhymed verse version in 1821 for *Desultory Thoughts on London*. Gerald Griffin's *Gisippus* was performed on the London stage in 1823 (see Wright, ibid., pp. 137–42, 280–84, 426–29, 464–68). Jones (*Boccaccio*, pp. 39–40) lists thirty other versions, including two by Sachs, *Die getruen heiden* (1531), and *Titus und Gesippus* (1546); John Lydgate, *Fabula duorum mercatorum* (1425); Timoneda, *Patrañuelo;* Thomas Underdoone [*sic*, the translator of the *Aethiopica*], *Titus and Gesyppus* (1592, now lost); Greene, *Philomela;* Lope de Vega, *La Boda entre das maridos* (1614); John Fletcher, *Monsieur Thomas* (1620). Jones (ibid.) lists twenty-seven versions before 1642. Louis Sorieri (*Boccaccio's Story of "Tito E Gisippo" in European Literature* [New York, 1937]) names more than one hundred works in Latin, French, Italian, English, Spanish, and German which derive in one degree or another—directly or indirectly—from the tale. Many relate primarily to the friendship motif, but many retain the Greek romance elements in varying degrees.

Munro (*Brooke's "Romeus,"* pp. xviii–xix, n. 3) says that Boccaccio's novels of "Ferondo" (III, 8), in which the hero is buried alive after taking a drug; and "Girolamo . . . [and] Salvestra" (IV, 8), in which the hero is shipwrecked and saved by an old woman; and the story of "Messer Gentil de' Carisendi" (X, 4), in which a woman is buried alive, are also related to the plot of *Romeo and Juliet*, and ultimately to the Greek romances. (See also R. A. Saner, "Da Porto, Boccaccio, and the Romeo Legend," *Romance Notes*, VII, ii [1965], 198–202.)

Warren (*History*, p. 81) thinks "Three Young Men Love Three Sisters" (IV, 3) has a Greek romance source. If this is so it is shadowy. Arthur Tieje in an unduly harsh review of Wolff (*The Greek Romances, Journal of English and Germanic Philology*, XIII [1914], 484), asserts that the Greek romance materials could have been known in England through the Greek plot of the *Clareo y Florisea* and the typical Greek psychology and rhetoric of the *Fiammetta*, known in Spain by 1492, in France by 1534, and in England by 1587.

Although Greek romance elements in Boccaccio usually seem to filter at secondhand or thirdhand through traditional sources, a firsthand link may exist in the *Ninfale fiesolano* (1477): A shepherd falls in love with a nymph of Diana. Penitent at breaking her vow of chastity, the nymph deserts him. The shepherd kills himself on the bank of a stream where they had been happy together. The nymph, after bearing a son, is turned into another stream. Eventually the streams converge. Hutton (*Giovanni Boccaccio*, p. 94) believes this tale derives in part from Ovid's *Metamorphoses* and in part from the myth of Rhodopis and Euthynicus, Book VII of Achilles Tatius.

[39] Other distinguished Renaissance Italians have left evidence that they knew the Greek romances. Giacopo Sannazzaro in the *Arcadia* (1504) describes a method of trapping birds like that in Longus, Book III (noted by Walter W. Greg, *Pastoral Poetry and Pastoral Drama* [New York, 1959], p. 49). This may be evidence that *Daphnis and Chloe* had a continuing literary history, for the romance was not available in print before the Amyot translation of 1559.

A number of scholars have noted that Torquato Tasso in his *Aminta*, I, ii (1573), borrowed the strategy of a pretended bee sting to gain a kiss, from Book II of Achilles Tatius, in print since 1544. Greg thinks the innocent child love of Silvia and Aminta derives from *Daphnis and Chloe* (see pp. 181, 184, 190). Warren (*History*, p. 228) thinks the presumed death of Silvia derives from the Greek novels. The circumstances of Clorinda's miraculous white birth to the Queen of Ethiopia and her subsequent abandonment and nurture in Canto XII of *Gerusalemne liberata* (1575) derive directly from Chariclea's early history in the *Aethiopica* (in print since 1534). (See Michael Oeftering, *Heliodore und seine Bedeutung für die Litterature* [Berlin, 1901], pp. 114–15.) Clorinda's nurture by a tigress reminds one of the nurture of infants by animals in the Longus romance.

Battista Guarini imitates the same Heliodoran details at the conclusion of the *Pastor fido* (1585). He also borrows from Longus, Book I, the device of hunting with dogs a person disguised in a wolfskin (see Homer Smith, "Pastoral Influence in the English Drama," *PMLA*, XII [1897], 365, n. 1). Oeftering (*Heliodore*, pp. 163–64) thinks the plot situation—Amarilli's betrothal to a priest's son, a man she does not care for, her concealed love for Mirtillo, and the desire of the voluptuous Corsica for Mirtillo—parallels the situation in Books III and IV of the *Aethiopica* in which we find Chariclea betrothed to the nephew of her guardian, a priest of Apollo, but secretly in love with Theagenes. Later in Book VII, Theagenes is sought by the voluptuous Arsace.

[40] See Ben E. Perry, *The Ancient Romances: A Literary-Historical Account of Their Origins* (Berkeley, Calif., 1967), pp. 64–65.

[41] A French translation *"par feu* M. Jacques Vincent de Crest

Arnault en Dauphine" appeared in 1554 at Paris. Evidence exists that before 1545 Francisco de Vergara made a Spanish translation, now lost, of Achilles Tatius (see Ruth Horne, "Lope de Vega's *Peregrino en su patria* and the Romance of Adventure in Spain before 1604" [Ph.D. diss., Brown University, 1946], p. 162).

[42] George Ticknor (*History of Spanish Literature* [New York, 1849], I, 24–25) believes it derives from the *Gesta Romanorum*. It has been translated in English as *The Book of Apollonius* by Raymond L. Grismer and Elizabeth Atkins (Minneapolis, Minn., 1936).

[43] Augustin Collado del Hierro turned the story of the *Aethiopica* into verse some time before 1630. It was not published, but is noted by Pellicer de Salas y Tobar in *El Fénix* (see Horne, "Lope de Vega's," p. 162).

[44] "The Greek Romance in the *Siglo de Oro*," *South Central Bulletin*, XXI, No. 4 (1961), 46.

[45] See W. G. Crane, *Wit and Rhetoric in the Renaissance*, Columbia University Studies in English and Comparative Literature, No. 129 (New York, 1937), p. 163.

[46] Published in 1604 at Seville, Madrid, and Barcelona; followed by editions at Barcelona, 1605; Brussels, 1608; Paris, 1614 (?); Madrid, 1618. French translations were published at Paris in 1615 and 1660. An English translation appeared in London in 1621, 1623, 1628, 1632. A German translation came out at Eisenstadt in 1629 and 1630 (see Horne, "Lope de Vega's," pp. 273–74).

[47] Ibid., pp. 181–96, 252. See Gerding, p. 46, and Rudolph Schevill, "Studies in Cervantes: 'Persiles y Sigismunda,' I and II," *Modern Philology*, IV (1907), 21. As to other examples, the *Historia de los honestos amores de Peregrino y Ginebra* (c. 1548) of Hernando Díaz is a translation of an Italian work by Jacopo Caviceo, *Il peregrino* (1508), an imitation Greek romance in which imaginary pilgrimages, separated lovers, slavery, persecutions, imprisonments, and a journey to Alexandria, occur in an atmosphere of sensuality. The greater part of the work, however, is given to details of courtship. The travel details are slight and only the hero goes away. Caviceo's work is a model for *Selva de aventuras* (1565) of Jerónimo de Contreras, a work characterized by morality, decorum, and an idealistic attitude toward love. In Antonio de Lofrasso's *Los diez libros de fortuna de amor* (1573), a vow of chastity, an elopement in shepherd's disguise, sea voyage, battle, and unjust imprisonment of the hero, carry on the tradition. The *Poema trágico del español Gerardo y desengaño del amor lascivo* (1615–1617) of Gonzalo Céspedes y Meneses utilizes the Heliodoran structure of separation plot, story within story, and "flashback." The adventure motifs are traditional for the Greek romance genre, but the

word *trágico* indicates that it does not move completely within the conventions (see Gerding, "The Greek Romance," pp. 46–47; and Horne, "Lope de Vega's," pp. 136–37, 167, 246).

[48] Lope de Vega, "La dama boba," *Obras* (Madrid, 1929), XI, 591. See also Rudolph Schevill, "Studies, II," p. 687.

[49] De Vega, "La dama boba," p. 619.

[50] *Novelas a la Señora Marcía Leonarda*, ed. John D. Fitz-Gerald and Leora A. Fitz-Gerald (Erlangen, 1913), p. 4. See also Gerding, "The Greek Romance," p. 47. Other Renaissance Spanish writers give evidence of knowing the Greek romances: Francisco de Lugo y Dávila in *Teatro popular* (1622), following the *Decameron* type framework for a collection of stories, makes one of his characters discuss *Teágenes y Cariclea* and *Leucippe y Clitophonte*. In the second novella of the collection the stock events of the Hellenistic novel are employed. In "La hermosa Aurora" of Juan Pérez de Montalbán's *Sucesos y prodigios de amor* (1625) the stock Greek romance motifs are reversed: The lovers are first joined by shipwreck and conceal their identity from each other, but not from the other characters. They are separated and reunited eventually. José Camerino's *Novelas amorosas* (1642) is an imitation of a Greek romance set in time and place that approximates the originals. Francisco de Quintana, *Experiencias de amor y fortuna* (1626), has no central pair of lovers, but murder, highway robbery, rape, abduction, treason, as well as the conventional disasters make up the entertainment. Horne ("Lope de Vega's," p. 256) thinks it is a kind of "degenerate version of *El peregrino*" and that a good case could be made for considering it a parody of the genre if both Quintana and Lope de Vega had not discussed it seriously in their prefaces. Quintana's *La historia de Hipólito y Aminta* (1627) includes the stock motifs of Greco-Byzantine romance with a central pair of lovers. There is a dramatic tomb rescue along with picaresque motifs: gypsies, beggars, mule stealing, horse theft, floods, drunks, adultery, faked murder through mutilation of a body, bull fights, duels, and real murder, all material more or less suitable for the *novela cortesana*. Horne (ibid., p. 257) thinks it descends from *El peregrino* rather than from Heliodorus (see Gerding, "The Greek Romance," pp. 47–48, and Oeftering, *Heliodore*, pp. 107–9).

[51] See René Pruvost, *Matteo Bandello and Elizabethan Fiction* (Paris, 1937), pp. 208–9.

[52] See William C. Atkinson, "The Enigma of the *Persiles*," *Bulletin of Spanish Studies*, XXIV (1947), 242–53, and E. C. Riley, *Cervantes's Theory of the Novel* (Oxford, 1962), pp. 51–53. According to Pinciano "los amores de Teágenes y Cariclea, de Heliodoro, y los de Leucipo y Clitofonte, de Aquiles Tacio, son tan épica como la *Ilíada* y la *Eneida*; y todos esos libros de ca-

ballerías, cual los cuatro dichos poemas, no tienen, digo, diferencia alguna esencial que los distinga, ni tampoco esencialmente se diferencia uno de otro por las condiciones individuales" (ibid., p. 52).

If Atkinson is correct in assigning the influence of Pinciano's work a major role in the composition of Cervantes's *Persiles,* the conclusions of Mack Singleton on the dating of *Persiles* are not valid. (See note 54, p. 175.)

[53] Scaliger may have been the first to call Heliodorus's work a model for epic poets. But Greek romance was less popular than *Amadis of Gaul* had been, except with the cultivated intellectual (see Riley, *Cervantes's Theory,* pp. 51–53).

[54] *Persiles y Sigismunda,* the last of Cervantes's published works, was issued by his family shortly after his death. On the basis of internal evidence, Mack Singleton ("The 'Persiles' Mystery," *Cervantes Across the Centuries,* ed. Angel Flores and M. J. Benardete [New York, 1947], pp. 227–38) assigns its composition to a period in Cervantes's life contemporary with the *Galatea* (1585), the first known published work.

The first edition of *Persiles* was issued at Madrid in 1617 by Juan de la Cuesta, who had published *Don Quixote* and the *Novelas exemplares.* A second edition appeared in Madrid that same year, as well as editions in Barcelona, Lisbon, Pamplona, Paris, and Valencia. By 1629 at least ten editions had been published, but after that year, no more until 1719. In 1618 two French translations, one by François de Rosset, another by le Sieur D'Audiguier, were published at Paris. D'Audiguier's work was reissued twice in 1626 and again in 1628 at Paris. *The Travels of Persiles and Sigismunda: A Northern History* translated from the French was published by "H. L. for M.[atthew] L. [ownes]" at London in 1619. *Persiles and Sigismunda: A Celebrated Novel,* translated from the original, was published in two volumes at London in 1741. L.[ouisa] D.[orothea] S.[tanley] published an English translation, *The Wanderings of Persiles and Sigismunda: A Northern Story,* at London in 1854. An Italian translation by Francesco Ellio Milanese appeared at Venice in 1626. I know of no German translation before 1746. *The Custom of the Country* (*c.* 1619), a play by Fletcher and Massinger, derives its main plot and underplot from *Persiles y Sigismunda.*

Galatea is a pastoral romance in prose and poetry after the model of Jorge Montemayor's *Diana* (*c.* 1542–1558/9) rather than of Longus; that is, it descended from the Vergilian pastoral tradition through the *Ameto* of Boccaccio, the *Arcadia* of Sannazzaro, the *Pastor fido* of Guarini. Rudolph Schevill ("Studies," p. 696) believes the "machinery of adventure" in *Galatea* is derived from the *Aethiopica* and that there are some verbal echoes as well. D. P. Rotunda ("A Boccaccian Theme in the

Galatea of Cervantes," *The Romanic Review,* XX [1929], 245) notes that the first half of Cervantes's story of Timbrio and Silerio in the *Galatea* is markedly similar to the latter part of the story of "Gisippus . . . and Titus" (X, 8) of *The Decameron,* a story with Greek romance roots.

The story of Felismena in Montemayor's *Diana* derives, according to Warren (*History,* p. 262), from Eustathius Makrembolites's *Hysmine and Hysminias.* It employs the motif of a girl disguised as a page boy and serving her beloved. The theme appears also in works by Matteo Bandello, François de Belleforest, Barnaby Riche, Nicolo Secchi, Curzio Gonzaga, Philip Sidney, and in Shakespeare's *Twelfth Night.* See *Twelfe-Night, or, What You Will: A New Variorum Edition of Shakespeare,* ed. Horace H. Furness (Philadelphia, 1901), pp. 326–77. Dunlop (*History,* II, 369–70) and T. P. Harrison ("Concerning *Two Gentlemen of Verona* and Montemayor's *Diana,*" *Modern Language Notes,* XLI [1926], 252) think that the story of Proteus and Julia in *Two Gentlemen of Verona* derived from the *Diana,* probably through the English translation of Edward Paston or a fragment by Barnabe Googe (1563).

As to the construction of the *Diana*—the action advancing quickly, then being stopped at times by anecdotes—Juan B. Avalle-Arce ("The *Diana* of Montemayor: Tradition and Invention," *PMLA,* LXXIV [1959], 1–6) believes that it derived from the narrative technique of the Byzantine novel crossbred with the folklore motif of the trip. Joseph S. Kennard (*Italian Romance Writers* [New York, 1922], pp. 9–10) speaks of *Daphnis and Chloe* as the "model" of the *Diana.* Oeftering (*Heliodore,* pp. 111–13) notes plot motifs in Gaspar Gil Polo's continuation of the *Diana,* the *Diana enamorada,* which derive from the *Aethiopica.* In *La Novela Pastoril Española* (Madrid, 1959), p. 107, Avalle-Arce says the model of the story of Ismenia is the story of Cnemon in the *Aethiopica.* Horne ("Lope de Vega's," p. 166) thinks the story of Marcelio and Alcida—sea journey and separation—derives from Heliodorus. Dunlop (*History,* II, 370) thinks also that the story of Felismena suggested the disguise in Beaumont and Fletcher's *Philaster.*

[55] Miguel de Cervantes Saavedra, *Novelas Exemplares,* ed. Rodolfo Schevill y Adolfo Bonilla (Madrid, 1922), I, 23.

[56] Rudolph Schevill ("Studies I and II," pp. 1–24, 677–704 and "Part III," *Connecticut Academy of Arts and Sciences,* XIII [1908], 457–548) is to my knowledge the best study in English of the sources of *Persiles.* I have drawn on this work for the discussion which follows.

[57] Gerding ("The Greek Romance," p. 48) thinks the *Historia de las fortunas de Semprilis y Genorodano* (1629) of Juan

Enrique de Zúñiga is an obvious imitation of *Persiles y Sigismunda.*
It includes an opening *in medias res,* royalty, desert islands, lost heirs, and exotic settings. Gerding notes that the century of imitation of Achilles Tatius and Heliodorus (1607–1701) that began with Lope de Vega's *El peregrino* ended with *La historia da Lisseno y Fenissa* (1701) of Francisco de Párraga Martel de la Fuente. In *La Novela Pastoril Española,* Avalle-Arce notes that Jacinto de Espinal Adorno's *El premio de la constancia y pastores de sierra Bermeja* (1620) imitates the Greek romance in its interrelated histories and in form of presentation (p. 166). J. A. Van Praag ("*Eustorgio y Clorilene: Historia Moscovia* [1629] de Enrique Súarez de Mendoza y Figueroa," *Bulletin Hispanique,* XLI [1939], 240) says the form Súarez de Mendoza gives to *Eustorgio y Clorilene* is imitated from *Persiles y Sigismunda,* thus at secondhand from Greek romance. He says further that it "*es mucho más que una mala imitacion 'Persiles y Sigismunda.'*" (See also Oeftering, *Heliodore,* pp. 109–11.)

[58] According to Avalle-Arce (*La Novela Pastoril Española,* pp. 163–64), the setting of Jerónimo de Covarrubias Herrera's *Eliséa* (1549) in the "*margenes*" of the Nile derives from the description of the isle of shepherds in Book I of the *Aethiopica.*

[59] Schevill ("Studies, II," pp. 698–704) demonstrates in detail the similarities between the *Aethiopica* and the *Persiles.* I have drawn on this material for the discussion which follows.

[60] Thomas Roscoe (*The Life and Writings of Miguel de Cervantes Saavedra* [London, n. d.], pp. 252–53) discusses this aspect of *Persiles* at some length.

[61] See Walter Boelich, "Heliodorus Christianus: Cervantes und der Byzantinische Roman," *Freundesgabe für Ernst Robert Curtius* (Bern, 1956), pp. 106, 113–14.

[62] "Studies." See especially *Modern Philology,* IV (1907), 1–24, 677–704.

[63] Ibid., especially pp. 19–21.

[64] Ibid., Part III, 501–5.

[65] See William J. Entwistle, *Cervantes* (Oxford, 1940), p. 18.

[66] C. Carroll Marden, "Introduction," *Libro de Apolonio: An Old Spanish Poem.* Part I, in Elliot Monographs, VI (Baltimore, Md., 1917), pp. xxxii–xxxix. Perry (*The Ancient Romances,* p. 304) notes the essential similarity between Books I and IV of the *Aeneid* and the Apollonius story.

[67] The first edition (Madrid, 1613) was issued by Juan de la Cuesta. In 1614 editions appeared at Madrid, Pamplona, and Brussels; in 1615 at Pamplona and Milan. Between 1616 and 1665 there were at least seventeen more at Venice, Madrid, Pamplona, Lisbon, Seville, Brussels, Barcelona, and Zaragoza.

F. De Rosset and Sr. D'Audiguier published a French translation at Paris in 1615, reissued at least nine times at Paris between 1620 and 1678. A German translation by Nicolas Ulenhart was published at Augsburg in 1617. An abbreviation by G. P. Harsdörffer was published at Frankfurt in 1650 and 1652. Two Italian translations were published, one by Guglielmo Allesandro de Novilieri Clavelli at Venice in 1626, 1628, and 1629; the other by Donato Fontana Milanese at Milan in 1627 and 1629. F.[elix] v.[an] S.[ambix] published a Dutch translation at Delft in 1643, and in Amsterdam in 1653. Three early English translations are known: *Exemplarie Novells in Six Books* by Don Diego Puede-Ser (a pseudonym for James Mabbe) appeared in 1640 and again in 1654 at London; *The Spanish Decameron: or, Ten Novels*, translated by R.[oger] L.[estrange], was published in 1687 at London; *Select Novels: The First Six Written in Spanish by Miguel Cervantes Sayavedra*, translated by "Dr. Pope," appeared in London in 1694. Numerous translations of the *Novelas exemplares* in Bohemian, Catalan, Danish, Dutch, English, French, German, Italian, Latin, Portuguese, and Swedish are listed by Jeremiah Ford and Ruth Lansing in *Cervantes: A Tentative Bibliography* (Cambridge, Mass., 1911), pp. 85–94.

[68] Sadie Trachman (*Cervantes' Women of Literary Tradition* [New York, 1932], pp. 138–40) says the resemblance between Preciosa and Tharsia derives from Juan de Timoneda's adaptation of *Apollonius of Tyre*, no. XI of *El Patrañuela* (1576), or from "Tarsiana" of the "Libro de Apolonio."

[69] Trachman notes (*Cervantes'*, p. 47) that Halima of "El amante liberal" as well as Zahara of the *Trato de Argel* and Halima of *Bañas de Argel*—all Moorish women who love Christian slaves—are reminiscent of Arsace who pursues Theagenes in the *Aethiopica*.

[70] Fletcher borrowed freely from *Novelas exemplares:* "La Señora Cornelia," and "Los dos doncellas" furnished material for *The Chances* (*c.* 1615) and *Love's Pilgrimage* (1635), respectively. The lost highborn child motif from "La illustre fregona" appears in *The Fair Maid of the Inn* (1626) and suggested portions of *The Beggar's Bush* (1622). "El amante liberal" contributed to *The Scornful Lady* (1616). See Douglas H. Orgill, "The Influence of Cervantes on the Plays of John Fletcher" (Ph.D. diss., University of Southern California, 1960) (University microfilm no. 60–2784), passim.

The question of whether the play *A Very Woman, or the Prince of Tarent* (*c.* 1634/5), ascribed to Philip Massinger, has its source in "El amante liberal" is discussed by Baldwin Maxwell, *Studies in Beaumont, Fletcher, and Massinger* (Chapel Hill, N.C., 1939), pp. 182–89.

[71] In *Don Quixote* knowledge of Heliodorus may be reflected

in the references to the gymnosophists. (See Schevill, "Studies, I," p. 21, n. 2.) Schevill ("Ovid and the Renascence in Spain," *University of California Publications in Modern Philology*, IV [1913–1916], 167) thinks the Greek romance manner is reflected in the wildly emotional behavior of heroines in Renaissance fiction: for example, in the Spanish Ovid of Bustamente—the lamentations of Daphne, Hecuba bewailing her daughter, and Thisbe weeping over the body of Pyramus.

The popularity of Heliodoran material is further attested by Roxas Zorilla's play *Persiles y Sigismunda* (1636), based on Cervantes's work. It was followed by Juan Pérez de Montalbán's *Los Hijos de la fortuna, Teagene y Clariquea* (*c.* 1638), a much garbled dramatization of the *Aethiopica,* in which Princess Sinforosa from *Persiles y Sigismunda* is also involved. (See George W. Bacon, "The Life and Dramatic Works of . . . Montalván [1620–1638]," *Revue Hispanique*, XXVI [1912], 120–24.) Calderón de la Barca treated the material in *Los Hijos de la fortuna* shortly after Montalbán. (See also Oeftering, *Heliodore*, pp. 155–62.)

[72] See Riley, *Cervantes's Theory*, p. 53.

[73] A parallel interest can be observed in French writers of the seventeenth century. The open tomb of the *Babylonica* reappears in the *Histoire africaine* (1627) of le Sieur de Gerzan, an expansion of Heliodorus, as does the old standby poison plot of the *Ephesiaca* utilized by Gilbert du Verdier in the *Nymphe solitaire* (1624), by the anonymous "Perrochel" in *Climandor* (1628), de Moreau in the *Filles enleveés* (1643), and by L'abbé René de Ceriziers in the *Illustre Amalazonthe* (1645). (See Maurice Magendie, *Le Roman Français au XVII*ᵉ *Siècle de "l'Astrée" au "Grand Cyrus"* [Paris, 1932], pp. 14–16.) Georges de Scudéry's *Almahide* (1660) is a kind of classic example of the potpourri of Greek elements—especially from Heliodorus and Achilles Tatius—which can be traced in similar works, such as Honoré d'Urfé's *Astrée* (1607–1627); Marin LeRoy de Gomberville's *Polexandre* (1619–1638) and *Cythérée* (1640–1642); Georges and Madeleine de Scudéry's *Ibrahim* (1641), *Le Grand Cyrus* (1649–1653), *Clélie* (1654–1660); and Gautier de Costes de la Calprénède's *Cassandra* (1642–1650), *Cléopâtre* (1647–1658), and *Faramond* (1662). *Almahide* (like the *Aethiopica,* the *Astrée, Clélie, Le Grand Cyrus,* and *Ibrahim*) begins *in medias res* and contains interpolated histories. Pirates, storms, disguises, oracles, and magic ride hand in hand with love at first sight, love sickness, attempted suicide, ekphrases of gardens and works of art, extended itineraries and interest in geographical details. (See Jerome W. Schweitzer, "Georges de Scudéry's *Almahide:* Authorship, Analysis, Sources, and Structure," *Johns Hopkins Studies in Romance Literature and Languages*, XXXIV [1939],

47–53. Heinrich Koerting's "Zweites Kapitel," *Geschichte de Franzosischen Romans in XVII Jahrhundert* (Oppeln und Leipzig, 1891), pp. 22–47, discusses this topic. Note also George Saintsbury, *A History of the French Novel to the Close of the Nineteenth Century* (London, 1917), I, 3, 153–54; and Warren, *History*, pp. 81–84. Philip A. Wadsworth's *The Novels of Gomberville: A Critical Study of "Polexandre" and "Cythérée"* (New Haven, Conn., 1942), is valuable. Magendie (*Le Roman*, p. 20) makes clear that *La Caritée, Mélante, Albanie et Sicile, l'Histoire africaine, l'Histoire asiatique, l'Histoire négrepontique, Ariane, Amelinte, Polexène, Ibrahim, Prazimène, Scanderberg, Hermiogène, Bérénice, and Cléopâtre* were influenced by Heliodorus.)

Oeftering (*Heliodore*, pp. 57–87) lists works reflecting Greek romance materials. Maillon (Heliodorus, *Les Éthiopiques* [*Théagène et Chariclée*], ed. R. M. Rattenbury and T. W. Lumb, trans. T. Maillon [Paris, 1935], p. xcviii) adds to the list a tragedy of Gabriel Gilbert, *Théagène* (1662). H. C. Lancaster ("Two Lost Plays by Alexandre Hardy," *Modern Language Notes*, XXVII [1912], 129–31) thinks the decapitation of the woman aboard ship in *Leucasie* (c. 1629–1631) is a clue to its source in *Clitophon and Leucippe*. Pierre Du Ryer's *Clitophon* (c. 1628) is based on the same source. A play by Balthazer Baro, *Le Prince fugitif* (1647), is the story of *Apollonius of Tyre*. (See R. C. Knight, "Racine et la Grèce," *Études de Littérature Étrangér et Comparée* [Paris, 1950], XXIII, 100.) Alfred Harbage, *Cavalier Drama* (New York, 1964), p. 29, relates Henri Vital d'Audiguier's *Lysandre et Caliste* (1616), and Jean Desmarets de Saint-Sorlin's *Ariane* (1631) to a base "in Greek fiction." Harbage quotes John Davies in his preface to Charles Sorels's *Le Berger Extravagant* (1627) as saying: "the Damosel certainly to be relieved upon the point of ravishing, a little child carried away out of his cradle, after some twenty years discovered to be the son of some great Prince, a girl after seven years wandering and cohabiting, and being Stole, confirm'd to be a Virgin, either by a Panterb, Fire, or a Fountain: and lastly all ending in marriage, and that all of a day, and in the same place, where to make up the number, somebody must be fresh discovered, . . . and others rise as it were from the dead" (ibid., p. 35).

Typical of the French interest in Greek romance is the reference in François Rabelaise to the *Aethiopica:* In a ship off the island of Chaneph "Pantagruel was . . . slumbering and nodding on the quarter deck . . . with a Heliodorus in his hand" (IV, lxiii). (See *The Works*, etc., trans. Thomas Urquhart and Peter A. Motteux, ed. Albert J. Nock and Catherine R. Wilson [New York, 1931], II, 753.)

Michel de Montaigne writes that Heliodorus "rather chose to

lose the dignity, profit, and devotion of . . . a prelacy, than to lose his daughter [the *Aethiopica*]; a daughter that continues to this day very graceful and comely, though a little too curiously and wantonly set off, and too amorous, for an ecclesiastic and sacerdotal daughter." (See "Of Recompenses of Honour," *Works,* etc., trans. [Charles Cotton], ed. W. Hazlitt and O. W. Wright [Boston, 1859], II, 72–73.)

Racine is said in his youth to have memorized most of the *Aethiopica*. It is known that he planned a drama based on the romance and that the plan was finally accomplished by Dorat. (See Dunlop, *History,* I, 36.) Knight ("Racine," pp. 244–45) asserts that by 1659–1663 Racine was *"an helléniste en herbe . . . sous les auspices d'Héliodore, non d'Euripide."* Aloys Tüchert (*Racine und Heliodore* [Zweibrucken, 1889]) and Maurice Lange ("Racine et le Roman d'Héliodore," *Revue d'Histoire litéraire de la France,* XXIII [1916], 145–62) discuss the relationship of the *Aethiopica* to a number of Racine's works. *Bajazet* is Lange's chief consideration. Fernand Baldensperger ("Racine et la Tradition Romanesque," *Revue de Littérature Comparée,* XIX [1939], 650) relates the subject matter of *Phèdre* to the Damaente material of Book I of the *Aethiopica*. He notes also that Racine names Heliodorus in his work on the *Odyssey*.

There is obvious reference to Longus in Henri Estiénne's eclogues of 1555 (see Alice Hulubei, "Henri Estienne et le Roman de Longus: *Daphnis et Chloé,*" *Revue de Sezième Siecle,* XIII [1938], 324–40). Greg (*Pastoral Poetry,* p. 13) says Longus's romance "finds its true descendant" in Jacques Henri Bernardin de Saint-Pierre's *Paul et Virginie* (1789). In Germany the *Idyllen* (1756) of Solomon Gessner are comparable.

CHAPTER THREE

[1] Frederick G. Fleay, *A Chronicle History of the London Stage: 1559–1642* (New York, 1909), p. 20. John P. Collier (*The History of English Dramatic Poetry to the Time of Shakespeare* [London, 1831], I, 198–99) notes a play called *Theagines and Chariclea,* performed *c.* June 9, 1572, as part of the entertainment of the Duke de Montmorency, Paul de Faix, and Bertrand de Salingers just after the conclusion of a league with France. We suspect it is the same play.

[2] Two of John Lily's plays contain lines which Samuel Lee Wolff (*The Greek Romances in Elizabethan Prose Fiction* [New York, 1912], p. 248, n. 1) considers allusions to the *Aethiopica*. See *Campaspe* (1580), I, i, 64–65, 79–80; and *Mother Bombi* (1590), I, i, 26–28. In *Gallathea* (1592), I, i, 28–34, the description of the flood is "unmistakably" from Achilles Tatius, IV, xii.

[3] See Wilhelm Creizenach, *The English Drama in the Age of*

Shakespeare, trans. Cécile Hugon from *Geschichte des neueren Dramas*, Books I–VIII (London, 1916), pp. 17–18. Creizenach (p. 28) says further that the plot materials of Cavalier plays derive from Greek fiction. Fletcher's *Sea Voyage* (1622) smacks of Greek romance in its themes of sea storm, shipwreck, and castaways. Adolphus Ward (*A History of English Dramatic Literature* [London, 1899], III, 29) has called Massinger's *The Emperor of the East* (1632) an *"incredible Greek romance."*

⁴ See Wallace A. Bacon, "Introduction," to William Warner's *Syrinx, or a Sevenfold History*, ed. Wallace A. Bacon (Evanston, Ill., 1950), p. xiv; and D. T. Starnes, "Barnabe Riche's 'Sappho Duke of Mantona': A Study in Elizabethan Story Making," *Studies in Philology*, XXX (1933), 455–72. The influence can be seen by 1579 if we consider Lyly's *Euphues*, derived from Greek Romance through Boccaccio.

⁵ Starnes ("Barnabe Riche's," pp. 457–72) also relates the story to the Medieval legend of St. Eustace, extant versions of which are known after the tenth century in almost all European languages. Latin versions are in the *Aurea Legenda* and the *Acta Sanctorum*. The legend seems to be adapted from the traditional separation plot: During a journey to Egypt, Eustace and his family are separated, the children apparently devoured by a lion and a wolf. Eustace labors as a common worker. Later, on a military campaign, he finds his wife and sons. The story is somewhat like *Apollonius of Tyre*. The anonymous drama *The Weakest Goeth to the Wall* (1600) also takes its materials from Riche's "Sappho" (ibid.).

⁶ Reissued London, 1589, 1592, 1596, 1597, 1602.

⁷ See Wallace A. Bacon, "Shakespeare's Dramatic Romances" (Ph.D. diss., University of Michigan, 1940), pp. 123–24. Bacon also finds relationships between Greek romance and Nicholas Breton's *The Strange Fortune of two excellent Princes* (1600) and the romances of Emanuell Forde: *Ornatus and Artesia* (before 1598?), *Parismus* (1598), *Parismenos* (1599), *Montelione* (earliest extant edition 1633). (Ibid.)

⁸ Reissued at London in 1593, 1598, 1599, 1605 twice, 1613, 1621, 1622, 1623, 1627, 1629, 1633, 1655, 1662, 1674. A French translation by I. Baudoin was published at Paris twice in 1624. Another by Geneviefve Chappelain appeared at Paris in 1625. A German translation by Martin Opitz was issued at Franckfurt on Main in 1629; reissued there in 1638, 1643, and at Leyden in 1646. A Dutch translation by Felix van Sambix was published at Delft in 1642.

⁹ Wolff, *The Greek Romance*, pp. 344–45.

¹⁰ See Marcus S. Goldman, "Sir Philip Sidney and the *Arcadia*," *University of Illinois Bulletin*, XXXII, no. 16 (1934), 125.

¹¹ Wolff, *The Greek Romances*, pp. 262–366.

[12] See p. 353. Wolff says further that even before the *Arcadia* was revised it contained much Heliodoran material (ibid.).

[13] See R. W. Zandvoort, *Sidney's Arcadia: A Comparison Between the Two Versions* (Amsterdam, 1929), pp. 195–97 and Richard A. Lanham, *The Old Arcadia* (New Haven, Conn., 1965), pp. 385–87. But Mary Patchell (*The "Palmerin" Romances in Elizabethan Prose Fiction* [New York, 1947], pp. 115–27) discusses parallels of many of Sidney's themes and motifs in the Palmerin cycle, at the same time admitting their universality. See also Kenneth O. Myrick, *Sir Philip Sidney as a Literary Craftsman* (Cambridge, Mass., 1935), p. 192 and passim.

[14] Wolff, *The Greek Romances*, pp. 367–68.

[15] See ibid., pp. 370–74.

[16] See ibid., pp. 376–408. Wolff (ibid., pp. 408–32) also indicates in Greene allusions to Heliodorus, borrowings of many incidental situations, motifs, tags, and bits of ornament, and suggestions for *"ensemble"* scenes and the development of female characters. In *Carde of Fancie* (1584) one of the heroines is "Lewcippa" and her father is "Clerophontes," a variant of "Clitophon." Other characters are "Thersandro" and a widow "Melytta," paralleling "Thersander" and "Melitte" of Achilles Tatius. *Morando* (1584) has many verbal echoes of Achilles Tatius; *Philomela* (1592) and *A Groat's-worth of Wit* (1592) similarity in incidents. *Philomela* and *Carde of Fancie* borrow incidents and phrases from Heliodorus, the final scenes imitating the great denouement of the *Aethiopica*. Scenes in *Tullies Love, Philomela,* and *Pandosto* probably derive from Heliodorus's great trial scene (ibid., passim.).

[17] Ibid., pp. 444–45.

[18] Ibid., pp. 433–38. Thomas H. McNeal ("The Literary Origins of Robert Greene," *Shakespeare Association Bulletin,* XIV [1939], 177–79), summarizes Wolff's conclusions, but wonders "if Greene might not have obtained a plot or device . . . from some other and more likely source."

[19] Thomas M. Parrott, "Notes," *The Plays of George Chapman,* ed. Thomas M. Parrott (New York, 1961), II, 674.

[20] Josephus tells this as the story of Herod's passion for his murdered wife Mariamne. A similar tale is told of an Arabian calif, of a king of Denmark, and of Harold Fairhair of Norway. The most famous predecessor is, of course, Charlemagne. See ibid., II, 775–76.

[21] The history of *Apollonius of Tyre* in English may also account in part for the second section of the late fifteenth-century play *Mary Magdalene* (Bodleian Digby MS. 133): The saint and the king and queen of "Marcylle" journey to the Holy Land. During the voyage the queen gives birth in the midst of a great tempest and apparently dies. The "dead" queen and the child are

placed on a rocky island. On the return journey the king stops by the island and finds the child alive. The queen wakes from a deep trance and all in joy return to "Marcylle." St. Magdalene had miraculously preserved the queen and her child. A similar theme of a scattered family reunited appears in *The Life of St. Clement* (see L. S. Salinger, "Time and Art in Shakespeare's Romances," *Renaissance Drama* (Evanston, Ill., 1966), ix, 9.

22 See *Narrative and Dramatic Sources of Shakespeare,* ed. Geoffrey Bullough (New York, 1957), I, 9–10, 50–54.

23 The lost child recovered theme not only appears in Shakespeare's late romances, but is an old constant in literature. Alfred Harbage (*Cavalier Drama: An Historical and Critical Supplement to the Study of the Elizabethan and Restoration Stage* [New York, 1964], p. 33) points to it in the pastoral *Florimene,* and plays by Hausted, Wilson, Carlell, Killigrew, Suckling, Rutter, Peaps, Cowley, Quarles, Jaques, Davenant, Shirley, Brome, Nabbe, Gough, Willan, and Forde, as well as in *The White Ethiopian.* Between 1632 and 1642 an average of two new plays each year contained this theme.

24 Shakespeare's shipwreck separation of the family is a substitution for the device in *Apollonius of Tyre* of placing the wife, apparently dead at sea from childbirth, in a sealed casket, casting it overboard where it will be washed ashore and the wife found and revived by the skill of a great physician. The child is lost when it is left to be reared by treacherous foster parents. The hero of *Apollonius of Tyre* suffers shipwreck elsewhere in the romance. The source is revised to economize on a means to complete the separation of parents and four infants. The medical skill of the physician who saves the wife is transferred in the play to the lost wife.

25 A play by Plautus, the *Rudens,* contains shipwreck, a daughter lost by her father and eventually reunited with him, and a priestess of Venus who helps the girl. (See R. A. Foakes, "Introduction," in the Arden Edition of *The Comedy of Errors* [Cambridge, Mass., 1962], p. xxxii).

26 *The Complete Works of Shakespeare,* ed. W. J. Craig (Oxford, 1943). All further citations of Shakespeare are to this edition unless otherwise noted.

27 Discussed at length by R. A. Foakes, ibid. and "Appendices," *Comedy of Errors,* pp. xxix and 113–15.

28 I have drawn on Foakes's discussion of *The Comedy of Errors* (*ed. cit.,* pp. xxiv–xxxiv, xxxix–li, 113–15) as well as T. W. Baldwin (*On the Compositional Genetics of "The Comedy of Errors"* [Urbana, Ill., 1965], pp. 92–93, 120–21), C. L. Barber ("Shakespeare's Comedy in *The Comedy of Errors,*" *College English,* XXV [1964], 493–97), and Bertrand Evans (*Shakespeare's Comedies* [Oxford, 1960], pp. 7–8).

²⁹ See *Shakespeare's Early Comedies* (New York, 1965), p. 47. See also L. C. Salinger, "Time and Art," pp. 9–10.

³⁰ Ibid., p. 16.

³¹ The similarity between the Aegeon-Aemilia plot and *Apollonius of Tyre* was pointed out in 1879 by Paul Wislicenus, "Zwei neuentdeckte Shakespeare-quellen," *Jahrbuch der Deutschen Shakespeare-Gesellschaft*, XIV, 87–96. De Perrot's essay is "Die Vorgänge im Heiligtum der Artemis zu Ephesus bei Achilles Tatios und in der Abtei daselbst bei Shakespeare," *Germanisch-Romanische Monatsshrift*, III [1911], 247–48.

³² See Robert Adger Law, "On the Dating of Shakespeare's Plays," *Shakespeare Association Bulletin*, XI (1935), 46–51. This is a convenient table of varying opinions of the dates of the plays. All further citations of the dates of Shakespeare's plays derive from it.

³³ See "Noch eine eventuelle Quelle zum Heiligen Dreikönigsabend," *Jahrbuch der Deutschen Shakespeare-Gesellschaft*, XLVI (1910), 118–20. De Perrot also sees the influence of Achilles Tatius in *The Two Gentlemen of Verona*, in the swift reconciliation of the banished Valentine and the Duke of Milan, father of Valentine's beloved, believing that this was suggested by the reconciliation of the pirate Callisthenes and Hippias. The parallel is reconciliation between an outlaw and the father of an outlaw's beloved, but Valentine of the play is a "Robin Hood" type, Callisthenes of the novel a pirate transformed by love into a good man. Further, *The Two Gentlemen of Verona* is usually dated *c.* 1591–1594. Shakespeare would have had to read Achilles Tatius in Italian, French, or Latin to know the novel.

Michael Oeftering (*Heliodore und seine Bedeutung für die Litterature* [Berlin, 1901], pp. 156–58 suggests that Heliodorus influenced act IV, scene i of *The Two Gentlemen of Verona*. Here the banished Valentine falls into the hands of a band of outlaws. Impressed by his appearance and valor, they offer to make him their captain. Valentine accepts, provided that the crew "do no outrages / On silly women, or poor passengers" (IV, i, 71–72). This situation Oeftering likens to the story of Thyamis in the *Aethiopica* who, as leader of a band of outlaws "never did wrong to women." (Heliodorus, *An Aethiopian History*, trans. Thomas Underdowne, ed. W. E. Henley [London, 1895], p. 29). The motif, however, is duplicated not only in chivalric romance, but by the Robin Hood legend—a far more familiar figure to an Englishman than Thyamis—and since Robin Hood is mentioned when Valentine is made chief: "By the bare scalp of Robin Hood's fat friar, / This fellow were a king for our wild faction!" (IV, i, 36–37), I think Heliodorus is an unlikely source.

³⁴ First acted at Siena in 1531. Reissued at Venice in 1538, 1540, 1543, 1550, 1562, 1563, 1585, 1595, 1609.

[35] Published in 1543 as *Le Sacrifice* and in 1549 and 1556 at Paris as *Les Abusés.*

[36] First acted in 1547. Reissued at Florence in 1568, 1615; Venice, 1562, 1566, 1582, 1585, 1587, 1600, 1602, 1610, 1627.

[37] Another Spanish play related to *Gl'Ingannati* is the anonymous and undated *La Española de Florencia.* See William B. Holden, "Appendix B: Sources," W. Shakespeare's *Twelfth Night; or, What You Will,* ed. William B. Holden (New Haven, Conn., 1954), p. 141.

[38] *Gl'Inganni* (Venice, 1604) by Domenica Cornaccini bears little resemblance to *Twelfth-Night.* (See Sir Arthur Quiller-Couch, "Introduction" to W. Shakespeare's *Twelfth-Night; or, What You Will,* ed. Sir Arthur Quiller-Couch and John Dover Wilson [Cambridge, Eng., 1949], p. xii.)

[39] The authors may have been George Meriton and/or George Mountaine. (See G. C. Moore Smith, "Introduction," *Laelia: A Comedy,* ed. G. C. Moore Smith [Cambridge, Eng., 1910], pp. viii–xvi.)

[40] Parts I, II, III appeared in the first edition. Part IV was published at Lione in 1573. Later editions appeared at Milan in 1560; Venice, 1566; Salamanca, 1589; Madrid, 1596.

[41] Reissued at Monte Regale in 1565; Venice, 1566, 1574, 1580, 1584, 1593, 1608.

[42] Reissued at Turin in 1571; Paris, 1580; Rouen, 1604; Lyon, 1616.

[43] Reissued at London in 1583, 1594, and in 1606. (See Thomas M. Cranfill, "Introduction," [Barnaby] *Riche's Farewell to Military Profession* [Austin, Tex., 1959], pp. lx–lxxix.) A dramatic version of "Apolonius and Silla," *Tugend und Liebesstreit,* was performed at Schloss Bevern in Germany in 1608, published in 1677. It seems likely that the earlier versions were enacted at Graz in 1608, at Dresden in 1626, and at Güstrow between 1654 and 1663 (ibid., pp. xliii–xliv).

[44] "Introduction," pp. xiii.

[45] Another bit of literary tradition that created an analogue between Shakespeare and Greek romance and Shakespeare and Cervantes may be recognized in the Birnam Wood episode of *Macbeth:* Shakespeare's immediate source for the deception was probably Raphaell Holinshed's *Chronicles of England, Scotlande, and Irelande* (London, 1586), although the motif appears also in Achilles Tatius's *Clitophon and Leucippe:* "After they perceived that *Charmides* approached . . . they devised this stratageme . . . : they appointed all the old men to go formost . . . carrying in theyr hands Olive branches . . . in signe of peace: they commanded . . . their youth to follow . . . well armed, and placed in battell array. So determining that the olde men . . . should shaddow the Armie of men comming behinde

with theyr boughs, the young men dragged theyr weapons . . .
that they might not be seene. . . . in this order, they went forward to meete *Charmides*, desiring him that he would take pittie
on theyr olde age, and spare theyr whole Cittie, . . . but *Charmides* . . . would not graunt them their requests, . . . wherefore
the spies seeing them come neere, plucked downe the bankes
[of the Nile], so that the Water began to overflow amaine, and
in an instant the old men got themselves away, the yong men
which dragd their weapons behind them, beganne to rush upon
them" (trans. Burton, ed. Gaselee and Brett-Smith, pp. 75–76).
The motif also appears in Judges 9: 48–49 (fourth or fifth century B.C.); in the *Alexander* romance (*c.* seventh century A.D.); in
an Arabian account written shortly after the death of Moham-
med; in the *Historia Danica* (*c.* 1208) of Saxo Grammaticus (see
N. W. Hill, "The Wood of Birnam," *Modern Language Notes*,
XXIV [1909], 229–30); in the *Liber Historiae Francorum* (eighth
century A.D.); the *Speculum Historiale* (thirteenth century) of
Vincent of Beauvais; the *Original Chronicles* (*c.* 1420) of Andrew
of Wyntoun; the *Scotorum Historiae* (1527, completed 1574) of
Hector Boèce (see Pauline Taylor, "Birnam Wood: A.D. 700–
A.D. 1600," *Modern Language Notes*, XXXIX [1924], 244–49); and
in *Persiles y Sigismunda* of Cervantes: "we discerned . . . a
forrest of mouing trees, which crossed the riuer from one side
to the other. But comming neere, we knew that that which
seemed a forrest of trees vvas boats couered with boughes,"
trans. M.[atthew] L.[ownes], p. 152.

[46] Barnaby Riche, "Riche his Farewell to Military Profession,"
ed. Geoffrey Bullough, *Narrative and Dramatic Sources of
Shakespeare* (New York, 1958), II, 346.

[47] In further support of his view that Achilles Tatius is a possible source for *Twelfth-Night*, De Perrot ("Noch eine eventuelle
Quelle zum Heiligen Dreikönigsabend," p. 119) cites passages
from *Clitophon and Leucippe* which seem to have parallels in
the play.

[48] J. J. Munro ("Introduction to [Arthur] Brooke's *"Romeus
and Juliet"* Being the Original of Shakespeare's *"Romeo and
Juliet*," ed. J. J. Munro [New York, 1908], pp. ix–xviii) discusses
this relationship.

[49] The Legend of Romeo and Juliet has even been described as
true history. (See *La pietosa morte di Giulia Cappelletti e Romeo
Montecchi*, etc., ed. Alessandro Torri [Livorno, 1831].) A tomb
said to contain the bodies of the lovers is in Verona. (See
Charles T. Prouty, *The Sources of Much Ado About Nothing:
A Critical Study* [New Haven, Conn., 1950], p. 6.)

[50] After the Masuccio version (reissued Mediolani, 1483; Venice, 1484, 1492, 1503, 1510, 1522, 1531, 1535, 1539, 1541, 1590?, another
dated 1525 with no place reference; another sixteenth- or seven-

teenth-century edition undated) and the Da Porto account (re-issued Venice, 1535, 1539, 1553; another dated 1535 with no place reference) the Romeo and Juliet legend appeared in versions by Adrian Sevin, the tale of Halquadrich and Burglipha in the "Epistle Dedicatory" of his translation of *Philocopo* (Paris, 1542) [a free adaptation of the legend in French]; "Clitia" [Gherardo Bolderi?], *L'Infelice Amore dei due Fedelissimi Amanti Giulia e Romeo* (Venice, 1553) [a poem in ottava rima]; Matteo Bandello, "Giulietta e Romeo" in Vol. II of the *Novelle* (Lucca, 1554); Pierre Boaistuau, "Histoire . . . De deux Amans, etc." in Vol. I of the *Histoires Tragiques* (Paris, 1559, 1564, 1572, 1580; Anvers, 1567; Lyon, 1571, 1578, 1596, 1616; Turin, 1570, 1582; Rouen, 1603); Arthur Brooke, *Romeus and Iuliet* (London, 1562, 1582, 1587); William Painter, "Rhomeo and Iulietta" in Vol. II of *The Palace of Pleasure* (London, 1567); Luigi Groto, *La Hadriana* (Venice, 1578, 1583, 1586, 1599, 1612) [a play]. The climax was of course the Shakespeare play (c. 1591–1598). There are early Spanish versions of the legend by Lope de Vega (*Los Castelvines y Monteses*, composed c. 1606–1612) and Don Francisco de Rojas (*Los Bandos de Verona*, composed c. 1640), both based on the Bandello version. A Dutch play in alexandrine couplets by Jacob Struijs, *Romeo en Juliette* (Amsterdam, 1634), agrees more or less with the Boaistuau version. A Latin manuscript, Sloane 1775, dated as of the early seventeenth century, in the British Museum, is a draft of a tragedy, *Romeus et Julietta*. A German play, *Romeo und Julietta* (c. 1624), is based on Shakespeare's text. (See Munro, "Introduction," xxv–xlvii.) The best work on the subject is Olin H. Moore's *The Legend of Romeo and Juliet* (Columbus, Ohio, 1950).

[51] An interesting variation of the potion plot occurs in the fifth story of the third decade of Cinthio's *Hecatommithi:* A man wishing to murder his wife in order to marry another begs poison from a physician, who himself sincerely loves the endangered wife. The physician substitutes a sleeping draught which the husband administers, thinking it is poison. The wife apparently dies and is buried. The physician, at the tomb as she awakens, takes her to his home. In spite of the husband's evil and the physician's love, she retains her honor. Friends of the wife press charges against the husband; he is tried and condemned to die. On his day of execution the faithful wife appears and his life is spared. The tale was translated by Barnaby Riche, the sixth novelle in his *Farewell to Military Profession* and dramatized as *How a Man May Chuse a Good Wife From a Bad* (London, 1602), ascribed variously to John Cooke, Ioshua Cooke, and Thomas Heywood. (See A. E. H. Swaen, "Introduction," *How a Man May Chuse a Good Wife From a Bad,* ed. A. E. H. Swaen [Louvain, 1912], pp. v–xvi.)

In *The Knight of Malta* (*c*. 1616–1619) by Fletcher, and perhaps Nathaniel Field or Massinger, a sleeping potion is administered to the heroine by a jealous husband. She awakens in the tomb and is visited there by the husband and two suitors. In the *Humorous Lieutenant* (1625) by Fletcher, a father who is a rival for his son's beloved declares the lady dead. The son despairs. In spite of a love philtre, the heroine remains firm in her virtue. A procuress in the play is named Leucippe. (The original "Leucippe" of Achilles Tatius downs a love philtre.) In *The Night Walker, or the Little Thief* (1639) by Fletcher, a girl is saved from live burial by the robbery of the coffin in which she has been contained as the result of seeming death. In disguise she settles the complications of the plot. Live burial is linked with adulterous love in a series of analogues cited by Archer Taylor, "The Buried Lover Escapes," *Studies in Medieval Literature in Honor of Professor Albert C. Baugh* (Philadelphia, 1961), pp. 209–17.

[52] Throughout the Renaissance the legend of the slandered bride was widely known through the work of Ariosto. Jean G. T. Gräesse, *Trésor de Livres Rares et Précieux* (Dresden, 1859), 8 vols., alone lists fifty-seven different editions of *Orlando Furioso* published between 1516 and 1596, some reissued several times. Gräesse (pp. 200–202) also lists French translations: one probably by Jean des Gouttes or Jean Martin (Lyon, 1543; Paris, 1543, 1545, 1552, 1555, 1571); Jean Fornier de Montaulban (Paris, 1555; Anvers, 1555 [verse]); Gabriel Chappuys (Lyon, 1576, [1577], 1582, 1583; Rouen, 1610, 1611, 1617, 1618); François de Rosset (Paris, 1615, 1644); a Spanish translation by D. Jeron. de Urrea (Anvers, 1549, 1554, 1558; Leon, 1550, 1556; Venice, 1553, 1575; Medina del Campo, 1572; Salamanca, 1577, 1578; Toledo, 1583, 1586; Bilbao, 1583); English translations by Sir John Harrington (London, 1591, 1607, 1634) [verse]; Temple Henry Croker [or William Huggins], [1755], 1757; John Hoole (London, 1783, 1791, 1799, 1807); W. Stewart Rose (London, 1825–1831); a translation in German "Poesie" by Dietrich von dem Werder (Liepzig, 1632–1636, 1634–1636, 1851; Jena, 1804–1809, 1827–1828; Halle, 1818, 1839); and a Polish translation by P. Kochanowskiego (Krakow, 1799). A French translation of the Genevra episode was begun by Mellin de Saint Gelais and completed by Jean-Antoine de Baïf (Paris, *c*. 1558–1572). There were numerous adaptations and parodies throughout the sixteenth and seventeenth centuries. Charles T. Prouty (*The Sources of Much Ado About Nothing: A Critical Study* [New Haven, Conn., 1950], p. 15) notes a French verse translation by Guillaume Landré (Paris, 1571) and a Latin translation (1570) by Visito Maurizi.

[53] John C. Dunlop (*History of Prose Fiction*, ed. Henry Wilson [London, 1911], p. 398) believes the work was composed about

1400. Other editions of *Tirante el blanco* were published at Barcelona, 1497; Valladolid, 1511; and Venice, 1538. An Italian translation appeared in 1538; a French translation was published in London about 1737. (See *A New Variorum Edition of Shakespeare; Much Ado About Nothing*, ed. Horace H. Furness [Philadelphia, 1927], p. 345.)

[54] Reissued at London in 1596, 1609, 1611, 1613?, 1617, 1679.

[55] Vol. III of Belleforest was reissued at Paris twice in 1568; at Lyon twice in 1594 and in 1581; Rouen, 1604. Sometime between 1593 and 1605 Jacob Ayrer dramatized the Bandello version in *Die schoene Phaenecia*, published in his *Opus Theatricum* (Nueremberg, 1618). Jan Jansen Starters's dramatization in Dutch, *Timbreo de Cardone ende Fenicie van Messine* (Leeuwarden, 1618), also followed Bandello. (See *Much Adoe About Nothing*, ed. Furness, pp. 311–39, and ed. Prouty, pp. 11–26.) Claude de Taillemont published at Lyon *La Tricarite*, "Le conte de l'infante Genevra." Three lost plays seem also to have dealt with the subject: On February 13, 1564, a play on the Fenicia legend was presented at Fontainebleau. On New Year's 1574/5, Leicester's company played "the matter of Panecia," a corruption of "Fenicia." On February 12, 1583, *Ariodante and Genevora* was performed by the boys of the Merchant Taylors' School. In *Two Italian Gentlemen* (1585), an adaptation of Luigi Pasqualigo's *Il Fedele* (1579), the deception is similar to that of *Much Ado About Nothing*. Abraham Fraunce's Cambridge Latin comedy *Victoria* (*c.* 1580–1583) is a translation of *Il Fedele*. *Fedele and Fortunio . . . Two Italian Gentlemen* (1585) by "M.A." [Anthony Munday?], performed in 1584, adapts Pasqualigo's work. *Gli duoi fratelli rivali* (Venice, 1601) of Giambattista della Porta sets the Bandello version in Spain. (See Prouty, ibid., and Geoffrey Bullough, "Introduction: *Much Ado About Nothing*," *Narrative and Dramatic Sources of Shakespeare*, II, 61–81.) A seventeenth-century manuscript entitled *The Partial Law*, by an unknown author, discovered about 1900, embodies the slandered bride theme through the Ariosto version. (See T. M. Parrott, "Two Late Dramatic Versions of the Slandered Bride Theme," *Joseph Quincey Adams Memorial Studies*, ed. James G. McManaway *et al.* [Washington, D.C., 1948], pp. 537–51.)

[56] See Konrad Weichberger, "Die Urquelle von Shakespeare's 'Much Ado About Nothing,'" *Jahrbuch der Deutschen Shakespeare-Gesellschaft*, XXXIV (1898), 339–45.

[57] The problem is reviewed in *A New Variorum Edition of Shakespeare: Othello*, ed. Horace H. Furness (Philadelphia, 1914), pp. 389–96. See also *The Oxford English Dictionary*, VI (M), 645, cl. 2.

[58] "Was Othello an Ethiopian?" *Harvard Studies and Notes in*

Philology and Literature, XX (1938), 3–14. I have drawn on this article for some of the discussion of *Othello.*

[59] See II, iii, 171–76; III, iii, 90–92, 362, 373; V, ii, 25ff, 31–32, 63–65, 86–87.

[60] See p. 9.

[61] See Heliodorus, trans. Underdowne, p. 73.

[62] Giraldi Cinthio, "Un Capitano Moro piglia per mogliera una cittadina Venetiana, etc." *Othello,* ed. Furness, p. 377.

[63] Heliodorus, trans. Underdowne, pp. 118–19.

[64] See Eldred Jones, *Othello's Countrymen: The African in English Renaissance Drama* (London, 1965).

[65] In this case it would follow that John Upton's emendation of the much disputed line: "[Othello] Like the base Indian, threw a pearl away" (V, ii, 346), to: "[Othello] Like the base Egyptian, threw a pearl away" is to be given more attention than it has had in the past. The quartos and the folios carry the word "Indian," but this was amended to "Judian" by Theobald and Warburton because of the general failure to explain satisfactorily the meaning of the reference. Upton suggested "Egyptian" because he believed "Indian" a misprint and the line an allusion to Thyamis of the *Aethiopica.* Thyamis is an Egyptian thief who loved Chariclea, but killed her—or thought he did—when he could not have her. (See John Upton, *Critical observations on Shakespeare* [London, 1746], pp. 255–56.) The entire problem is reviewed in *Othello,* ed. Furness, pp. 327–31.

[66] Reissued at London in 1592, 1609, 1612, 1634, 1642.

[67] Wolff (*The Greek Romances,* pp. 459–60) discusses Lodge's allusions to the *Aethiopica* in *Forbonius and Prisceria* (1584) and in *The History of Robert, Second Duke of Normandy* (1591). He does not recognize Lodge's utilization of the Longus stock plot. On the other hand, it is Wolff's opinion (pp. 432–33) that the Elizabethan tradition of "escape" literature—from city or court to the country, from the active life to the life of contemplation—and the employment of the pastoral setting as a solution to turbulence created in court or city, as in Sidney's *Arcadia;* William Warner's story of Argentile and Curan in *Albion's England* (1586); Greene's *Pandosto* (1588), *Tullies Love* (1589), and *Menaphon* (1589); Lodge's *Rosalynde;* and Shakespeare's *As You Like It* (c. 1599–1600) and *The Winter's Tale* (c. 1610–1611), is closely related to the Longus romance and may derive from it.

[68] See Bullough, *Narrative,* II, 143–45.

[69] Wolff (*The Greek Romances,* pp. 312–13) believes that the Gloucester plot of *King Lear* is another Greek romance plot in Shakespeare, derived like *As You Like It* at secondhand, in this case from the story of the *"unkinde* [unnatural] *King"* of Paphlagonia in Sir Philip Sidney's *Arcadia.*

CHAPTER FOUR

[1] Philip Edwards's valuable essay "Shakespeare's Romances: 1900–1957" (*Shakespeare Survey,* II [1958], 1–18) discusses the changing critical estimates of the last plays in interesting detail and with much insight. I have drawn on his essay for this short review.

[2] See Ben E. Perry, *The Ancient Romances: A Literary-Historical Account of Their Origins* (Berkeley, Calif., 1967), pp. 74–75. Erwin Rhode (*Der Griechische Roman und Seine Vorläufer,* ed. Wilhelm Schmid, 3d ed. [Leipzig, 1914], p. 376) cites examples.

[3] See T. W. Baldwin, *William Shakspere's Small Latine and Lesse Greeke* (Urbana, Ill., 1944).

[4] See Hereward Price, "Shakespeare's Classical Scholarship," *Review of English Studies,* New Series, IX (1958), 54–55.

[5] See F. D. Hoeniger, "Introduction" to the Arden edition of *Pericles* (Cambridge, Mass., 1963), pp. lxv–lxix.

[6] See Gerard A. Barker, "Themes and Variations in Shakespeare's *Pericles,*" *English Studies,* XLIV (1963), 402.

[7] See Elizabeth H. Haight, *More Essays on the Greek Romance* (New York, 1945), p. 179.

[8] See Albert H. Smyth, *Shakespeare's Pericles and Apollonius of Tyre* (Philadelphia, 1898), p. 69, and Hoeniger, "Introduction," p. xviii.

[9] See pp. xix, lxxxviii–xci. See also L. S. Salinger, "Time and Art in Shakespeare's Romances," *Renaissance Drama* (Evanston, Ill., 1966), IX, 20–23.

[10] John Gower, "The Story of Apollonius of Tyre," *Shakespeare's Library,* ed. John P. Collier and W. C. Hazlitt (London, 1895), IV, 181.

[11] See Haight, *More Essays,* p. 175.

[12] See Smyth, *Shakespeare's Pericles,* p. 70, and Samuel Singer, *Apollonius von Tyrus* (Halle, 1895), pp. 32–67.

[13] In 1607 or 1608 George Wilkins published a novel based on Shakespeare's *Pericles: The Painful Adventures of Pericles, Prince of Tyre.* It has at times been described as a source for Shakespeare, although few now hold that opinion. (See Hoeniger, "Introduction," pp. xl–xlix, lix–lxii.) Two later plays also reflect *Apollonius of Tyre:* In Thomas Heywood's *The Captives, or the Lost Recovered* (1624), two cousins, daughters of wealthy brothers, are held by a brothel keeper. Sea journey and shipwreck liberate them. Unrecognized by the father of one, they are protected for the sake of his lost child. Finally identified by infant clothes and trinkets, they are honorably married. *The City Night Cap* (1624) of Robert Davenport similarly contains brothel scenes which suggest *Pericles,* and thus ultimately may be related to *Apollonius of Tyre.*

[14] In *The Crown of Life* (London, 1947), p. 73.

[15] (London, 1949), pp. 174ff.

[16] J. M. Nosworthy in the "Introduction" to the Arden edition of *Cymbeline* (London, 1955), pp. xl–xlviii, reviews critical opinion.

[17] *Crown of Life*, pp. 129–202.

[18] Ibid., p. 166.

[19] See Robert G. Hunter, *Shakespeare and the Comedy of Forgiveness* (New York, 1965), pp. 176–82.

[20] A little later than Montreuil's poem is a manuscript in the Bibliothèque Royale, "dou roi Flore et de la bielle Jehane" (XIII century); another Medieval French analogue is the *Roman du Compte de Poitiers*. (See *A New Variorum Edition of Shakespeare: The Tragedy of Cymbeline*, ed. Horace H. Furness [Philadelphia, 1913], 470–74). Karl Simrock (*Die Quellen des Shakespeare in Novellen, Märchen, und Sagen*, Neue Ausgabe [Bonn, 1872], p. 276) believed that the Boccaccio version and *Ein Liepliche history und Warheit von vier Kaufmendern* (undated), an old German folk book, have probably arisen from a Latin original, perhaps like the Latin version of *Apollonius of Tyre*, a translation of a Hellenistic Greek romance.

[21] *Illustrations of Shakespeare and of Ancient Manners* (London, 1807), II, 199.

[22] See "Shakespeare's Pastorals," *Studies in Philology*, XIII (1916), 139–40.

[23] Professor Nosworthy ("Introduction," pp. xxv–xxvi) thinks the source of the pastoral material is the play *The Rare Triumphs of Love and Fortune* (1589). This would not conflict with the identification with the Longus stock plot which was doubtless traditionally derived.

[24] Achilles Tatius, *The Loves of Clitophon and Leucippe*, trans. Thomas Burton, ed. Stephen Gaselee and H. F. B. Brett-Smith (Oxford, 1923), p. 87.

[25] Ibid., p. 83.

[26] Cf. *Achilles Tatius of Alexandria: The Adventures of Leucippe and Clitophon*, ed. and trans. Stephen Gaselee (London, 1917), pp. 3–5, and "Daphnis and Chloe by Longus," *Three Greek Romances*, trans. Moses Hadas (New York, 1953), p. 1.

[27] See *An Aethiopian History written in Greek by Heliodorus*, Englished by Thomas Underdowne, ed. W. E. Henley (London, 1895), p. 117.

[28] Ibid., pp. 287–88.

[29] Ibid., pp. 188–89.

[30] Ibid., Book X.

[31] Ibid., p. 274.

[32] Ibid.

[33] Ibid., p. 103.

[34] Ibid., Book X.

[35] Ibid., p. 234.

[36] Ibid., pp. 181–82.

[37] Ibid., p. 264.

[38] Ibid., pp. 267–68.

[39] *Cymbeline*, III, iii, 1–8, 12–26, 45–55; IV, ii, 24–27, 203–8.

[40] Trans. Underdowne, p. 260.

[41] Ibid., p. 285.

[42] Ibid.

[43] Ibid., p. 289.

[44] The idea that the peace tableau at the conclusion of *Cymbeline* might have been suggested by the *Aethiopica* does not contradict Emrys Jones's belief ("Stuart Cymbeline," *Essays in Criticism*, XI [1961], 89) that it refers to King James I's "strenuous peace-making policy" and "presents . . . the stillness of the world awaiting the appearance of the Christ-child," born during the reputed reign of Cymbeline.

[45] J. M. Nosworthy ("Appendix A: Sources," in the Arden edition of *Cymbeline*, p. 197) points to a song in Underdowne's *Aethiopica* as echoing the last act of *Cymbeline* and bearing on the controversial vision of Act V, scene iv. Nosworthy reprints the song, ibid., pp. 211–12.

[46] Nosworthy ("Introduction," pp. xxviii–xxxvii) reviews the problem of mixed authorship of *Cymbeline* and decides against it. Knight (*Crown of Life*, pp. 168–202) emphatically awards the vision sequence to Shakespeare.

[47] Bacon ("Shakespeare's Dramatic Romances," Ph.D. diss., University of Michigan [1940], p. 26) lists twenty details in *Cymbeline* which can be found in *Pericles*, thus deriving more or less from *Apollonius of Tyre*. Most appear in the other Greek romances. He recognizes in *Cymbeline* the general structure of Greek romance (pp. 269–92). F. D. Hoeniger ("Irony and Romance in *Cymbeline*," [Rice University] *Studies in English Literature*, II [1962], 222) links several ironic situations in *Cymbeline* to the examples of Achilles Tatius and Heliodorus. At least two other plays of the period employ the separation plot and motifs: Fletcher's *Monsieur Thomas* (*c.* 1609) and *The Hector of Germany* (*c.* 1613) by Wentworth Smith.

[48] The British Museum manuscript of *The White Ethiopian* (*c.* 1625 to 1675), a play which seems never to have been acted or published, recounts the story of the *Aethiopica*, and draws on Underdowne's translation. This has been edited by Arthur D. Matthews, "The White Ethiopian: A Critical Edition" (Ph.D. diss., University of Florida, 1951), who describes it as four dreary acts preserving Heliodoran structure in an atrocious singsong style (pp. vii–xx). Matthews mentions several other plays as being dependent on the *Aethiopica: The Inconstant Lady* (1633)

of Arthur Wilson, *The Goblins* (1638) of Sir John Suckling, *Arviragus and Philicia* (1636) of Ludowick Carlell, and *The Strange Discovery* (1640) of John Gough (pp. xxix–xxxiv).

CHAPTER FIVE

[1] Reissued 1592, 1595, 1607, 1614, 1632, 1636, 1648, 1688, 1696, 1703.
[2] *The Greek Romances in Elizabethan Prose Fiction* (New York, 1912). See also Jerry H. Bryant, *"The Winter's Tale* and the Pastoral Tradition," *Shakespeare Quarterly*, XIV (1963), 387–89. English pastoral drama draws heavily on Greek romance: for example, the anonymous *Maydes Metamorphosis* (1600) (ibid., p. 30). Ben Jonson's *Sad Shepherd* (composed *c.* 1614) contains a motif from the stock pastoral plot. *The Faithful Shepherdess* (*c.* 1608–1610) by Beaumont and Fletcher includes "Daphnis and Chloe" as well as a chastity trial which Homer Smith ("Pastoral Influence in the English Drama," *PMLA*, XII [1897], 365) considers a direct borrowing from Achilles Tatius. *The Shepherd's Holiday* (*c.* 1634) of Joseph Rutter has a stock pastoral plot with incidents reminiscent of Heliodorus. James Shirley's *Arcadia* (1640) and *Andromana* (1640) include Greek romance elements derived from Sidney's *Arcadia*. The "Phaedra" story in *Andromana* derived from the "Cnemon" episode of Book I of the *Aethiopica* through the *Arcadia*. Beaumont and Fletcher's *Cupid's Revenge* (1615) is an earlier adaptation of the "Cnemon" story, again through Sidney. Many of the horrors of John Webster's *Duchess of Malfi* (1623) have been credited to the *Arcadia*. (See Felix Schelling, *Elizabethan Drama: 1558–1642* [Boston, 1908], I, 36.) Wolff (*The Greek Romances*, pp. 316–17) has traced these same elements to Achilles Tatius. The pastoral elements of the *Arcadia*, absent in Webster, appear again later in Allen Ramsey's *The Gentle Shepherd* (1725): During the Cromwell disturbance a highborn boy and girl are reared in pastoral seclusion by an old shepherd and a nurse. The children grow up to love each other. When their high births are revealed they are betrothed. Daphnis and Chloe again!
[3] Wolff, *The Greek Romances*, pp. 447–55. A table of correspondences in Day's translation of *Daphnis and Chloe*, Greene's *Pandosto*, and *The Winter's Tale* appears on pp. 448–50.
[4] Ibid., pp. 452–55.
[5] Longus, *Daphnis and Chloe: The Elizabethan Version from Amyot's Translation by Angel Day* (London, 1890), p. 74.
[6] *The Greek Romances*, pp. 410, 422; [Robert] *Greene's "Pandosto" or "Dorastus and Fawnia,"* etc., ed. P. G. Thomas (London, 1907), p. 30.
[7] See *An Aethiopian History written in Greek by Heliodorus,*

Englished by Thomas Underdowne, ed. W. E. Henley (London, 1895), p. 108.

[8] Greene, *Pandosto*, p. 21.

[9] Wolff (*The Greek Romances*, pp. 452–55) discusses the problems of causation in *The Winter's Tale* as it relates to *Pandosto*.

[10] See George C. Taylor, "Hermione's Statue Again: Shakespeare's Return to Bandello," *Shakespeare Association Bulletin*, XIII (1938), 82–86.

[11] Matteo Bandello, *La Prima Parte de le Novelle del Bandello* (London, 1740), I, 154.

[12] See E. A. J. Honigmann, "Secondary Sources of *The Winter's Tale*," *Philological Quarterly*, XXXIV (1955), 27–38.

[13] Various opinions and interpretations are reviewed by J. H. P. Pafford in the "Introduction" to the Arden edition of *The Winter's Tale* (Cambridge, Mass., 1963), pp. xxxvii–xliv. G. Wilson Knight (*The Crown of Life* [London, 1947], pp. 76–128) writes on *The Winter's Tale* as an allegory of "great creating nature."

[14] See *A New Variorum Edition of Shakespeare: The Tempest*, ed. Horace H. Furness (Philadelphia, 1920), pp. 324–41, for a discussion of the coincidences and a reprint of Ayrer's play.

[15] E. K. Chambers (*William Shakespeare: A Study of the Facts and Problems* [Oxford, 1930], I, 493–94) reviews the theory.

[16] J. M. Nosworthy, "The Narrative Sources of *The Tempest*," *Review of English Studies*, XXIV (1948), 282.

[17] Ibid., pp. 383–84.

[18] Ibid., pp. 287–93.

[19] See C. J. Sisson, "The Magic of Prospero," *Shakespeare Survey*, II (1958), 76.

[20] Reviewed in *The Tempest*, ed. Furness, pp. 308–15, 320–24. A recent survey of source studies of the play is in Sharon L. Smith, "The *Commedia dell'Arte* and Problems Related to Source in *The Tempest*," *The Emporia State Research Studies*, XIII (1964), 11–23.

[21] See "Appendices" of the Arden edition of *The Tempest*, ed. Frank Kermode (London, 1954), pp. 145–50.

[22] See "Introduction," *The Tempest*, ed. Kermode, p. lx.

[23] For example, see "Daphnis and Chloe by Longus," *Three Greek Romances*, trans. Moses Hadas (New York, 1953), pp. 21, 30, 36, 58–59; and *The Tempest*, I, ii, 337–38; II, i, 49–56; II, ii, 173–74; III, ii, 147–50.

[24] Longus, trans. Day, p. 58.

[25] Ibid., pp. 55, 57, 59 passim.

[26] See Nelson S. Bushnell, "Natural Supernaturalism in *The Tempest*," PMLA, XLVII (1932), 690; and W. S. Johnson, "The Genesis of Ariel," *Shakespeare Quarterly*, II (1951), 205–10.

[27] *The Tempest*, ed. Furness, p. 64, reviews the question.

[28] Longus, trans. Day, p. 23.

[29] Ibid., pp. 74–77. My italics except *"Arme Arme."*

[30] My italics except *"Fer."*

[31] Longus, *Les Amours Pastorales de Daphnis et Chloé*, trans. [Jacques Amyot] (n.p., 1731), pp. 61–64.

[32] I have been unable to obtain this edition for examination.

[33] See IV, i. 110–17.

[34] Longus, trans. Hadas, p. 97.

[35] Longus, trans. Amyot, pp. 156–57.

[36] Robert A. Law ("On the Dating of Shakspere's Plays, *The Shakespeare Association Bulletin*, XI [1935], pp. 46–51.) dates *The Winter's Tale* between 1610 and 1611.

[37] See James E. Phillips, *"The Tempest* and the Renaissance Idea of Man," *Shakespeare 400: Essays . . . on the Anniversary of the Poet's Birth*, ed. James G. McManaway (New York, 1964), pp. 148–50.

[38] Kermode ("Introduction," to *The Tempest*, pp. lxxxi–lxxxviii) reviews the more important interpretations.

[39] Shakespeare's contemporary Robert Burton made frequent allusions to Greek romance in *The Anatomy of Melancholy* (Oxford, 1621, 1624, 1628, 1632; Edinburgh, Oxford, and London, 1638, 1651, 1660, 1676). Bacon ("Shakespeare's Dramatic Romances," [Ph.D. diss., University of Michigan, 1940], p. 19) lists in the sixth edition and the final from Burton's hand, one allusion to Antonius Diogenes, three to Longus, thirteen to Achilles Tatius, fourteen to Heliodorus, and two to the Byzantine imitations of Greek romance. Often the allusions relate to symptoms and effects of love or the depiction of beauty (ibid., pp. 124–27). Robert Burton's brother William was a translator of Achilles Tatius. Richard Crashaw included a poem called "The Beginning of *Heliodorus*" in *The Delights of the Muses* (London, 1646, 1648, 1670). Nahum Tate published a second edition of *The Triumphs of Love and Constancy: A Romance containing the heroic amours of Theagenes and Chariclea*, etc. at London in 1687, reissued 1753.

[40] *Anatomy of Criticism: Four Essays* (Princeton, N.J., 1957), pp. 187–88.

APPENDIX

[1] *The Anglo-Saxon Version of the Story of Apollonius of Tyre*, ed. and trans. Benjamin Thorpe (London, 1834). *Apollonius of Tyre* is listed in a catalog of books of the abbey of St. Wandrille in Normandy, A.D. 747. See A. J. Tieje, "The Critical Heritage of Fiction in 1579," *Englische Studien*, XLVII (1913–1914), 437, n. 1.

[2] *A new boke about Shakespeure and Stratford-upon-Avon.* This is reprinted in Albert H. Smyth, *Shakespeare's Pericles and Apollonius of Tyre* (Philadelphia, 1898), pp. 249–55.

[3] *The Romance of "Kynge Apollyn of Thyre," reprinted in facsimile by E. W. Ashbee from the unique original* (London, 1870).

[4] Reprinted by Smyth, *Shakespeare's Pericles*, pp. 293–312.

[5] Ed. Tycho Mommsen (Oldenburg, 1857). See also H. D. Sykes, *Wilkins' and Shakespeare's Pericles, Prince of Tyre* (Stratford-upon-Avon, 1919).

[6] See Smyth, *Shakespeare's Pericles*, pp. 225–47, and Peter Goolden, *The Old English Apollonius of Tyre*, ed. Peter Goolden (Oxford, 1958), p. xiii.

[7] Goolden (ibid.), Joseph Raith (*Die alt-und mittelenglischen Apollonius Bruchstücke mit dem Text der Historia Apollonii nach der Englischen Handschriftengruppe*, ed. Joseph Raith [Munich, 1956]), and Elemar Klebs (*Die Erzählung von Apollonius aus Tyrus* [Berlin, 1899]) discuss the manuscripts. See also Smyth, *Shakespeare's Pericles*, pp. 17–23.

[8] Smyth, *Shakespeare's Pericles*, p. 17, who says further (ibid.) that Moritz Haupt of Berlin in 1857 knew of more than one hundred manuscripts of the Latin *Apollonius*.

[9] "Socratis Scholastici," *Patrologia cursus completus, seu Bibliotheca Universalis . . . Series Graecae . . . a S. Barnaba ad Photium*, ed. J. P. Migne (Petit-Montrouge, 1859), LXVII, col. 63.

[10] *Bibliotèque*, ed. and trans. in French by René Henry (Paris, 1959), I, 147.

[11] "Nicephori Callisti Xanthopuli Ecclesiasticae Historiae," ed. J. P. Migne, *Patrologia*, CXLVI (1865), col. 860.

[12] See "Introduction" to Heliodorus, *An Ethiopian Romance*, trans. Moses Hadas (Ann Arbor, Mich., 1957), pp. ix–x. Freese (*The Library of Photius*, trans. John H. Freese [London, 1920], p. 120, n. 1) believes that the historian Socrates wrongly identified Heliodorus with a Bishop of Tricca during the reign of Theodosius. The latter was probably confused with Theodosius, father of Heliodorus. Maillon (Heliodorus, *Les Éthiopiques* [*Théagène et Chariclée*], ed. R. M. Rattenbury and T. W. Lumb, trans. J. Maillon [Paris, 1935], I, xv) believes that Heliodorus was a Syrian influenced by the local sun cult and by neo-Pythagoreanism, but was finally converted to Christianity and became a bishop. See also Thomas R. Goethals, Jr., "The *Aethiopica* of Heliodorus: A Critical Study" (Ph.D. diss., Columbia University, 1959), pp. 231–62.

[13] The manuscript history is traced by Rattenbury, Lumb, and Maillon (*trans. cit.*, I, xxiv–xlvii). See also Heinrich Dörrie, *De Longi Achillis Tatii Heliodori Memoria* (Gottingen, 1935). This is a study of the manuscript tradition of the Greek erotica.

[14] See W. R. M. Lamb, "Introduction," Heliodorus, *Ethiopian Story*, trans. W. R. M. Lamb (London, 1961), p. xxi.

[15] Paul Bonnefon ("Note Préliminaire," *Une Traduction Iné-*

dite de Premiere Livre de Théagène et Chariclée in *Annuaire de Association pour l'encouragement des études grecques en France,* XVII [1883], 327–33) calls attention to MS. 2143 in the Bibliothèque Nationale: "Le Premier livre d'Héliodore de l'histoire d'Aethiopie, translaté de grec en français par [Lancelot de] Carle," Bishop of Riez, on internal and biographical evidence is dated somewhat earlier than the Amyot version of 1547. It follows the Greek text of Obsopoeus (1534) (ibid., p. 331).

[16] Lamb, "Introduction," p. xxi.

[17] F. A. Wright, "Introduction," *Heliodorus: An Aethiopian Romance* (London, n.d.), p. 5.

[18] Lamb, "Introduction," p. xxi.

[19] Ruth Horne, "Lope de Vega's *Peregrino en su patria* and the Romance of Adventure in Spain before 1604" (Ph.D. diss., Brown University, 1946), p. 162.

[20] See T. W. Baldwin, *William Shakspere's Small Latine & Lesse Greeke* (Urbana, Ill., 1944), pp. 219, 312, 535.

[21] *Histrio-Mastix: the Player's Scourge, or, Actors Tragedy* (London, 1633), pp. 916–17.

[22] See *Achilles Tatius of Alexandria: The Love Adventures of Leucippe and Clitophon,* ed. and trans. Stephen Gaselee (London, 1917), p. vii, and F. A. Todd, *Some Ancient Novels* (Oxford, 1940), p. 10.

[23] Ebbe Vilborg ("Testimonia" in *Achilles Tatius "Leucippe and Clitophon,"* ed. Ebbe Vilborg [Stockholm, 1955], pp. 163–68) lists early references to Achilles Tatius. See also Gaselee, *Achilles Tatius,* pp. vii–xi.

[24] Vilborg ("The Sources of the Text," *Achilles Tatius,* pp. xv–lxxi) discusses the manuscript tradition.

[25] Todd, *Ancient Novels,* p. 35.

[26] See M. Schoell, *Histoire de la Littérature Grecque Profane,* 2d ed. (Paris, 1824), VI, 238. Ben E. Perry (*The Ancient Romances: A Literary-Historical Account of Their Origins* [Berkeley, Calif., 1967], pp. 350–51, n. 17) discusses the identification.

[27] J. M. Edmonds ("Introduction" to *Daphnis and Chloe by Longus,* trans. George Thornley, ed. J. M. Edmonds [Cambridge, Mass., 1935], pp. xiiff) discusses the manuscript tradition. See also Longus, *Pastorales (Daphnis et Chloé),* ed. and trans. Georges Dalmeyda (Paris, 1934), pp. xlv–lv. As to the lacuna, Alice Hulubei ("Henri Estienne et le Roman de Longus Daphnis et Chloé," *Revue de Seizième Siecle,* XVIII [1938], 329) gives evidence that although the complete Longus was generally lost to scholars before 1809, Henri Estienne knew the missing material and displays the knowledge in the Latin eclogues of *Chloris* and *Rivales* of 1555, four years before the Amyot version was published.

[28] Georges Dalmeyda, "Introduction," Xénophon D'Éphèse, *Les Éphésiaques ou le Roman D'Habrocomès et D'Anthia,* trans. and ed. Georges Dalmeyda (Paris, 1926), p. ix.

[29] Francis Douce, *Illustrations of Shakespeare and of Ancient Manners* (London, 1807), II, 199.

[30] Marcus Landau, *Die Quellen des Dekameron* (Stuttgart, 1884), p. 296; and A. Collingwood Lee, *The Decameron: Its Sources and Analogues* (London, 1909), p. 32.

[31] Konrad Weichberger, "Die Urquelle von Shakespeare's 'Much Ado About Nothing,'" *Jahrbuch der Deutschen Shakespeare-Gesellschaft,* XXXIV (1898), 339–45.

[32] Rudolph Blum, "La Biblioteca Della Badia Fiorentina e I Codici di Antonio Corbinelli," *Biblioteca Apostolica Vaticana: Studi e testi* (Città del Vaticano, 1951), CLV, 18 and 88. Cataloged today as "Codex Abbazia Fiorentina 2728, Conventi Soppressi, 627."

[33] Perry (*The Ancient Romances,* p. 345) notes several fifteenth- and sixteenth-century references to the manuscript.

[34] J. J. Munro ("Introduction" to [Arthur] *Brooke's "Romeus and Juliet" Being the Original of Shakespeare's "Romeo and Juliet,"* ed. J. J. Munro [New York, 1908], pp. ix–xlvii) discusses the relationship.

[35] Pietro Bembo addressed a letter to him on June 9, 1534, mentioning "la bella vostra Novella." The second edition of Da Porto's novel was dedicated to Cardinal Bembo. See P. A. Daniel, "Introduction," Arthur Brooke, *Romeus and Iuliet,* ed. P. A. Daniel; New Shakespeare Society, Series III; Originals and Analogues, Part I (London, 1875), p. v; and Maurice Jonas, *Romeo and Juliet: A Photographic Reproduction of Luigi Da Porto's Prose Version of Romeo and Guilietta . . . with a Literal Translation into English,* etc. (London, 1921), p. xix.

[36] Very little is known of Masuccio (*c.* 1420–1474–1476) beyond publication details of his work and that he was secretary to Roberto Sanseverino, a prominent Neapolitan. One of his novels was dedicated to Antonio Beccadelli, known as "Il Panormita," a leading humanist and professor of history at Milan.

[37] *The Elizabethan Stage* (Oxford, 1923), IV, 402.

Achilles Tatius of Alexandria: The Adventures of Leucippe and Clitophon, ed. and trans. Stephen Gaselee. London, 1917. Loeb Classical Library.

Achilles Tatius "Leucippe and Clitophon," ed. Ebbe Vilborg. Stockholm, 1955.

Achilles Tatius. *The Loves of Clitophon and Leucippe,* trans. William Burton, ed. Stephen Gaselee and H. F. B. Brett-Smith. Oxford, 1923.

The Anglo-Saxon Version of the Story of Apollonius of Tyre, ed. and trans. Benjamin Thorpe. London, 1834.

Historia Apollonii Regis Tyri, ed. Alexander Riese. Leipzig, 1893.

Bacon, Wallace A. "Introduction" to William Warner's *Syrinx, or A Sevenfold History,* ed. Wallace A. Bacon. Evanston, Ill., 1950. Pp. xi–lxxxv.

Baldensperger, Fernand. "Was Othello an Ethiopian?" *Harvard Studies and Notes in Philology and Literature,* XX (1938), 3–14.

Baldwin, T. W. *William Shakspere's Small Latine & Lesse Greeke.* 2 vols. Urbana, Ill., 1944.

Bandello, Matteo. *La Prima Parte de le Novelle del Bandello.* 3 vols. London, 1740.

Boccaccio, Giovanni. *The Decameron . . . Translated into English anno 1620,* ed. Edward Hutton. 2 vols. New York, 1940.

————*Il Filocolo,* ed. Ettore de Ferri. 2 vols. Torino, 1927.

[Arthur] *Brooke's "Romeus and Juliet" Being the Original of Shakespeare's "Romeo and Juliet,"* ed. J. J. Munro. New York, 1908.

Bullough, Geoffrey, ed., *Narrative and Dramatic Sources of Shakespeare.* New York, 1957–1958. Vols. I, II, VI.

Cervantes Saavreda, Miguel de. *Novelas Exemplares,* ed. Rodolfo Schevell y Adolfo Bonilla. 2 vols. Madrid, 1922.

———*The Exemplary Novels,* trans. Walter K. Kelly. London, 1908.

———*The Travels of Persiles and Sigismunda: A Northern History* [trans. Matthew Lownes]. London, 1619.

Charitonis Aphrodisiensis. *De Chaereas et Callirhoe Amatoriarvm Narrationvm Libri Octo,* ed. Warren E. Blake. Oxford, 1938.

Chariton's Chaereas and Callirhoe, trans. Warren E. Blake. Ann Arbor, Mich., 1939.

Da Porto, Luigi. *Romeo and Juliet: A Photographic Reproduction . . . with a Literal Translation into English,* etc., trans. Maurice Jonas. London, 1921.

Du Meril, Édelstand, "Introduction" to *Floire et Blancheflor: Poèmes de XIIIᵉ Siècle,* etc. Paris, 1856.

Dunlop, John Colin. *History of Prose Fiction,* ed. Henry Wilson. 2 vols. London, 1911.

Gaselee, Stephen. "Appendix on the Greek Novel" in *The Love Romances of Parthenius and Other Fragments,* trans. Stephen Gaselee. London, 1935. Pp. 403–14. Loeb Classical Library.

Gerding, Jess. "The Greek Romance in the *Siglo de Oro,*" *South Central Bulletin,* XXI (1961), 45–48.

Gräesse, Jean George Theodore, *Trésor de Livres Rares et Précieux.* 8 vols. Dresden, 1859–1869.

[Robert] *Greene's "Pandosto" or "Dorastus and Fawnia" Being the Original of Shakespeare's "Winter's Tale,"* ed. P. G. Thomas. London, 1907.

Greenlaw, Edwin. "Shakespeare's Pastorals," *Studies in Philology,* XIII (1916), 122–54.

Greg, Walter W. *Pastoral Poetry and Pastoral Drama: A Literary Inquiry, with Special References to the Pre-Restoration Stage in England.* New York, 1959.

Haight, Elizabeth H. *Essays on the Greek Romances.* New York, 1933.

————*More Essays on the Greek Romances.* New York, 1935.

Heliodorus. *An Aethiopian History Written in Greek by Heliodorus Englished by Thomas Underdowne anno 1587*, ed. W. E. Henley. London, 1895.

————*Les Éthiopiques (Théagène et Chariclée)*, trans. J. Maillon, ed. R. M. Rattenbury and T. W. Lumb. 3 vols. Paris, 1935.

Horne, Ruth Nutt. "Lope de Vega's *Peregrino en su patria* and the Romance of Adventure in Spain before 1604." Ph.D. diss., Brown University, 1946.

Iamblichi Babyloniacorum Reliquiae, ed. Elmar Habrich. Leipzig, 1960.

Kermode, Frank. *William Shakespeare: The Final Plays.* London, 1963.

Knight, G. Wilson. *The Crown of Life.* London, 1947.

Landau, Marcus. *Die Quellen des Dekameron.* Stuttgart, 1884.

Lavagnini, Bruno. *Le Origini del Romanzo Greco.* Pisa, 1921.

Law, Robert Adger. "On the Dating of Shakspere's Plays," *The Shakespeare Association Bulletin,* XI (1935), 46–51.

Lee, A. Collingwood. *The Decameron: Its Sources and Analogues.* London, 1909.

Lodge, Thomas. "Rosalynde: Euphues Golden Legacie," in *A New Variorum Edition of Shakespeare: As You Like It*, ed. Horace H. Furness. Philadelphia, 1890. Pp. 316–87.

Longus. *Daphnis and Chloe: The Elizabethan Version,* etc., trans. Angel Day, ed. Joseph Jacobs. London, 1890.

————"Daphnis and Chloe by Longus," *Three Greek Romances,* trans. Moses Hadas. New York, 1953. Pp. 17–98.

————*Les Amours Pastorales de Daphnis et Chloé,* [trans. Jacques Amyot]. N.p., 1731.

————*Longus Pastorales (Daphnis et Chloé)*, trans. and ed. Georges Dalmeyda. Paris, 1934.

Moore Smith, G. C. "Introduction" to *Laelia: A Comedy*, ed. G. C. Moore Smith. Cambridge, Eng., 1910. Pp. vii–xxviii.

Munro, J. J. "Introduction" to [Arthur] *Brooke's "Romeus and Juliet" Being the Original of Shakespeare's "Romeo and Juliet,"* ed. J. J. Munro. New York, 1908.

"The Ninus Romance," in *The Love Romances of Parthenius and Other Fragments*, trans. and ed. Stephen Gaselee. Cambridge, Mass., 1935. Pp. 382–97. Loeb Classical Library.

Oeftering, Michael. *Heliodore und seine Bedeutung für die Litteratur.* Berlin, 1901.

Perry, Ben E. *The Ancient Romances: A Literary-Historical Account of Their Origin.* Berkeley, Calif., 1967.

Photius, *Bibliothèque,* ed. René Henry. 3 vols. Paris, 1959.

———*The Library of Photius,* trans. John Henry Freese. London, 1920.

Prouty, Charles T. *The Sources of Much Ado About Nothing: A Critical Study,* etc. New Haven, Conn., 1950.

Reinhold, Joachim-Henry. *Floire et Blancheflor: Étude de Littérature Comparée.* Paris, 1906.

Rohde, Erwin. *Der Griechische Roman und Sein Vorläufer,* 3d ed. Leipzig, 1914.

Schevill, Rudolph. "Studies in Cervantes: 'Persiles y Sigismunda,'" *Modern Philology,* IV (1907), 1–24, 677–704; *Connecticut Academy of Arts and Sciences,* XIII (1908), 475–548. (In three parts.)

The Arden Shakespeare, ed. Una Ellis-Fermor and Harold F. Brooks:

    The Comedy of Errors, ed. R. A. Foakes. Cambridge, Mass., 1962.

    Cymbeline, ed. J. M. Nosworthy. London, 1955.

    Pericles, ed. F. D. Hoeniger. Cambridge, Mass., 1963.

    The Tempest, ed. Frank Kermode. London, 1954.

    The Winter's Tale, ed. J. H. P. Pafford. Cambridge, Mass., 1963.

Shakespeare, William. *The Complete Works,* ed. W. J. Craig. Oxford, 1947.

Smyth, Albert H. *Shakespeare's Pericles and Apollonius of Tyre.* Philadelphia, 1898.

de Vega, Lope. "La dama boba," *Obras.* Madrid, 1929. XI, 587–633.

————*Novelas a la Señora Marcia Leonardo,* ed. John D. Fitz-Gerald and Leora A. Fitz-Gerald. Erlangen, 1913.

Wolff, Samuel Lee. *The Greek Romances in Elizabethan Prose Fiction.* New York, 1912.

Xenophon of Ephesus. *Les Éphésiaques au Le Roman D'Habrocomès et D'Anthia,* trans. and ed. Georges Dalmeyda. Paris, 1926.

————"An Ephesian Tale," *Three Greek Romances,* trans. Moses Hadas. New York, 1953. Pp. 101–72.

Index

This book has been set in Aster,
a type face designed by Francesco
Simoncini; with Eric Gill's Perpetua
for display.

Design by Jonathan Greene

Composed, printed, & bound
by Kingsport Press